Forecasting, Planning, and Strategy for the 21st Century

Forecasting, Planning, and Strategy for the 21st Century

SPYROS G. MAKRIDAKIS

THE FREE PRESS
A Division of Macmillan, Inc.
NEW YORK

Collier Macmillan Publishers
LONDON

The Free Press
A Division of Macmillan, Inc.
866 Third Avenue, New York, N.Y. 10022

Collier Macmillan Canada, Inc.

Printed in the United States of America

printing number
1 2 3 4 5 6 7 8 9 10

Library of Congress Cataloging-in-Publication Data

Makridakis, Spyros G.
    Forecasting, planning, and strategy for the 21st century / Spyros
    G. Makridakis.
        p.   cm.
    Includes bibliographical references.
    ISBN 9–02–919781–3
    1. Business forecasting.   2. Decision-making.
HD30.27.M343   1990
658.4'012—dc20   90–30733
                                                                         CIP

The definitions on page 143 are from the book, *Webster's New World Dictionary*, Second College Edition, © 1982. Used by permission of the publisher, Simon and Schuster, Inc., New York.

To Ari, Michelle, and Petros

Contents

Preface

Managers make many decisions each day, and the great majority of them refer to future events. Thus, knowing what is certain or likely to happen in the future can help management avoid wrong decisions and improve its chances for success. This book aims at increasing interest in the future and stimulating the search for a rational, pragmatic approach toward future-oriented decisions in business organizations. Its objective is to arm managers with a better understanding of and a realistic approach to the forces that influence the future, and to acquaint them with the types of thinking and actions required to face it as effectively as possible.

Management is a very young field in comparison with some other disciplines, but exaggerated claims are being made about its contributions in improving the efficiency of business organizations and the quality of managerial decisions. The consequences of such exaggerated claims are unrealistic expectations, which often are not fulfilled in practice. This book argues that the time has come to be realistic. The limitations, as well as the advantages, of the field of management must be understood and accepted. Moreover, we must search in other, more mature disciplines (e.g., military strategy) for relevant knowledge, which we can then apply to the field of management (e.g., in competitive business strategy). Most important, we must learn from our past mistakes and understand the reasons why they were made. We must accept the idea that all of us as individuals or as managers are prone to making similar mistakes in the future (because of the way our minds work), unless we are willing to make an effort to avoid them. But in order to succeed in the business world, it is not enough just to study the past. Future trends, including technological, economic, and other changes, must be predicted so that steps can be taken to deal with their effects. Facing up to the future and the uncertainty that surrounds it in an intelligent and pragmatic way is a critical necessity for today's manager. It requires accurate forecasting, effective planning, appropriate strategies, a great deal of creative thinking, an effective organization, and considerable implementation skills. The challenges involved are enormous. This book discusses such challenges as well as the difficulties and paradoxes facing managers in their quest to adapt their organizations to the changing environment of tomorrow and what it will take to succeed.

Introduction

I am interested in the future because I will spend the rest of my life there.

C. F. KETTERING, Seeds for Thought

Almost all decisions are intended for some future event or situation. Thus, we can never be sure how good they will be. This introduction discusses the importance, complexity, and difficulty of future-oriented decisions. It outlines some of the challenges involved and summarizes eight areas or tasks that must be covered when making future-oriented decisions.

On October 26, 1987, Arthur Kane, fifty-three, of Kendall, Florida, an investor, killed a Merrill Lynch vice-president and seriously wounded another, then shot and killed himself. Mr. Kane was a longtime customer of Merrill Lynch and had amassed a portfolio worth millions of dollars before the stock market crash of October 19, 1987. As the stock market fell, Mr. Kane was faced with a deadline for covering his margin losses; the deadline was approaching when he shot the two Merrill Lynch brokers and himself. A day later, on October 27, another investor, Vernon Lamberg of Wantoma, Wisconsin, who had reportedly lost $500,000 in the stock market, committed suicide in a motel room after his broker demanded payment of loans. A few days later Ansgar Schmetzer, thirty-seven, of Hollywood Hills, was found dead by his wife. Police said he was distressed over losing millions of dollars in the market's recent drops. Schmetzer's wife stated that he was still worth millions despite his stock market losses.

Killings and suicides are extreme actions that sometimes make headlines. There were millions of other cases of serious financial loss or at

1

least severe anxiety when the stock market lost 40 percent of its value (about $1 trillion, or the combined annual GNP of France and Italy) over a period of three weeks. The killings and the emotional stresses could have been avoided if stock market investors had followed some basic principles of forecasting and decision-making, but they chose instead to ignore available knowledge. The stock market is characterized by strong cyclical swings, along with a secular long-term trend. The market has gone up and down in the past and will continue to do so, since there have been no fundamental changes in the economy or the structure of corporations to suggest that cyclical fluctuations have been eliminated. Downturns in the stock market are therefore inevitable. The one on October 19 should have surprised no one. Because it did, panic developed, and the stock market fell much more than it would have otherwise.

That was not the first time the stock market had fallen by a percentage larger than expected, nor will it be the last. The problem is that people have a short memory (psychologists call this the *recency bias;* see Chapter 2). They forget that the stock market has gone down many times before and that it is as likely for stock prices to go down as it is for them to go up (see Chapter 3), in particular when stock values have been increasing for more than six years.

Thus, investors overextend themselves (buying on margin, mortgaging their houses in order to play the market, and so forth) in the hope of making a killing. Some, however, end up killing themselves or others or seeing their lifetime savings evaporate, as in October 1987. Investors should have contemplated the implications of a steep decline in the stock market and its consequences for their savings, as well as their future earnings. Obviously, many people did *not* consider the uncertainty involved in playing the stock market. Past evidence was ignored, and excessive optimism overruled objective thinking. The shocking return to reality, costly to many people, could have been avoided.

Obviously, one must invest his or her savings. However, the uncertainty, risks, and potential returns of each investment choice must be clearly understood so that the right choices, consistent with one's needs and preferences, can be made. Such choices should be based not on undue optimism or wishful thinking but on sound facts and objective, rational decisions. Otherwise, surprises and hardship might result, as they have in the stock market many times in the past (see Chapters 3 and 4).

Stock market investors are not the only ones who can make serious mistakes with decisions concerning future events. Business people as well as government officials make similar errors, causing hardship or even untold misery. Can such mistakes be avoided, or is it at least possible to anticipate their potential negative consequences so as to avoid unpleasant surprises? As with stock market investing, it is indeed possible to improve future-oriented decision-making. Eight tasks are required:

1. The first step is to acquire knowledge of the forces that shape the future and the extent of their predictability. This necessitates understanding which events can be predicted and which cannot, as well as the chances of being right in forecasting forthcoming events (see Chapters 3, 4, and 5).

2. Future uncertainty must be understood and taken into account in all future-oriented decisions. Such uncertainty must be dealt with by operating at a level of risk consistent with one's preferences and by taking appropriate actions (e.g., buying insurance) or elaborating strategies to cushion the impact of bad surprises and events different from those predicted and planned for (see Chapters 3, 8, and 9).

3. Decision-makers must be aware of the biases and limitations that characterize their judgment. Effective ways of avoiding or minimizing the negative consequences of such biases and limitations must be found (see Chapter 2).

4. The factors that contribute to success and those that delay or avoid failure must be understood and exploited (see Chapters 11 and 12).

5. The advantages and limitations of planning as a way of preparing to deal with future events must be comprehended, and the implications involved when the future turns out differently from what was planned for must be accepted (see Chapter 7).

6. More realistic and effective approaches for formulating strategies, both competitive and noncompetitive, must be developed and put into practice (see Chapters 8 and 9).

7. Creative new ways of solving existing problems and generating original ideas must be constantly sought and implemented (see Chapter 10).

8. In addition, managers must be aware of the value of management theories and the help to be derived from such theories in better managing their organizations. When forecasting, planning, formulating strategies or making major decisions, they also need to understand fully the limitations of managerial theories and the mistakes made in the past. Such understanding is essential to avoid making similar mistakes in the future (see Chapter 1).

It is highly likely that the future will be different from today. It is just as probable that the importance of technology and the rate of technological change will increase in the near and distant future. Computers, robotics, biochemistry, genetic engineering, medical breakthroughs, lasers, expert systems, cheap communications, cheap and fast transportation, and plentiful and affordable products will become widespread by the twenty-first century. At the same time new technologies—not yet discovered—will also appear. What can businesses do to be ready to face the future? How can they best plan? What strategy should they follow to keep up with new technologies? How can they adequately compete? What do they need to do to improve their chances of survival or their ability to succeed?

Planning for the introduction of new products or services, acquiring and using new technologies, expanding into new markets, and similar decisions must be made well in advance. That requires forecasting as accurately as possible. But this is not enough; managers must realize that competitors will also study the future and attempt to gain maximum benefits from the opportunities it might present. Forecasts and strategies must therefore take into account the possible plans of competitors and their strategies.

Uncertainty and risks do not disappear when the future is considered scientifically. On the contrary, an important aspect of dealing with the future is understanding and accepting the entire range of future uncertainty and the risks associated with it. This allows different individuals and organizations to operate at different levels of uncertainty, risk, and potential returns. The fact remains, however, that high returns can seldom be achieved unless one is willing to take correspondingly high risks. The challenge therefore lies in intelligently assessing future uncertainty and not taking more than the necessary risks to achieve one's own objective in terms of potential returns. This is where an appropriate strategy becomes indispensable.

In order to visualize the extent of change between now and the year 2001, consider the magnitudes of these changes in the United States between the beginning of this century and, say, the middle 1950s: the shift from agricultural to manufacturing jobs, the replacement of unskilled or semiskilled workers by automation, the replacement of skilled workers (e.g., shoemakers, tailors, carpenters, masons) by machines, or the change in the type of work performed by engineers and their importance.

Many agricultural jobs were lost as people crowded the cities in search of work in factories. In 1900, two-thirds of the population was in agriculture and less than 20 percent in producing goods. In 1955, 12 percent worked in agriculture and 32 percent producing goods. In 1989 the corresponding figures were 2 percent and 18 percent. A big change that has caused a lot of dislocation. Many unskilled or semiskilled tasks have been automated, bringing a lot of hardships and unemployment among those doing such jobs. Skilled jobs, learned after many years of training and requiring many more years of experience, have become obsolete over a period of a few decades. Machines have been designed and built to do the same jobs as well or better, much faster, and at a fraction of the cost. Even the engineers, the architects of the industrial revolution, who designed, built, and repaired the machines that brought the large changes between 1900 and today, saw their jobs and importance change too.

Managerial and organizational skills became more important than engineering ones. Not only did building, repairing, and running machines become routine tasks, but such tasks were also standardized and automated. The new stars became the professional managers, whose numbers increased exponentially (there was hardly any MBA education in 1955; thirty-five years later there were close to 70,000 MBAs graduating each year) as they replaced the engineers, whose ranks declined.

How will things change between now and the year 2001? Which jobs will be reduced or will disappear? Will middle managers exist at all in the year 2001? What about blue-collar workers or typists? Will there still be secretaries? If so, what will their job look like? These and similar questions are very important at the personal level (what advice to give your children on study or career for example), among government administrators, and for business executives. Answering these questions is critical and must be done with the utmost of care. This book will consider these questions as well as the most likely answers in the context of forecasting, planning, and strategy.

1

The Rise and Fall of Management Theories

*T*hat which has always been accepted by everyone, everywhere, is almost certain to be false.

PAUL VALÉRY, *Tel Quel*

A manager must decide whether existing or new knowledge can be introduced to help run his or her organization more efficiently. This requires a critical evaluation of existing or new management theories (or, if none are appropriate, his or her own). The challenge is to avoid making costly mistakes (by selecting an inappropriate theory or wrongly implementing an appropriate one) and instead to benefit by using the correct existing or new theory. This chapter describes problems with management theories, mistakes managers have made in the past in using them, and what can be done to improve chances of success by identifying the right issues and adapting the right theory.

The book *In Search of Excellence* was published in 1982. It became an instant commercial success, selling several million copies. Through research conducted between 1961 and 1980, its authors, Tom Peters and Robert Waterman, identified thirty-six excellent companies and presented throughout the book the factors[1] that contributed to such "excellence." The purpose of the book can best be captured by its subtitle, *Lessons from America's Best-Run Companies*. Could others have learned, however, from America's best? An answer might suggest itself if we look at what has happened to those thirty-six "excellent companies" since 1980.

In October 1987, *Business Week* published a study identifying the "Top 46" of "America's leanest and meanest companies."[2] Among those forty-six companies, only seven were from the thirty-six applauded in *In Search of Excellence*. A few months later *Fortune* published its annual survey of America's most admired companies.[3] Among the top ten, six were not even listed in *In Search of Excellence*. The book's favorite, IBM, had slipped into thirty-second place, and Wang Labs, an "excellent" company according to Peters and Waterman, had slipped to the bottom of Fortune's 300 or so companies; in 1988 its profits were down 97 percent from 1987, while in 1989 it incurred a loss of close to half a billion dollars. If the vast majority of the excellent companies from before 1980 did not manage to meet that definition less than ten years later, can they really offer lessons on excellence to others?

Another commercially successful book published in 1982 (more than 3 million copies sold), was *The One-Minute Manager*. It offered a handful of recipes for one-minute praise, reprimand, and goal-setting to those wishing to become effective managers in sixty seconds. It has been followed by other one-minute management books, which will probably be succeeded in their turn by *The One-Minute Inventor, The One-Minute Planner, The One-Minute Strategist,* and so on. After all, if one can manage in sixty seconds, why not do everything else in that amount of time?

In Search of Excellence and *The One-Minute Manager* cover the two extremes of management literature. The former, according to its authors, represents twenty years of research as well as an extensive review of existing management literature. It was written by two top consultants, one of whom was teaching at the Stanford Business School at the time the book was written. The second book can be *read* in nearly sixty seconds. It does not make any claims to superior methodology and long years of research. Its authors do not come from a known consulting firm or a famous business school. Yet both books were read by millions of managers and the overwhelming majority of business students at the time.

Today both books are out of fashion, replaced by new favorites. The advice they gave for success does not seem to be working today. Peters, a co-author of *In Search of Excellence*, admits this in his new book,[4] where he writes, "IBM is declared dead in 1979, the best of the best in 1982, and dead again in 1986. People Express is the model 'new-look' firm, then flops twenty-four months later. . . . Excellent firms don't believe in excellence—only in constant improvement and constant change."

In Search of Excellence and *The One-Minute Manager* are not the only books on management to become popular for a time and then slowly fade away. They were chosen as highly visible examples of the fads and fashions that characterize the field of management. Exhibit 1–1 shows

Exhibit 1–1 Major Management Theories I Have Come Across Since 1965

Management Theory	Brief Description	Problems or Assumptions Violated
Management by Objective	Setting goals through negotiations between superior and subordinates and then evaluating performance on how well such goals were accomplished	People play the game of setting low objectives easy to achieve. Too much paper work. Too time-consuming
Theory X and Theory Y	Authoritarianism (theory X) should give way to participative management (theory Y)	Participative management can reduce efficiency of decision-making and dilute responsibility
T-Groups	Encounter groups for managers aimed at increasing their sensitivity to others and making them less authoritarian	Sensitivity gained during T-groups did not last. Some participants remain hostile toward their co-workers
Management Science	Using quantitative tools and computers to improve decision-making and actual operations	Many decisions (notably those involving people and strategy) cannot be quantified
Matrix Management	A form of organization where an individual can have more than one boss	Problems of conflict and split alliances can develop
Diversification	To maintain high growth, companies must diversify to promising industries or new markets	Difficulty in accurately forecasting promising industries/markets
Decentralization	Decision-making is placed in the hands of line managers	Without effective coordination, decision-making can become ineffective
Conglomerates	Acquiring dissimilar businesses under a single corporation	By definition the most conglomerates can achieve is average returns
Optimal Investment Portfolios	The risk of investing can be minimized by selecting stocks that do *not* go up and down at the same time	Past patterns in the movement of various stocks do *not* also hold for the future

The Systems Approach	The whole is much more important than the sum of its parts. Decisions must therefore be made having the whole—not the parts—in mind	Complexity increases beyond human capability if it is assumed that everything relates with everything else
The Managerial Grid	Classifying a manager based on his/her concern toward people and/or production	Managers cannot be classified into nice boxes. Their behavior and motives are complex
Econometric Models	Statistical models capable of capturing the relationship(s) among complex phenomena in order to use it to predict future situations	Past relationships do not necessarily hold true into the future
Long-Range Strategic Planning	Extrapolate long-term trends in sales, demand, etc., and plan capital investments and other expansions accordingly	The established growth in sales, demand, etc., cannot be guaranteed into the future
S-Curves and Product Life Cycles	The life cycle of products (and technologies) follows a logistic or S-curve, which can be predicted beforehand	No S-curve can be predicted, although self-fulfilling prophecies can make it seem such prediction is possible
Zero-Based Budgeting	Start from scratch in making next year's budget	Too much uncertainty for longer-range planning
Portfolio Matrix	Products or business units are classified as dogs, cows, question marks, and stars. The objective is to get rid of dogs and to promote stars, financing them with cash generated from cows	It assumes future stars can be identified. It ignores synergies. It can drop profitable products. It disregards competitive action and learning
Experience Curves	As production doubles, nondirect costs decrease by a constant percentage	It might work for mass production. But bureaucracy can wipe out economies of scale
PIMS	An empirical database containing company-supplied information whose purpose is to discover the relationship between profitability and other factors	Too many methodological problems and tautologies to make the results reliable and useful

Exhibit 1-1 (*Continued*)

Management Theory	Brief Description	Problems or Assumptions Violated
Centralized Corporate Strategy	Strategy must be formulated at the top, where the whole picture of corporate goals and long-term visions is available	Individual managers have little or no say in determining the strategy for their units/departments
Limits to Growth	Natural resources are limited, thus their price will increase indefinitely as the size of population keeps increasing	Technology has lifted the Malthusian fears to growth. Products are cheaper in real prices now than in the past
Intuitive/Analytic Management	Managers who predominantly think in the right hemisphere are intuitive, those who think mostly on the left are analytic. Such a dichotomy can be used to facilitate training and improve decision-making	Empirical research has shown no help in training or improvements in decision-making by exploiting the left/right hemispheres
Searching for Excellence	Through empirical research, identify the factors common to excellent companies and use them to become excellent too	Past excellence cannot be used to achieve excellence in the future
One-Minute Management	Balancing praise and criticism in sixty seconds	Gimmicks do not change managers' or employees' behavior
Management by Walking Around (MBWA)	Visiting the line people and customers to obtain first-hand information	MBWA imposes formidable time constraints. Information can be gathered much more effectively
Restructuring	Getting rid of unprofitable businesses or those that do not fit the corporate identity	The challenge is to know what businesses to get rid of

Entrepreneurship	Encourage entrepreneurial spirit (and projects) within the corporation	The challenge is how to achieve entrepreneurship. This is not trivial
Competitive Strategies	Analyze the competitive situation in your industry and learn to read competitive signals	The challenge is to predict future competition, not analyze past or existing ones
Theory Z	Adopt Japanese style of management (life employment, job enrichment, product quality, long-term goals)	It is difficult to adopt without a Japanese culture. In France, life employment has not increased productivity
Quality Circles	Form groups, or committees, within the firm to discuss and promote ways of improving product or service quality	Helpful if quality can be improved without wasting too much time
Strategic Alliances	Form alliances (if necessary even with your arch-rival(s)) to improve your competitive position	Long-term effects can be detrimental, as they provide a false sense of security
Global Rationalization	The market place is the world. Thus, production, marketing, finance and R&D decisions must be made with such a view in mind	How do you know future conditions? A change in exchange rates, for instance, can make all plans useless
The Management of Chaos	The environment is unpredictable and fast-changing. To deal with it, therefore, requires flexible organizations that can constantly change and adapt	The challenge is to create flexible organizations and to know when, what, and how to change
The New Future Theory	There is *one certainty*. There will be *many* new theories, although I cannot predict what they will advocate, how popular they will be, or how long they will last	Only through critical evaluation can you avoid the same mistakes managers made in the past by adopting fashionable theories

some major theories[5] that, like fashion in clothing, became popular at some point but were then put into the closet, to be worn only occasionally in special circumstances.

The theories listed in Exhibit 1–1 cover the period from 1965, when I started my PhD studies at New York University, to the present. Those at the top of Exhibit 1–1 were popular when I was a student. The others became popular at some time in the intervening years. Each theory, when it appeared, gave rise to a surge in the number of papers and books written on the topic, courses offered at business schools, and consultants trying to sell its ideas to business firms. Those theories inevitably then became unpopular as experience with their application or empirical investigation showed no visible benefits or, in some cases, extensive damage. Today only a handful of the theories listed in Exhibit 1–1 are taught to business students; the rest are all but forgotten. Some of these theories, notably the portfolio matrix proposed by the Boston Consulting Group, brought huge losses to those who used them.

Exhibit 1–2 lists eight individuals (along with the essence of their theories) whom the majority of my academic colleagues agree to have been the most influential management thinkers in this century. From the eight, only Alfred Chandler, Peter Drucker, and Herbert Simon are still alive, and only Peter Drucker is still being read by a large number of business students and executives. Although some of his theories (e.g., management by objectives) have gone out of fashion, his work has been the opposite of faddish.

The point behind both exhibits is this: The question of how a manager is to evaluate existing or new theories is important and must be carefully considered.

EVALUATING MANAGEMENT THEORIES

A theory can be descriptive, normative, or predictive. A descriptive theory, as the name implies, attempts to describe a phenomenon, event, function, or job. It can explain, for instance, how organizations become bureaucratic and another how chief executive officers make decisions. Normative theories describe how things ought to work under ideal conditions. In economics, for instance, it is often assumed that consumers are rational, their preferences are stable, information is ideally disseminated, and perfect competition exists. Given those assumptions, one can develop a theory that explains prices in different conditions of supply and demand.

Predictive theories, finally, aim not only at describing and explaining

Exhibit 1–2 Eight Individuals (and Their Theories) Who Have Had a Lasting Effect on Management Thought and Practice in the West

Individuals	Essence of Theory	Reasons for Importance of Theory
1. Henri Fayol 1841–1925	General principles for managing organizations more effectively	General principles are still needed and used in managing organizations
2. Frederick Taylor 1856–1915	Management can be made into an exact science	Some aspects of management (notably those involving routine, repetitive tasks) can be analyzed and dealt with more effectively using formal, management science techniques
3. Alfred Sloan 1875–1966	Lessons from managing General Motors	An illuminating account of how strategy was applied and how a large organization was managed
4. Elton Mayo 1880–1949 (with Fritz Roethlisberger)	Attention to employees is the single most important factor in improving productivity	The importance of people in organizations was demonstrated, starting the human relations movement that is still valid today
5. Chester Barnard 1886–1961	Good managers shape the informal side of their organizations	Excellent insights of a practitioner about the importance of the informal side of organizations and its influence on long-term survival
6. Alfred Chandler 1918–	Structure follows strategy	Unless an appropriate structure can be installed, strategy cannot succeed.
7. Herbert Simon 1916–	The satisfying (as opposed to optimizing) manager	Contrary to popular belief managers (like human beings in general) are limited in their capacity for making decisions by their inability to optimize such decisions Critical implications for how decisions are made and organizations are run
8. Peter Drucker 1909–	Critical evaluation and good insights on topics of current concern	Identification of major concerns and critical evaluation of them—the opposite of fashionable, although dealing with current topics

the past but also at predicting the future. This means their assumptions must be realistic and must hold true in the conditions of the future, which might differ from those existing when the theory is proposed. A recent example of a theory with high predictive value concerns the launching and trajectory of Voyager 2, which on August 24, 1989, after having traveled twelve years and 2.8 billion miles, arrived at its rendezvous with Neptune within a few thousand miles and a few seconds from the intended place and time estimated theoretically twelve years earlier.

Descriptive and normative theories provide insights that can help managers understand themselves and their organizations by studying and explaining the past. It must be understood, however, that descriptive theories refer to specific situations and periods of time. It must also be clear that normative theories are based on restrictive assumptions that often have little or nothing to do with reality. Therefore, any attempt to generalize from descriptive or normative theories and to use such theories for predictive purposes involves a risk, as the conditions in the future will in all likelihood be different. Interestingly enough, all eight theories listed in Exhibit 1–2 are descriptive. Such theories do *not* tell us how to improve future-oriented decisions. Instead, they describe strategies, operations, organizations, or people. No predictive theories seem to have lasted.

Nevertheless, predictive theories are of special value to the field of management, because, in addition to describing or explaining the past, they can also provide us with the means of making most effective decisions concerning future situations. A theory must predict future events accurately; otherwise, its value is no greater than that of history, which supplies us with an understanding of the past so that we can avoid repeating past mistakes.

A serious problem develops when descriptive or normative theories are confused with predictive ones. There would have been nothing to complain about, for instance, had the subtitle of *In Search of Excellence* been *A Historical Description of America's Best-Run Companies, 1960–1980*. The problems develop when descriptive or normative theories are used as the basis for future-oriented decisions, when the circumstances in all likelihood will have changed, and when idealized or unrealistic assumptions do not hold true in practice.

Theories in the field of management are a mixture of descriptive, normative, and predictive. Descriptive and normative theories, however, are rarely labeled as such, while the assumptions and limitations of predictive theories are rarely stated.

A limitation of descriptive theories in management is that their forecasts are often like those of the stock market. Future prices of individual stocks and market indices can be predicted through a high-powered and accurate descriptive theory. But don't raise your hopes of becoming rich,[6] as such a theory tells us that the best forecast of future prices is today's value (see Chapter 3). Thus, although there is a predictive theory, its benefits do not come from its forecasts. If the best forecast for the future price of stocks is its price today, everybody has access to such a "best forecast." Nobody can benefit more than anyone else since everybody can use the best forecast to maximize his or her benefits by buying stocks. There are advantages to be gained by accepting and using such a predictive theory. The most obvious one is not paying a fee to those who pretend that they can forecast stock market prices better than "today's" price.

There are some reasons why predictive theories in management are similar to those of the stock market:

1. *The Zero-Sum Game of Excellence.* Unfortunately, the number of companies that can be excellent in a certain industry is limited. Excellent companies will, by definition, excel, thus forcing their competitors into also-ran status. At the same time, the competitors of excellent companies will not be capable of uprooting them unless they can come up with imaginative new methods, whether in marketing, production, or provision of services.

Now consider a new theory. It is perfect. It provides seven easy steps for a company to become excellent. Can such a theory have any real value? Obviously not. If it is so easy and so perfect, competitors, including the excellent company, will also use it. In that case nothing much will change. Now suppose manager X uses it first. It is highly unlikely that competitors, including the excellent company, will not realize that he or she is using a new theory. They will soon follow, erasing whatever advantages the innovator might have gained since he or she started using the perfect magic formula. After all, the theory is simple and highly effective. Thus, what has worked for the innovator will necessarily work for them too.

2. *Shifting the Real Issues.* Theories are often presented in the form of a claim that it is easy to succeed if you do A and B. They do not say, however, how A and B, frequently restatements of the real issue, can be achieved. In the field of strategy, for instance, one is told that to be successful opportunities and threats in the environment must be recognized. Once that is done, the opportunities must be exploited while steering clear of the threats. No one is ever told, however, *how* to find and

exploit opportunities or *how* to predict and avoid threats (the "easy" things are left unsaid).

3. *Ignoring Constraints*. Managers are told that successful leaders must be great communicators and great motivators, must manage by walking around, must be available to be seen by everybody, must be present at all meetings, must send thank-you notes—or better yet make personal telephone calls—to everyone who has done something clever, must be active in public relations, and, at the same time, must free themselves from mundane tasks so that they can do the strategic thinking indispensable for the long term well-being of their organization. However, there is no advice on how to become Superman or Superwoman or how to learn to manage with no more than a couple of hours of sleep at night.

4. *Change and Innovation, the Ultimate Buzzwords*. The newest advice for becoming successful is to create an organizational climate that thrives on constant change and innovation. We are not told, however, how such an organization can be created, or what type of change and innovation will be beneficial. Business firms, and life in general, would be trivial to manage if all change and innovation produced positive results. IBM has tried for the last few years to change and innovate, but somehow its competitors have managed to change and innovate even more successfully. In 1987, for instance, IBM's profits increased 10 percent (the lowest in its industry) while those of Apple increased by 80 percent, and Compaq Computer's an astonishing 218 percent. In 1988 IBM's profits increased only 4 percent (below the 6 percent industry average), leaving it far behind Apple and Compaq Computers, which grew 50 and 87 percent, respectively.

In 1978 General Motors was earning a record $3.5 billion while holding more than a 48 percent share of the U.S. market. In 1987 its market share had fallen to 36 percent (an enormous 12 percent drop in an industry where each percentage point is worth more than $2 billion), while its earnings were $1.1 billion below those of Ford, although GM spent close to $70 billion to change and innovate.

5. *Heisenberg's Uncertainty Principle*. Heisenberg, a Nobel Prize–winning physicist, showed that the mere act of observing a particle affects the outcome of the observation. Thus, it becomes impossible to determine with high accuracy the position of a particle if we observe its momentum, or its momentum if we measure its position. The same phenomenon applies to management theories. Observation affects the outcome and in the process reduces or nullifies a theory's value or its predictions. Con-

sider, for instance, the one-minute manager. He or she is not the only one who has read the little book that describes how to become such a manager or is aware of its approach. Thus, an employee will know when he or she gets one-minute praise, a one-minute reprimand, or is asked to describe half a dozen goals to be read in under a minute. The employee will therefore play the one-minute game. Or, better, as André and Ward suggest in their book, employees can get a one-second jump on their managers by predicting and taking advantage of the One-Minute Manager's behavior.[7]

THEN WHAT?

The single most important task currently being neglected in management is learning. We must learn from our past mistakes as well as from those made in other disciplines when they were young and inexperienced, as the field of management is today. This is where a critical evaluation of management theories becomes useful, for learning is not possible without understanding and correcting mistakes. The following is a list of relevant mistakes (made in both the field of management and other disciplines) we must avoid if we are to advance the field of management.

1. *Fashionableness of Theories*. It has been demonstrated that the vast majority of managerial theories do not last long. A manager must therefore view theories as temporary fads unless they can be proved otherwise with convincing, indisputable evidence. As a matter of fact, even in a hard science like physics new theories are proposed to replace existing ones that become obsolete in explaining the physical reality.[8]

2. *Oversimplicity of Theories*. The purpose of management theories is to help create mental models of reality (reality itself being too complex to deal with). Such models are subsequently used to guide the thinking process and to facilitate or improve decision-making. Of necessity a theory must be simple, otherwise it would be hard to grasp and use as a mental model. Reality, on the other hand, is extremely complex; it cannot be simplified beyond a certain point and still be represented accurately by the theory. Thus, as Einstein cleverly pointed out, a theory should not be more complex than is necessary, but it cannot be less complex than the minimum level required to be realistic.

There is a tendency to oversimplify theories, and not only in the field of management. It is tempting to provide easy explanations of reality. For instance, in the area of psychology "behaviorism" explained human behavior in simple terms. Desired behavior was to be achieved through immediate rewards, while undesired behavior was to be extinguished through lack of rewards or through mild punishment. Although such a theory is simple, it cannot explain the complexity of human behavior or the factors that motivate people. Nevertheless, "behaviorism" was the most popular theory for more than twenty-five years, and it still appeals to some.[9]

In management one can mention many theories that fall into the same category—the portfolio matrix, the One-Minute Manager, the Managerial Grid, and so on. Although attractively simple, such theories cannot be expected to explain the complex reality of management or the best way of dealing with people. Worse, they cannot be expected to have much predictive value.

3. *Inappropriate or Incorrect Basic Principles or Assumptions.* A theory can be logically consistent but be based on a wrong premise. Consider, for instance, the Ptolemaic astronomy, which assumed that the universe turned around the earth—an obviously (by now) incorrect basic axiom. That did not prevent the Ptolemaic system from being used for almost 1,800 years as the prevailing theory or from helping astronomers in their work. Moreover, its predictions were reasonably accurate and certainly much better than those of previous theories, even though its basic premise was certainly wrong.

Discontent with theories develops as observation does not agree with theoretical predictions. This necessitates new theories to explain and correct the discrepancies. By the sixteenth century the Ptolemaic system was so cumbersome and inaccurate that it had become a nightmare to predict when winter would arrive (at times it was late by more than a month). This obsolescence provided the momentum to reject the Ptolemaic theory and to advance that of Copernicus.[10]

Management theories have followed a pattern similar to that of Ptolemy. With use, their deficiencies in predicting accurately become obvious. They are subsequently modified to improve their performance until they become highly complex but still unable to predict adequately, at which point they are abandoned.

In addition, theories must make several assumptions in order to simplify reality. Alfred North Whitehead, in an excellent book published in 1925, gives the following advice, "one's whole trouble is with the first chapter, or even with the first page. For it is here, at the very outset, where the author will probably be found to slip up in his assumptions. Further, *the trouble is not with what the author does say, but with what he does not say. Also, it is not with what he knows he has assumed, but with what he has unconsciously assumed.*"[11] A serious problem complicating the evaluation of management theories is that their assumptions are rarely made explicit, even those of which authors are aware.

4. *Demand Creates Its Own Supply*. Demand for theories creates an ample supply, not necessarily motivated by a desire to advance knowledge or to improve management, particularly when monetary rewards await those creating or selling theories. In medicine, for instance, "mankind suffered cruelly for centuries from lack of medical knowledge. . . . Doctors can follow more false trails than Inspector Clouseau. They can become so fond of dead doctrines, they resemble a procession of ostriches with their heads in the sand."[12] Those are the words of a doctor, who goes on to point out how in the past doctors applied disastrous treatments, for which they should have been ashamed, to diseases of which they knew little. Only since the beginning of this century have *scientific* advances in medicine, along with the extensive use of antibiotics, established the effectiveness of medicine on an objective basis. At present management theories are at the same point as medical theories were before this century, which means that a critical assessment of the theory's concrete advantages is required before deciding to use it.

5. *General Truths Versus Detailed Predictions*. The fact that a theory is valid does not automatically mean that it can be used to arrive at precise predictions. Consider, for instance, the theory of relativity. Present knowledge indicates that it is correct. However, sending a spacecraft to Neptune requires much more than espousing the theory of relativity. Spacecraft technology must be available. Financial and human resources must be found. A huge number of specific computations must be made to determine the spacecraft's trajectory. In addition, effective monitoring of its actual path is necessary to discover errors, which must subsequently be corrected to achieve a successful approach and landing. Although an accurate theory is a necessary condition before a successful rendezvous can even be considered, that theory is not by itself a sufficient condition for success. The same principle applies to management theories, which, even if valid, need an appropriate organization, adequate resources, specific directions, ways of monitoring results, and effective procedures for taking corrective actions. In management, unlike physics, paths cannot be established in a precise quantitative manner, accurate feedback cannot be provided at will, and corrective actions are often of limited usefulness when changes in established courses become necessary. Thus, the value

of a theory should not be overestimated, even if one is convinced that it is valid, without also considering questions of organization, resources, and implementation.

6. *The Constantly Changing Tomorrow.* Unlike physics, where established patterns and relationships do not—for any practical purposes—change, the business world is characterized by rapid change. This creates a serious problem. Past observation and current measurement are not sufficient to verify the predictive ability of a theory. Theories cannot be used, therefore, until it is established how future changes will affect their predictions. Such future changes have to include learning based on theoretical predictions, contrarian moves, and actions taken as a result of learning and previous actions, as well as governmental (e.g., the Federal Reserve Board) or other interference. Hence the predictive value of even the best theory is limited. It becomes imperative to consider the extent of a theory's predictability under various scenarios (or forecasts) of future change, competitive actions and reactions, and environmental conditions. At present, the advocates of theories do not refer to their limitations or their inabilities to predict future events when conditions will, in all likelihood, be different from today's. These are important concerns, however, which must be examined before deciding whether or not to use a theory.

THE PARADOXES

1. A manager must use a management theory to guide his/her thinking and facilitate or improve his/her decision-making, yet past experience indicates that the great majority of theories in management are short-lived and of doubtful value (see Exhibit 1–1).
2. A manager needs a predictive theory, yet in management few, if any, theories are predictive.
3. A manager needs a simple theory which he/she can easily understand and which can tell him/her how to succeed, yet no such theories can be found in the public domain.

THE CHALLENGE AHEAD

Management theories are indispensable. Practice without theory is a dangerous exercise, no less perilous than an inappropriate theory. However, much can be done to improve a theory's contribution to more effectively dealing with the reality of business. This conclusion should hardly surprise anyone. The management of large business organizations is, after all, a new field. If it took astronomy, medicine, and other disciplines many centuries to achieve their present state, it cannot be expected that management can reach an equally high level of accomplishment in less than 100 years. On the other hand, learning can be accelerated if we recognize and are willing to accept our past mistakes, as well as those mistakes made in other disciplines. This would require a critical evaluation of the achievements and drawbacks of managerial (and other) theories.

THE CHALLENGES AHEAD

1. Be a skeptic. Don't take anything for granted. There are many who try to sell ideas (including myself). Become selective and discriminating in finding the right theory.
2. Choose the issues (opportunities, problem areas, dangers) that confront the given organization and those that lie ahead. This is as critical a step as searching for solutions.
3. Select a theory to deal with these issues. In all probability, the theory will have to be modified and tailored to your specific needs. If no formal theory exists, an informal one must be developed in your mind.
4. Evaluate the theory critically. Consider its costs, benefits, and possible dangers. Most important, understand the principles upon which it is based and the main assumptions (all theories are, by necessity, based on assumptions), their limitations, and how they restrict the value of the theory. Unless satisfied beyond a reasonable doubt, don't implement the theory.
5. It is highly likely that competitors will imitate a successful manager (the greater the success, the greater the imitation). He/she must, therefore, always change and adapt his/her theory in order to be one step ahead of competitors. He/she must constantly innovate.
6. Study the evolution of other disciplines more advanced than management. Learn from them and avoid the mistakes they have made.

Biases and Limitations of Our Judgment

*E*rrors of judgment are often systematic rather than random, manifesting bias rather than confusion. Thus, man suffers from mental astigmatism as well as from myopia, and any corrective prescriptions should fit this diagnosis.

D. KAHNEMAN AND A. TVERSKY, "Intuitive Predictions: Biases and Corrective Procedures," *TIMS Studies in Management Science, Vol. 12 (1979).*

A major part of a manager's job is devoted to making decisions. Unfortunately, these decisions cannot be assumed to be rational. Human judgment exhibits serious limitations and systematic biases. At present not much is done to deal with such limitations and biases, mostly because they are not well understood or accepted in the field of management. This chapter describes the judgmental biases that influence most future-oriented decisions. The challenge facing managers is to avoid the negative consequences of judgmental biases and to help their organization develop procedures that guard their members against such biases while making decisions.

All the best stories begin "once upon a time," and the following is no exception. However, this one is rooted firmly in reality, and its lessons are the focus of this chapter.

Once upon a time, in a faraway country, lived an absolute ruler. One day he was presented with a golden opportunity (in the form of an annual revenue of many billions of dollars), which conjured up a tantalizing vision of the future in his mind. He wanted to modernize his illiterate, barefoot country and raise its living standards to those of the West in ten years. "Do you think, sir," the journalist interviewing him asked, "you will be able to accomplish what took the West many generations in just ten years?" "Yes, of course," the despot replied confidently.

In fact, the absolute monarch was none other than the Shah Mohammed Reza Pahlavi, and his country was Iran. The time was 1973, just after the outbreak of the Arab-Israeli war, when the quadrupling of oil prices brought the Shah a minimum of $20 billion a year in revenue. What did he do with his golden opportunity? He endeavored to seize it in order to enrich the lives of his subjects, to protect and educate them, to modernize their way of life, and, through the spread of Western values and technology, to transform his underdeveloped kingdom into the fifth greatest power in the world. After all, he certainly had the money to do so, and everybody was willing (for a price) to help him translate his golden vision into reality.

As we know, the dream was never realized, and the story ended in tragedy for the Shah. The failure cannot be explained by saying that he was stupid (on the contrary, he was a highly intelligent and well-educated man) or inexperienced (he was a shrewd ruler for more than thirty years). Rather, his downfall was the result of faulty judgment, large-scale errors, and an unshakable belief in his own wisdom. Neither Savak, his omnipresent secret police, nor the CIA managed to avert his downfall. He lavishly attempted to give his subjects something they did not want, and he completely misjudged his opponent as a senile, uneducated mullah. With hindsight, it seems he did everything wrong—including closing his ears to any hint of evidence contrary to what he wanted to hear.

The Shah's sad story is not unique. Many rulers before him have had similar or worse experiences, and many will doubtless encounter the same in the future. The overthrow of the Tsar in Russia, for instance, is another famous case where the downfall of a dynasty was largely brought about by misjudgment. And myriad other examples of faulty decisions made by high-ranking government officials, generals, Popes, doctors, and individuals could be cited. After the Bay of Pigs invasion, President Kennedy was reported to have said, "How could I have been so stupid as to let them go ahead?" He should have asked, "How could we have made such a stupid decision?" because neither President Kennedy nor his staff were stupid. Probably the lowest IQ of those who decided to go ahead and invade Cuba was over 140.

In his book on military incompetence, Norman Dixon investigates some famous military disasters and concludes that such incompetence cannot be attributed to dullness of intellect on the part of those in charge. Instead, he lists ego-weaknesses, authoritarianism, ill-founded assumptions, the inability to act on military intelligence, and underestimating the enemy, rather than stupidity, as the main causes of military ineptitude.[1] Janis and Mann, in an excellently documented book, provide additional examples of disastrous decisions taken by otherwise highly intelligent government officials, military commanders, and other individuals.[2]

Business executives have made their share of faulty decisions. Companies go bankrupt; others fire thousands of people to cut costs; yet others pay exorbitant prices to silence dissent (as when General Motors paid H. Ross Perot $700 million to leave its board of directors) or do nothing in the face of overwhelming evidence of major technological changes— these and all sorts of similar mistakes abound. Such mistakes often escape public notice for two reasons: First, executives do their best to hide them, and unless they are uncovered they are not reported; and second, the public is much less interested in faulty decisions and mishaps than in brilliant moves and success stories, which are therefore reported more readily and widely publicized.

Shakespeare's view—''what a piece of work is man! How noble in reason! How infinite in faculty!''—has been shattered by a plethora of empirical evidence and laboratory studies. The ''paragon of animals'' has been revealed to be only too fallible when it comes to making decisions. The inevitable corollary of that discovery has serious implications for the way our organizations are run, since the biases and limitations of our judgment throw doubt on the validity of our decisions. Organizations ignore the existence of such faults of judgment (or what are known as judgmental biases) and their detrimental consequences. What should be done is to recognize the danger biases represent and to take appropriate steps to minimize their possible ill effects?

THE NATURE OF JUDGMENTAL BIASES AND LIMITATIONS

I doubt that many of us can remember the telephone numbers of our favorite restaurants or what we ate for lunch a month ago, and that we have memorized all our appointments for next week. Human beings are well aware of the limitations of their memories. They know they cannot remember everything, so they take steps to avoid the negative consequences. The names of people and businesses are written down in alphabetical order, along with addresses and phone numbers, in an address book in order to be able to retrieve them easily. For appointments there is an appointment book to enter the names of people to see, telephone calls to make, or meetings to attend, along with the times, under the correct date. A simple glance at such a book reveals the day's schedule.

The fact that we do not entrust these things to memory and take remedial action to compensate for its deficiencies and limitations does not mean that memory is deficient. On the contrary, the human memory is a superb organ, of infinite value. Even the most sophisticated computer cannot achieve even a tiny fraction of its marvelous workings. The human memory's complexity is estimated to be roughly the equivalent of sixty times that of the entire U.S. telephone system, and its capacity 500 times that of the entire *Encyclopaedia Britannica* (or 500,000 times if redundancies are counted). Yet even this enormous capacity would be filled in a few days if everything was indiscriminately stored. Thus, one of the most important functions of our memory (and mind) is to know what is important to remember and what can be ignored. Furthermore, it can determine when something stored has to be pushed back or be forgotten to accommodate new, more important information. It is because the memory is a superb mechanism that we should write down all the things that can be easily retrieved. The more it is relieved of the burden of storing trivial facts, the greater its capacity to store and easily retrieve more important information.

The ability of our brain to process information and make decisions is very similar to memory, on which it depends a great deal. There are many tasks our mind can do superbly. But, as with memory, there are other tasks it cannot accomplish as well or cannot do at all. Think for instance of finding the square root of 53591468115. Unless one is a computational genius, or more accurately a specialized idiot-savant, the task cannot be achieved directly in our brain alone. As with memory, our mind must make compromises in order to accomplish many different and often conflicting tasks. For instance, novel problem-solving and creativity require abilities at the opposite extreme from those needed to make computations or deal with routine, repetitive situations. Similarly, learning requires trial and error (it therefore necessitates making mistakes), which is dysfunctional in stable situations when no change is envisioned.

The big difference between memory and judgment is that while we accept the deficiencies and limitations of our memory (and so write down useful addresses or things we want to remember later on), we rarely do anything to remedy the deficiencies of our judgment, mainly because we are unaware or unwilling to accept that our judgment can be faulty or biased. Because they are almost never presumed to exist, it is extremely important to expose judgmental biases. Empirical evidence demonstrates beyond all reasonable doubt their existence and their negative, damaging consequences. Research shows that judgmental biases do not mean stupidity, for their presence is clearly discernable among highly intelligent people. Rather, they result from the way the mind operates and reflect its endeavors to achieve the optimal reconciliation of conflicting objectives.

Clearly, business executives, like everybody else, are not entirely rational beings.[3] More attention is required to deal with judgmental biases in managerial decision-making and to avoid or minimize their negative impact on the organization. In the remainder of this chapter those biases relevant to forecasting and future-oriented decisions are described, and ways of minimizing or neutralizing their negative impact are proposed.

JUDGMENTAL BIASES IN FORECASTING AND FUTURE-ORIENTED DECISIONS

Imagine for a moment that you work for Elco Electronics, a small-to-middle-size company with some 2,000 employees, as product manager for microcomputer printers, which account for about 40 percent of Elco's revenues. Competition in the microcomputer printer market is fierce, both from new entrants at home and from imports coming mostly from Pacific rim countries. The product manager must make many decisions concerning the product, ranging from how many units of each of twenty models of printers to produce and ship to distributors, to how much money to invest for R&D and new plants and equipment. Making those decisions is not easy. There is a great deal of uncertainty surrounding the microprinter market. Sales are linked very closely to microcomputer sales, which are hard to predict. For instance, there was a big slump in microcomputer sales around 1985, lasting almost two years, which nobody had predicted beforehand. Furthermore, new technology and new low-cost competitors can slash prices by as much as 30–50 percent a year, rendering estimates of revenues highly inaccurate. Yet every year in October–November managers must make budget forecasts and a rolling five-year long-range plan, which is sent to top management for approval. Moreover, budget resources must be allocated to different departments, pricing decisions made, R&D projects funded, and strategic directions and ways of achieving them formulated.

Exhibit 2–1 shows Elco's sales of microcomputer printers since 1982, when the printer division became a separate unit. There has been a healthy increase in sales during the past. However, the product manager's concern is the future. He needs to make a unit sales forecast (in addition to price, competition, and so on) for next year and for five years from now.

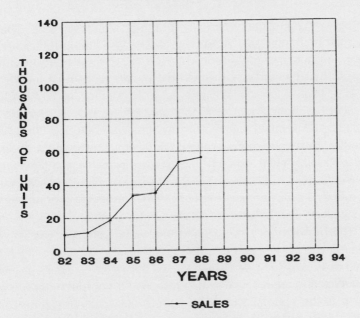

Exhibit 2–1 Yearly Sales of Microcomputer Printers for Last Seven Years

What will be the forecast? For planning purposes, he also needs to make another type of estimate which should include a low, pessimistic sales figure and a high, optimistic one. The estimates of the low and high figures have to be made in such a way that if the actual sales are above or below the values specified more than 5 percent of the time, management will be extremely surprised. Assuming for a moment that you are that beleaguered product manager, write down what your estimates of micro computer printers would be.

Forecast Sales of Microcomputer Printers for 1989 and 1993

Year	Low (Pessimistic) Forecast	Most Likely Sales Forecast	High (Optimistic) Forecast
1989	_____	_____	_____
1993	_____	_____	_____

In fact, there is no right or wrong forecast in predicting the sales of printers. Much will depend upon outside forces beyond the control of a rather small company like Elco Electronics. On the other hand, management and employees can move things in desired directions, in particular when the survival of their company and their jobs is at stake. The future will, in the final analysis, become an interplay of three forces: (1) competitors' attempts to gain as much of Elco's market share as possible; (2) Elco's efforts to counteract competitive moves to grab its market share, while at the same time increasing and strengthening its competitive position, and (3) events outside Elco's control, such as general economic conditions, the demand for microcomputers, the price of the dollar vis-à-vis other currencies, new technological developments, and so forth.

If a third party (like yourself) were asked to forecast Elco's sales, he or she would most likely predict a straight-line extrapolation from the past to the future. Thus, the most likely forecast, around which most answers will be located, will be about 65,000 units for 1989 and 100,000 units for 1993. That is because it is assumed that what has happened in the past will continue to happen in the future, that the various factors causing sales to go up or down will cancel themselves out as Elco and its competitors make moves and countermoves that effectively neutralize each other. At least that is the approach used by people making judgmental forecasts when no additional inside information is available, and when personal or political considerations are not at stake. Such an approach, although mechanistic, seems to work in practice better than other alternatives.

What is interesting, however, is how the forecasts change if those asked to respond are told that the data of Exhibit 2–1 represents a new (or, alternatively, a mature or old product). As can be seen in the graph shown in Exhibit 2–2, the answers vary widely, which demonstrates how often we ignore concrete data and instead forecast using stereotypes (the sales of a new product must increase, for example, while those of an old one must decrease). In fact, the differences in the forecasts for new, mature, and old products (in particular for 1993) are enormous, highlighting the need to exclude judgmental biases while forecasting. After all, a good percentage of new products do fail, particularly in the microcomputer industry, where competition is fierce. Clearly then, it cannot be automatically assumed that sales will increase in more than a straight line simply because a product is new. Yet this type of mistake is constantly made by people who are asked to predict the sales at Elco. Stereotypes are a good example of the consistent mistakes psychologists call biases. They are systematic errors (irrationalities) in our judgment that can produce mistakes (sometimes serious ones—think of the Shah) in the way we make decisions. Thus, it is imperative to know about them and to find effective ways of eliminating or reducing their negative impact.

The same data in Exhibit 2–1 were given to a group of product managers who were told it represented the past sales of a product belonging

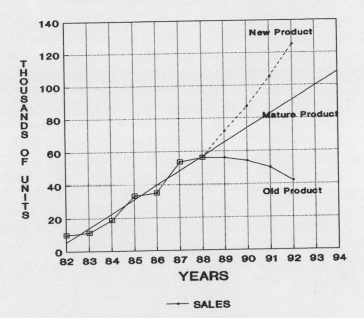

Exhibit 2–2 Forecasts When the People Were Told That the Product Was New, Mature, or Old

to their company. They extrapolated the figures to show an exponential *increase*. However, another group of product managers of the same company, provided with the same data but told that it related to a product belonging to their major competitor, forecast an exponential *decline*. Obviously, such differences in forecasting are caused by personal considerations, springing from optimism or wishful thinking, that have little or nothing to do with reality. However, forecasts influence future-oriented decisions—say, whether or not to build a new factory—and can have a substantial impact on the strategy adopted by a company and therefore on its future prosperity. That means it is absolutely vital to eliminate optimism and similar biases in order to come up with realistic forecasts. Stock market investors who overextend themselves and risk losing their life savings are another good example of the optimism bias.

In addition to biases related to stereotypes and those resulting from optimism or personal or political considerations, all respondents who saw Exhibit 2–1 considerably underestimated the uncertainty involved (the estimation of the interval between high and low forecasts). This was true in particular for 1993, at which time sales can be a great deal lower than the low interval and much higher than the high interval specified by the respondents. Many things can happen over five years, but respondents consistently underestimated future uncertainty regardless of their position

(MBA students, middle managers, top managers) or their background (MBAs, engineers, fine art students, or financial, marketing, or general managers). A realistic estimate (based on statistical theory) of the low and high sales value for 1989 is from 40,000 to 90,000 units. For 1993 the same figures are from 50,000 to 150,000 units. If, as product manager, you came close to those realistic intervals, you are exceptional; the vast majority of people estimate intervals less than half of those.

Thus, there is one thing we know with absolute certainty. We humans sometimes make foolish decisions not because we are stupid but because of the way our minds work. Worse, we rarely take corrective action to avoid making faulty decisions, because, unlike the well-known and accepted frailties of our memories, we are not sufficiently aware of the biases of our minds. Our logic supplies the rationale to explain or justify the irrationality of our decisions. My claim can be dismissed as alarmist, of course, or I can be cursed as the bearer of bad news. But shooting the messenger will not alter the overwhelming evidence in support of my claim. The implications must therefore be taken into consideration: Some decisions can be (rather, most likely are) biased. The best solution is to attempt to find ways of avoiding or minimizing their negative consequences.

Dealing with Judgmental Biases

The entire subject of judgmental biases could take one or more volumes to treat thoroughly.[4] Obviously, it cannot be covered here in great detail. I intend to be selective, discussing the aspects of judgmental biases that most critically and directly affect future-oriented decisions. I should emphasize that at the moment there is little direct knowledge of how judgmental biases apply to managerial decisions, nor has the best way of taking corrective actions been identified. Whatever I propose, therefore, comes from evidence in the area of cognitive or judgmental psychology and my own research work and experience with business organizations, managers, and MBA students.

Through the course of our lives, we all form beliefs and opinions. Everyone has his or her own ideas of what works and does not work and specific ways of doing things. Naturally, we cannot change our minds every five minutes about what does and does not work—that would make life impossible. Moreover, there is too much information around, so we have learned to be selective. Whenever some new information, such as the ideas in this chapter, is presented, we must decide whether we are going to believe it. Are we going to change our opinions, beliefs, and ways of doing things because of it?

In this chapter, and in most of this book, I provide what cognitive psychologists call disconfirming evidence, since it probably goes contrary to common opinions and beliefs. Strong empirical evidence shows that a book like this is less likely to be sought out and read. Furthermore, once it has been read, it is unlikely that the arguments will cause much changing of minds. On the contrary, people are more likely to select and read a book that supports their current opinions or beliefs and does not require changing their minds. Here is some concrete information about what I am describing: supportive and disconfirming evidence.

Wason, a cognitive psychologist, made it his life's goal to learn more about how people search for information and evidence.[5] He found that as much as 90 percent of all the information we are searching for aims at supporting views, beliefs, or hypotheses that we have long cherished. Thus, if a manager thinks that a certain promotional campaign will increase his sales he will look for supportive evidence to prove that that belief (or, more precisely, hypothesis) is correct. Unfortunately, however, it is practically impossible to prove the hypothesis that the promotional campaign is effective simply by observing that sales go up, for there are many factors other than promotions that can cause sales to rise. In this case, supportive evidence can *never* prove the hypothesis is right. That could be done by stopping the promotional campaign for a period of time, the equivalent of getting disconfirming evidence. If the sales then go down, the hypothesis can be proved to be right. If the campaign is stopped several times in several regions, and the outcome is always the same, it can then be ascertained with confidence that the decrease in sales is not due to chance but is influenced by the decrease in advertising. Although it might be impractical to stop promotions or advertising, from a scientific view it is the only way to prove, beyond any reasonable doubt, that the hypothesis that promotions increase sales is correct. People, however, do not look for disconfirming evidence.

Another problem associated with searching out and finding supportive evidence is that it increases confidence, which might be illusory. For many years I used to take vitamin C in the winter. I had read reports that it reduces the chances of catching a cold, and it did indeed seem to work. I was getting few if any colds. So I kept on taking it and every year became more convinced of its preventive qualities. Then I read Wason's studies and realized that my belief in the powers of vitamin C might be unjustified. There was an easy way to prove whether or not my confidence was justified: I could stop taking the vitamin for at least one winter.

I did so, and I continue to get few or no colds. The same holds true in almost all situations: Supportive evidence is of little or no help to prove a hypothesis, but it increases our confidence. Moreover, it is the kind of evidence we mostly search for.

There is another side to the picture. We tend to remember information that confirms our beliefs far better than information that disproves them. In experiments, believers have tended to remember confirming material with 100 percent accuracy, but negative material only about 40 percent of the time. Skeptics, on the other hand, have remembered both supportive and disconfirming evidence equally well—their accuracy was 90 percent in both cases. Thus, not only do we search for supportive evidence, but once we find it we tend to remember it more accurately. By contrast, we are more apt to forget negative evidence if we come across it sooner than supportive evidence. Consider the implications of these facts. If we believe something, we tend to search for information that proves our point of view. If we come across conflicting evidence, we are inclined to disregard it as irrelevant. Furthermore, our memories retain supportive evidence better than disconfirming evidence.

The higher up a manager is in the organization, the more the information he or she receives is filtered by several levels of subordinates, assistants, and secretaries. They know, or think they do, what the manager wants to hear and selectively present supportive information. No one in the Shah's immediate circle dared to tell him bad news, for it is well known that the bearers of bad news quickly fall from favor. Yet a fermenting revolution cannot be kept a secret—it is not something that can be organized in a backyard or from a small, faraway village. The informants of Savak and the CIA knew what was going on, and their information was passed to the first-level operatives of both organizations. But somehow this information was filtered on its way to the top and failed to reach the Shah, or if it did it was disregarded as nonsense. The same fate befell reports in the foreign press that talked about a grassroots revolution; such reports were dismissed as sensation-seeking propaganda. By the time disconfirming evidence was finally accepted it was too late. The revolution was unstoppable.

It is possible to minimize or avoid confirmation biases, that is, the search for and selective remembering of supportive evidence. It can be done by setting up procedures in an organization that encourage the search for disconfirming evidence. First of all, disconfirming, rather than supportive, evidence must be collected. It is not always a practical thing to do. For example, one cannot stop all advertising to find out whether or not sales will then go down. However, ways of getting around such problems can be devised. It would be possible, for instance, to stop all advertising selectively in a small geographical region not covered by nationwide TV stations. Similarly, the effectiveness of a certain department, or mode of operation, can be proved by abolishing it in a single region or a small country.

Disconfirming evidence must also be deliberately elicited in meetings or when new projects, ideas, or theories are considered. Encouraging someone to play the role of devil's advocate or always including people with opposing views in the same meeting are two examples. In other words, dissent must be encouraged rather than discouraged. When important decisions or projects are under consideration, it is possible even to go a step further. A manager can pretend that his choice is the opposite of what he really wants. If he can be convinced he is wrong, this would be the most effective and rational way of obtaining disconfirming evidence to prove that his belief or hypothesis is correct.

I do not underestimate the problems that might surface by encouraging people to play devil's advocate or by inviting to a meeting people who hold opposing views. Discontent might develop, the team spirit of the organization might suffer, and meetings will almost invariably take longer. Such problems should be anticipated and forestalled. Agreeing to disagree must be accepted as an organizational necessity that should not conflict with team spirit. Japanese companies are strong believers in encouraging varying points of view. Akio Morita, the president of Sony, made this point vividly in a dispute he had with Mr. Tajima, Sony's chairman of the board:

> Sir, if you and I had exactly the same ideas on all subjects, it would not be necessary for both of us to be in this company and receive a salary. Either you or I should resign in that case. It is precisely because you and I have different ideas that this company will run a smaller risk of making mistakes.[6]

In fact, our search for supportive evidence is not unreasonable in view of the sheer volume of information with which we are bombarded daily, much of it representing a wide variety of views and evidence, often conflicting. If we were to try and process all of it, our minds would suffer from information overload. Moreover, if we tried to change our minds every time some new evidence indicated that our beliefs were wrong, we would then suffer from severe inconsistency. And that evidence could be faulty or slanted to serve the political or personal purposes of whoever presented it. It is to protect ourselves from dangers like information overload and inconsistent behavior that our minds have developed such habits as the search for supportive evidence. As with memory flexibility, our minds must be simultaneously consistent and able to change if real reasons exist. However, they cannot be consistent and adaptable without making sacrifices, which sometimes results in inconsistencies or an inability to process disconfirming evidence and modify long-held and cherished beliefs.

Inconsistency is another human bias with serious negative consequences. It happens when we change our minds (or decisions) when there is no need to do so. Consider, for instance, a production manager who must decide how much to manufacture for each of ten products in the coming month. Bowman, back in the 1950s, found that production managers' decisions about how much to produce fluctuated from month to month for no apparently good reason, and that making their decisions consistent improved profitability.[7] Bowman's findings have been reproduced in a great number of studies. The conclusion is always the same. Repetitive, routine decisions can be improved if inconsistency is removed. People are often unable or unwilling to apply the same criteria or procedures when making similar decisions. Sometimes they forget; other times they are influenced by their mood of the day (think of a decision made the morning after a quarrel with one's wife and a sleepless night); still other times they might be bored and want to try something new; finally, they might believe that conditions have changed when they actually have not.

Production managers are not the only ones whose decisions are inconsistent. Meehl, in a small but influential book, concluded that decision rules using a few variables to predict do better than people, mostly because the models can consistently apply the same variables and decision criteria, while people are inconsistent in their choice of variables on which to base their decisions and in the criteria they employ.[8]

Meehl's conclusions have been confirmed by hundreds of additional studies. Decision rules in the form of simple statistical models have been found to outperform expert judges when repetitive, routine decisions were involved. These decisions included medical diagnosis, psychological predictions about people's personality traits, selection of students to be admitted to colleges or universities, predicting future earnings of companies, and so forth. There is hardly any evidence showing that expert decision-makers do better than decision rules. Obviously, these studies refer to repetitive, routine decisions, but even then their conclusions are surprising, as in the case of medical diagnosis. Garland, for instance, reported a study in which experienced X-ray specialists, when examining X-rays, failed to recognize the presence of lung disease that was definitely visible on the X-ray film about 30 percent of the time.[9] Similarly, studies found that radiologists changed their minds about 20 percent of the time *when given the same X-ray on two different occasions.*

Inconsistency can be avoided by formalizing the decision-making process (in our day it is called building expert systems). This would require deciding first what factors are important to consider in making a certain repetitive decision; second, how such factors should be weighted (one might be twice as important as another); and third, what objective should be optimized. The usefulness of decision rules derives from the fact that several people can get involved in determining them, thus making it possible to select the best factors, an optimal weighting scheme, and a viable objective. Since the rule will be used again and again, it makes sense to devote effort and resources to come up with the best one possible. The rule can subsequently be applied on a routine basis, freeing considerable human resources. Consider, for instance, when credit officers decide on a case-by-case basis whether or not a purchase by an American Express cardholder should be approved. This takes numerous credit officers and becomes an expensive operation. Now consider finding all important factors that are used by credit officers to decide whether or not to approve a credit request. Since many such officers can be consulted and a great deal of effort can be devoted to the process, the most relevant factors can be found and included in a statistical model, which would determine if such factors are indeed important and how much weight should be given to each. A decision rule will thus be established, allowing a clerk to enter the required information and let the model reach a decision. Credit officers would be consulted only in the exceptional case where the model indicates a gray area and cannot decide. Fewer officers are required, and decisions will be consistent (based on the decision rule accepted) and objective. Given today's computer technology and telecommunications capabilities, decision models of the type just described can be economically developed and profitably applied on a routine basis. American Express has indeed applied one such decision-making model (called an expert system) and has reported considerable improvements in efficiency and profits.

Obviously, decision rules cannot be used indefinitely. The environment changes, as does competition, new objectives might be set, and so on. Thus, it becomes important to monitor the effectiveness of the decision rules constantly to make sure they are still appropriate. That means learning must be introduced; otherwise, we run the risk of applying obsolete rules. Too much consistency can be as dangerous as inconsistency, for it excludes learning and leads to another bias, conservatism.

Exhibit 2-3 Common Biases in Future-Oriented Decisions and Proposed Ways of Avoiding or Reducing Their Negative Impact

Type of Bias	Description of Bias	Ways of Avoiding or Reducing the Negative Impact of Bias
Search for supportive evidence	Willingness to gather facts which lead toward certain conclusions and to disregard other facts which threaten them	• Induce disconfirming evidence • Introduce role of devil's advocate
Inconsistency	Inability to apply the same decision criteria in similar situations	• Formalize the decision making process • Create decision making rules to be followed
Conservatism	Failure to change (or changing slowly) one's own mind in light of new information/evidence	• Monitor for changes in the environment and build procedures to take actions when such changes are identified
Recency	The most recent events dominate those in the less recent past, which are downgraded or ignored	• Realize that cycles exist and that not all ups or downs are permanent • Consider the fundamental factors that affect the event of interest
Availability	Reliance upon specific events easily recalled from memory, to the exclusion of other pertinent information	• Present complete information • Present information in a way that points out all sides of the situation being considered
Anchoring	Predictions are unduly influenced by initial information which is given more weight in the forecasting process	• Start with objective information (e.g., forecasts) • Ask people to discuss the types of changes that are possible; also ask the reasons when changes are being proposed
Illusory correlations	Belief that patterns are evident and/or two variables are causally related when they are not	• Verify statistical significance of patterns • Model relationships, if possible, in terms of changes

Selective perception Regression effects	People tend to see problems in terms of their own background and experience Persistent increases might be due to random reasons which, if true, would increase the chance of a decrease. Alternatively, persistent decreases might increase the chances of increases	• Ask people with different backgrounds and experience to independently suggest solutions • Explain that when errors are random the chances of a negative error increases when several positive ones have occured
Attribution of success and failure	Success is attributed to one's skills while failure to bad luck, or someone else's error. This inhibits learning as it does not allow recognition of one's mistakes	• Do not punish mistakes, instead encourage people to accept their mistakes and make them public so they and others can learn to avoid similar mistakes in the future. (This is how Japanese companies deal with mistakes)
Optimism, wishful thinking	People's preferences for future outcomes affect their forecasts of such outcomes	• Have the forecasts made by a disinterested third party • Have more than one person independently make the forecasts
Underestimating uncertainty	Excessive optimism, illusory correlation, and the need to reduce anxiety result in underestimating future uncertainty	• Estimate uncertainty objectively. Consider many possible future events by asking different people to come up with unpredictable situations/events

This is the problem with biases—in trying to avoid one we might cultivate another. A bias in this case exists precisely because our minds must ensure consistency, but must also allow for learning. The challenge facing all of us, therefore, is to be consistent while at the same time introducing mechanisms to ensure learning and eventually changes in the decision rules to adapt to new conditions.

Can biases be avoided if decisions are made in groups? Unfortunately not—in fact there is evidence suggesting that groups amplify bias by introducing groupthink (a phenomenon that develops when group members become supportive of their leader and each other, thus avoiding conflict and dissent during their meetings).[10] Moreover, group decisions are more risky, as responsibility for the decisions taken cannot be attributed to any single individual.

Exhibit 2–3 describes those biases I have found (through my experience of working with companies and my research work) to be of critical importance for forecasting and future-oriented decision-making. It also provides suggestions to help prevent or mitigate their impact. A prominent example of one such bias, recency (remembering more vividly recent events, which consequently influence our judgment to a greater extent than less recent events), concerns oil prices between 1965 and 1988. During that period basic economic facts were ignored and many mistakes were made because of the recency bias, as organizations and governments overreacted to the latest price levels and made decisions assuming that such prices (or the trends involved) were going to last forever.

CONVENTIONAL WISDOM

Another type of judgmental bias that can threaten the effectiveness of decision-making is that of unfounded beliefs or conventional wisdom. We have grown up in a culture where we accept certain statements as true, though they may not be. For instance, we believe that the more information we have, the more accurate our decisions will be. Empirical evidence does not support such a belief. Instead, more information merely seems to increase our confidence that we are right without necessarily improving the accuracy of our decisions (see "Confidence and Accuracy" exercise at the end of this chapter). This is a finding reached by Oskamp[11] and many other researchers, who warn against devoting energy and resources to gathering a lot of information. In reality, the information found is usually redundant and provides little additional value.

Another example of conventional wisdom we are willing to accept is that we are capable of discriminating between useful and irrelevant information. Empirical research indicates that this is rarely the case. In experiments, subjects supplied with "good" and "bad" information are not capable of distinguishing between the two. In addition, the irrelevant information is often used, decreasing the effectiveness of decision-making (see exercise b at the end of this chapter).

Exhibit 2–4 summarizes relevant conventional wisdom, including the two examples already offered. It also lists the new evidence available through empirical and laboratory studies. As with the biases discussed, the conventional wisdom listed in Exhibit 2–4 can greatly influence our decisions. It is important to avoid the negative consequences by establishing procedures aimed at minimizing their impact through the use of empirical findings listed in Exhibit 2–4.

THE PARADOXES

1. The human mind is a superb organ of infinite complexity and exquisite value, yet it can produce "stupid," biased decisions.
2. Conventional wisdom, which we accept as true and use to guide our decisions, may decrease the value or accuracy of our decisions.

CONCLUSIONS

No one has yet discovered a method of changing the way the human mind works. Thus we must accept its biases in the same spirit as we accept its other limitations or the limitations of memory. The challenge for everyone, as human beings, and specifically for managers, is to find effective ways of avoiding or minimizing the impact of biases. In some instances it might even be possible to use them to advantage. Objective information (forecasts from statistical models, for example, or the outcome of decisions made with formal decision rules) can be given at the beginning of budget meetings to "anchor" the discussion, that is, to keep it focused on objective data.

If a manager accepts the human biases I have described in this chapter, he cannot assume rationality from his subordinates, superiors, or competitors. This complicates matters considerably, as all economic theories and the vast majority of managerial ones assume cold rationality. How,

Exhibit 2–4 Conventional Wisdom Versus Empirical Findings

Conventional Wisdom	Empirical Findings
1. The more information we have, the more accurate the decision.	The amount of information does not improve the accuracy of decisions, instead it increases our confidence that our decision will be correct.
2. We can distinguish between useful and irrelevant information.	Irrelevant information can be the cause of reducing the accuracy of our decisions.
3. The more confident we are about the correctness of our decision the more accurate our decision will be.	There is *no* relationship between how confident one is and how accurate his or her decision is.
4. We can decide rationally when it is time to quit.	We feel we have invested too much to quit, although the investment is a sunk cost.
5. Monetary rewards and punishments contribute to better performance.	Human behavior is too complex to be motivated by monetary factors only.
6. We can assess our chances of succeeding or failing reasonably well.	We are overly optimistic and tend to downgrade or ignore problems and difficulties.
7. Experience and/or expertise improve accuracy of decisions.	In many repetitive, routine decisions, experience and/or expertise do *not* contribute more value to future-oriented decisions.
8. We really know what we want, and our preferences are stable.	Slight differences in a situation can change our preferences (most people, for instance, prefer a half-full to a half-empty glass of water).

for instance, does a manager deal with a competitor who is driven by irrational motives? He cannot understand them or predict how they will influence the competitor's decisions. There is no way of doing so, since irrationality cannot be predicted. Thus, another challenge facing managers is to accept the possibility of irrationality and attempt to rationalize it. That is probably the hardest of all challenges a manager must face. Worse, the lack of rationality is not limited to competitors only but exists everywhere. Jealousy, excessive ambition, fighting for no apparent reason, breakdowns in communication, and similar irrational behavior abound in any organization and must be dealt with in a sensible manner in order to neutralize or reduce their negative effects as far as is possible.

The challenge is considerable, but it is one that must be confronted. We must move forward, although we know the road will not always be smooth.

THE CHALLENGES AHEAD

1. Keep making decisions while accepting that such decisions might be biased.
2. Understand judgmental biases and attempt to avoid or minimize their negative impact for both managers and the organization.
3. Dealing with biases is like being between a rock and a hard place, since avoiding one bias (e.g., inconsistency) can lead to another (e.g., conservatism).
4. As biases and their influence on managerial decision-making are not fully understood, it might be necessary to devote time and resources to developing ways to deal with them more effectively.

JUDGMENTAL EXERCISES

This section provides four exercises that can help better understand judgmental biases and verify their widespread existence. By using these exercises with friends or employees, a manager can be persuaded that the statements made in this chapter concerning judgmental biases are correct. I have been using these exercises (together with many others not included in this section) for more than ten years with MBA students, with executives at INSEAD's permanent education programs, and in company seminars. They have rarely failed to show the bias they intend to illustrate (except sometimes when given to small groups). Try them. It is the best way to recognize the extent and importance of judgmental biases and their widespread existence. To use these exercises, give version 1 to half of the people in the group and version 2 to the other half (do not mark them as version 1 or 2). Then compare the results, which are different, although they should not be.

THE ANCHORING BIAS

Version 1

AFRICAN NATIONS

What is the percentage of countries in the U.N. that are African? To make your estimate, I would suggest that you start with a value of 10 percent (this percentage was found in the computer by generating a random number between 0 and 100). First decide whether this value is too high or too low—then move upward or downward from that value to what you feel is the true value.

Your final estimate as to the true percentage of African nations in the U.N. is:

☐

Version 2

AFRICAN NATIONS

What is the percentage of countries in the U.N. that are African? To make your estimate, I would suggest that you start with a value of 65 percent (this percentage was found in the computer by generating a random number between 0 and 100). First decide whether this value is too high or too low—then move upward or downward from that value to what you feel is the true value.

Your final estimate as to the true percentage of African nations in the U.N. is:

☐

The difference between versions 1 and 2 is minimal. Version 1 says to start the estimate at 10 percent. In order to make sure that this number will not influence the answer, it is clearly stated that this 10 percent was generated randomly. Version 2 gives 65 percent as the starting number. Although the starting values of 10 percent and 65 percent should *not* have any influence on the final answer, they do. People to whom version 1 is given answer, on the average, that the percentage of African countries in the U.N. is 25%. On average those with version 2 answer 45 percent. The difference between 25 and 45 percent is highly significant and proves an *anchoring* effect (bias); that is, our judgment is influenced (anchored) by the 10 or 65 percent and cannot (because of this bias) move far away from such starting values. If the anchoring bias did not exist there should have been no difference between the answers given in versions 1 and 2, since from a rational point of view the starting values of 10 and 65 percent should have absolutely no influence on the answer (the reader is told they were generated randomly).

THE VALUE OF EXTRA INFORMATION
Version 1

ENGINEERS AND LAWYERS

A psychological test was administered to a group of 100 people. The group consisted of thirty engineers and seventy lawyers. If you had to place a bet on whether a participant in the test named Peter Jones was an engineer or a lawyer, what would you say?

Peter Jones is an engineer ☐

Peter Jones is a lawyer ☐

Please check the appropriate box.
Version 2

ENGINEERS AND LAWYERS

A psychological test was administered to a group of 100 people. The group consisted of thirty engineers and seventy lawyers. The following descriptions were obtained for Peter Jones.

Peter Jones is of high intelligence and exhibits a strong drive for competence. He has a need for order and clarity and for neat and tidy systems in which every detail finds its appropriate place. His writing is enlivened by somewhat corny puns and by flashes of imagination. He seems to have little feel and little sympathy for other people and does not enjoy interacting with others. Self-centered, he nonetheless has a deep moral sense.

If you had to place a bet on whether a participant in the test named Peter Jones was an engineer or a lawyer, what would you say?

Peter Jones is an engineer   ☐

Peter Jones is a lawyer   ☐

Please check the appropriate box.

In version 1 the answer should be a lawyer. Since there are seventy lawyers and only thirty engineers and no other information is available, it is obvious that one has to bet that the person chosen is a lawyer. The vast majority of answers do indeed say that Peter Jones is a lawyer. In version 2 some additional information about Peter Jones is given. This is supposedly a description of him, but it says absolutely nothing. However, people read traits of lawyers or engineers into this description (depending upon their stereotypes of lawyers and engineers) and answer the question based on such traits. In version 2, on the average 50 percent say that Peter Jones is a lawyer and 50 percent say he is an engineer. Thus the good information (70 percent lawyers and 30 percent engineers) is ignored and instead the irrelevant information (the useless description) is used and influences the answer.

As you read this you might think that my explanation is not correct because you are sure that the description of Peter Jones clearly indicates he is a lawyer (or engineer). Give it to some other people to read. You will see that half of them will think the opposite and will say you are wrong, as they will be convinced (like you) that Peter Jones is obviously an engineer (or lawyer).

THE CONSISTENCE OF OUR PREFERENCES
Version 1
You are the chief executive officer of a company faced with a difficult choice. Because of worsening economic conditions, 600

people will have to be fired to reduce payroll costs and avoid serious problems. Two alternative programs to combat the firings have been proposed to you. The estimates of the consequences of the programs are as follows:

- If program A is adopted, *200 jobs will be saved.*
- If program B is adopted, there is a two-thirds probability that *no jobs will be saved* and a one-third probability that 600 jobs will be saved.

Which of the two research and development projects would you select?

A ☐

B ☐

Please mark the appropriate box.

Version 2

You are the chief executive officer of a company faced with a difficult choice. Because of worsening economic conditions, 600 people will have to be fired to reduce payroll costs and avoid serious problems. Two alternative programs to combat the firings have been proposed to you. The estimates of the consequences of the programs are as follows:

- If program A is adopted, *400 people will be fired.*
- If program B is adopted, there is a one-third probability that *nobody will be fired,* and a two-thirds probability that 600 will be fired.

Which of the two research and development projects would you select?

A ☐

B ☐

Versions 1 and 2 are slightly different. In version 1 the preferences are expressed in terms of gains (200 jobs will be saved), in version

2 in terms of losses (400 people will be fired). The differences in people's preferences are considerable. Of those answering version 1, two-thirds prefer Project A and one-third Project B. In version 2 the preferences are reversed: one-third prefer A and two-thirds prefer B. Thus, a slight change in the formulation of the problem produces a substantial switch in people's preferences, showing that our preferences are not as well founded and stable as we might think.

CONFIDENCE AND ACCURACY

Version 1

FINISHED FILES ARE THE RESULT OF YEARS OF SCIENTIFIC STUDY COMBINED WITH THE EXPERIENCE OF YEARS

(Please do not read the above sentence again)

Please indicate the number of F's which appear in the above sentence.

How confident are you of your above answer? Indicate your confidence on a scale from 0 to 100 with 0 indicating no confidence and 100 indicating full confidence.

Version 2

FINISHED FILES ARE THE RESULT OF YEARS OF SCIENTIFIC STUDY COMBINED WITH THE EXPERIENCE OF YEARS

Please indicate the number of F's which appear in the above sentence.

How confident are you of your above answer? Indicate your confidence on a scale from 0 to 100 with 0 indicating no confidence and 100 indicating full confidence.

How many times did you read the sentence "FINISHED FILES . . . . . . OF YEARS"?

People who receive version 1 are told to read the sentence only once. Exhibit 2–5 shows some representative answers. From those answers it becomes clear that there is no correlation between confidence and accuracy (there are six F's). People who were 100 percent confident gave the wrong answer and people with little confidence guessed the number of F's correctly.

In version 2 people were not told to read the sentence only once. A question was put asking "How many times did you read the sentence "FINISHED . . . . . OF YEARS?"". Exhibit 2–6 shows some typical answers. Interestingly, the answers of people who read version 2 are not more accurate than those who had version 1. There is, however, a phenomenal increase in confidence. Those who had version 2 are mostly 100 percent confident that they found the right answer, although in reality they were not more accurate than those who read the sentence only once. Also, there is no correlation, as with those who answer version 1, between confidence in being accurate and correctness of one's answer. Disturbing, isn't it? How can you be sure someone is right? The evidence from this and many other studies indicates that timid people are as likely to be right as those who claim to be sure.

Exhibit 2–5. Answers of 550 MBAs and Executives on the Number of F's in the Sentence When It Was Read Only Once (Version 1)

Percentage Confidence in Answer	Number of F's indicated in answer								
	1	*2*	*3*	*4*	*5*	*6*	*7*	*8*	*TOTAL*
100		6	19	15	15	6			61
99		3	6	3	3	3			18
95–98		3		9	6	6			24
90–94			3		9	12	3		27
85–89			6	3	6	9			24
80–84		18	6	3	9	9	3		48
75–79		6	12	12	6	12			48
70–74		3	6	12	6	6			33
60–69		6	6	3	12	6	3		36
50–59		27	12	24	21	6		3	93
40–49	3	12	3	3	6				27
30–39		3	24	3	12				42
20–29			3	9	6	3			21
10–19		6	12	9	12	6			45
0–9							3		3
TOTAL	3	93	118	108	129	84	12	3	550

Exhibit 2–6. Answers of 552 MBAs and Executives on the Number of F's in the Sentence When It Was Read More than Once (Version 2)

Percentage Confidence in Answer	Number of F's indicated in answer								
	1	*2*	*3*	*4*	*5*	*6*	*7*	*8*	*TOTAL*
100		18	120	57	51	60	3		309
99		3	24	9	9	9			54
95–98		3	9	12	6	9		3	42
90–94			6	3	12	12			33
85–89			6	6	3	6			21
80–84			18	6	6	9			36
75–79			12	3		6			21
70–74			3		3	3			9
60–69			3		6	9			18
50–59			3			6			9
TOTAL		24	198	99	96	129	3	3	552

3

Predicting the Future: Myths and Reality

---

*T*he future isn't what it used to be.

ANONYMOUS

Human fascination with the future can be traced back to prehistoric times. People have always wanted to predict the future for psychological reasons (to reduce their fear and anxiety about the unknown). Concrete evidence shows that the human desire to foresee the future has been exploited by some for profit, fame, or power. There is a scientific basis to forecasting; but there are also serious limitations on our ability to predict future events and situations. This chapter shows how you can be convinced about someone's alleged abilities to predict the future and how it is necessary to avoid being misled into believing in prophecies. It becomes important to know precisely what can and cannot be predicted, and the advantages as well as the limitations of forecasting.

The temple of Delphi is in the middle of the Parnassus mountain range, on the southern part of the Greek mainland. The view from it is awe-inspiring; excellent visibility allows one to see a good part of the Gulf of Corinth and the northern Peloponnesus. The blue of the sky and the sea are perfectly blended with the green mountains to provide a unique, breathtaking image, difficult to forget. In such a setting the priests of Delphi operated the first institutionalized forecasting service.

To reach the temple required a long and tiring mountain climb, but the hospitable priests gave their guests a warm welcome. Good food and plentiful wine were made available to the exhausted travelers, who, while

49

eating and drinking, were encouraged to talk about themselves and about their needs, desires, and expectations.

The temple of Delphi became the richest institution in ancient Greece. Its power of prophecy was believed in by everyone, because it was attributed to Apollo, god of the Sun, who could see and therefore foretell the future for all those who could afford the services of his oracle. The oracle, or sibyl, gave her predictions in such a way as to make their invalidation difficult. Those seeking advice were often told what they were expecting to hear. If that was not possible, the prophecies were equivocal; their wording was obscure, they were general or they were impossible to check against reality.

EXAMPLES OF DELPHI PROPHECIES

1. *Telling what one wants to hear:* I do not know if you are a god or a human, but I see more of a god in you.
2. *Double meaning or conditional wording:* If you cross the river a great army will be destroyed (whose army is left unsaid).
3. *Obscure or general wording:* If you return to Athens you will gain the benefit of the law (but laws can condemn someone to death too).
4. *Cannot be checked against reality:* Sophocles is wise, Euripides is wiser; but Socrates is the wisest.

Delphi was not the only place selling prophecies. Since the dawn of civilization priests, astrologers, prophets, fortune tellers, and the like have sought to satisfy the human need to predict the future. The temple of Delphi became the best known and most successful of all because of the uncanny shrewdness of the priests who ran it. They were full-time employees, the first professional forecasters, who had an obvious interest in making people believe that their oracle could foretell the future. Their livelihood and prosperity depended on that accomplishment. Judging from the unquestioned acceptance of their prophecies, the richness of their holdings, and their lasting influence—more than 500 years—we must conclude that theirs was a success story, although nobody would doubt today that the predictive power of their prophecies was zero. Are things any different at present?

EXAMPLES OF PRESENT-DAY PROPHECIES SIMILAR TO THOSE
OF DELPHI

1. *Foretelling what we want to hear:* The Dow-Jones industrial average will hit the 3,500 mark by the middle of next year.
2. *Double meaning or conditional wording:* All evidence indicates that a great depression is in the making, and unless immediate remedial action is taken, the results will be catastrophic.
3. *Obscure or general wording:* To the uninitiated, markets can often seem perverse. But recent weeks have added a bizarre new twist. The faster the U.S. economy expands, the more anxiously Wall Street seems to worry that it will contract.
4. *Cannot be checked against reality:* Unless pollution is stopped, carbon dioxide will increase the earth's temperature resulting in the melting of the polar ice in 30,000 years.

Today forecasting is a multibillion dollar industry. All economic publications devote considerable space to economic forecasts; political writers hold forth on political trends and forthcoming government policies; stockbrokers and financial gurus foretell stock market trends, when to buy, and what stocks to select; and many others prophesy on such diverse topics as when the next ice age will come (or alternatively the melting of the polar ice), how to cope with the inevitable great depression of the 1990s, what to do when a barrel of oil costs $100 in 1995, or how to survive after a nuclear World War III. Unfortunately, many people believe such forecasts, prolonging the myth that somehow prophecies are possible. Even worse, there are people who seriously believe they possess divine powers enabling them to predict the future. Worst of all, reputable publishing houses and widely read business journals publish such forecasts, perpetuating the expectation and the myth that they can be usefully implemented to improve future-oriented decisions.

In the next section I shall show that even today superstitious beliefs about the future abound. The empirical evidence proves beyond any reasonable doubt that no one can consistently predict the future more accurately than his or her colleagues. Yet there are eminent forecasters and famous gurus who pretend to be capable of foreseeing the future.

STOCK MARKET FORECASTS:
THE MODERN VERSION OF DELPHI

Stock market investing is an important activity in our day. One can become rich if the right stocks are bought or can lose huge sums through the wrong choices. Today there are about 800 newsletters offering stock-picking advice. Every general financial publication offers daily advice about the stock market and individual stocks. *Value Line* analyzes all listed stocks and evaluates their performance; every major brokerage house employs its own gurus, and even small brokerage firms have at least one forecaster on their payrolls. All this generates a huge volume of stock market forecasts. Millions of people read them—some paying steep subscription fees to receive stock market newsletters—and act upon their advice. Obviously, a lot of the issuers of stock market forecasts become rich in the process, and the livelihood of many others depends upon their predictions. Yet the value of all these forecasts is zero. This sounds like Delphi, doesn't it? Is it possible that mass deception still exists in our day? I believe it does, and I propose to explain why.

THE RANDOM WALK THEORY

In 1965 Paul Fama of the University of Chicago published an influential paper in which he proved, using theoretical reasoning and empirical evidence, that predicting changes in stock market prices (increases or decreases from ''today's'' value), either as a whole or for any individual stock, could not be done any better than by using ''today's'' price (taking the closing stock prices reported on the financial pages of newspapers) as the forecast. This means it is impossible for investors to profit from so-called accurate forecasts of which stock prices will go up or down. Indeed, nobody can do so without inside knowledge, which cannot be used legally. Then why are there 800 newsletters and daily newspaper reports, and why are there stock market gurus? Obviously, their existence makes no sense from a rational point of view. Both the theoretical *and* the empirical evidence are indisputable: No one can predict stock market prices more accurately than by using ''today's'' price. Yet the overwhelming majority of investors (both individuals and institutions) still prefer a stock analyst or a professional manager to take care of their money. By sheer luck, some analysts or managers might do better than a market average for a certain period of time, but all evidence suggests that *consistent* above-average performance is virtually impossible. Thus, for example, you could hang the *Wall Street Journal* listing of NYSE stocks on the wall, throw ten darts to choose ten stocks, and your portfolio, on the average, will perform no worse than one selected by an expert. However, few people feel comfortable with such a random selection when investing their life savings.

The random walk (changes in stock prices are random, hence unpredictable) is a highly accurate predictive theory. If you read *Business Week, The Economist, Forbes,* and similar periodicals, you can find ample evidence of its accurate predictive value. What surprises me is that virtually all executives in the courses I teach are *not* aware of this evidence, although they also read *Business Week, The Economist, Forbes,* and the rest. So let me summarize some of the evidence.

If stock market experts could forecast better than you, I, or anybody selecting stocks at random, professionally managed portfolios and mutual funds would perform better than the market average. That is not true and has rarely been true since such comparisons were started in the late 1920s.[1]

Here are some recent statistics concerning average returns on stocks, collected from various 1987 *Business Week* issues:

	1986	Last Three Years	Last Five Years
Professionally managed funds	21.2%	25.6%	25.0%
Mutual funds	19.0%	22.7%	22.8%
Index funds (portfolios selected randomly)	26.1%	27.2%	26.6%
Average of S&P—500 stocks	26.1%	27.2%	26.6%

The same results can be found in average returns on money invested in bonds. Managed bond funds do *not* outperform the market average. Here are some recent statistics:

	1986	Last Three Years	Last Five Years
Index Bond Funds (bonds selected randomly)	5.6%	18%	16.8%
Managed Bond Funds	5.8%	17.1%	16.4%

One could say that the above comparisons are not fair because they include all professionally managed funds and all mutual funds. It might be true that some experts do better than the rest. *Forbes* regularly asks ten experts to recommend their favorite stock. The most recent available results when this chapter was written show that the ten stocks selected by the experts lost an average of 22 percent, against the market's overall loss of 4 percent.

The above evidence demonstrates the random walk theory. Random selection of stocks or bonds (which indicates average performance) outperforms selection by expert forecasters. The important question is whether or not John Q. Investor believes this evidence and will act upon it.

In the first chapter I recommended being a skeptic, which in this case necessitates a search for additional evidence. Paying careful attention to stock market and bond comparisons when reading financial publications clearly reveals that Delphi-type forecasts abound even in our day. Individuals and companies can save millions in fees by not using them.[2]

If the random walk is valid, how do some people get rich by playing the market? Some people also get rich by playing in casinos. Does that mean they can correctly predict the winning numbers? If there are millions of people playing the market, it is inevitable that some will make lucky choices. In 1966 the publishers of *Forbes* magazine selected twenty stocks by throwing darts at the stock market page of that day's *Wall Street Journal*. Fifteen years later their randomly selected portfolio had risen 239 percent, while the S&P 500 was up only 35 percent. Luck is possible even in random selections.

If someone places a bet on a roulette number, his or her chance of winning is one out of thirty-seven. Since a lot of people play, some will win. Suppose a winner puts all he or she won on another number. He or she will lose 36 out of 37 times, but since there are many people playing, someone will inevitably win twice in a row (the chances are that one person out of 1,369 will). But since large numbers of people play, someone can win three times in a row (the chances are that one out of 50,653 people will do so). Thus, depending on the upper limit permitted on a single number, he or she can become a millionaire. No skills are involved, just plain good luck.

Luck plays strange tricks. Robert E. Humphries, a truck driver, won two Pennsylvania lottery jackpots in a period of less than two years, which brought him net annual earnings of more than $250,000 for life. He spent only $45 a week on the game. Was Mr. Humphries skillful in picking the winning ticket? Although the chance of winning two jackpots in such a short time is more than one in a billion, someone is bound to win, since extremely large numbers of people buy lottery tickets. Again, no skills are involved, just plain good luck.

Does the fact that stock market predictions are of little value mean that forecasting is useless? The answer is a categorical no. Forecasts are useful in a wide range of applications. However, it is important to know why forecasts are needed and when they can be used to gain concrete benefits, or at least to understand the uses, advantages, and limitations of forecasting.

WHY ARE FORECASTS NEEDED?

Forecasts are made with a purpose and an audience in mind. There are three principal uses of forecasting:

1. *Satisfying Curiosity*. Some forecasts aim to satisfy simple curiosity. Horoscopes, astrology, and fortune-telling fall into this category. So do science fiction and the vast majority of forecasts whose purpose is to describe distant future worlds and what they might be like. Writings about interplanetary travel, intelligent robots, and brand new energy sources fall into this category. For managers, such types of forecasts provide little of direct value. However, if superstitious beliefs can be separated from objective, rational projections, there might be some indirect value, because such forecasts might help see the future in a clearer way. Managers could better anticipate the future by establishing long-term visions and formulating general strategic directions that could help their organizations change in order to cope better with what is ahead. But nothing is certain; no one can be sure whether, and most importantly *when,* the forecasts will become reality.

2. *Improving Decision-Making*. Some forecasts aim at improving the value of decision-making. Stock market predictions, the start and beginning of the next recession, the number of cars to be sold in the last quarter of next year, and the party that will win the next election are forecasts whose accuracy can benefit or, should they be wrong, damage the person or organization using them as a basis for decisions. In the introduction, I talked about suicides and murders directly related to false expectations (forecasts) about the stock market. Forecasts in this category are not neutral. They can be harmful as well as beneficial, and great care must be taken while using them. It is therefore necessary to know how accurate they are. In addition to being accurate, forecasts must also be reliable. A forecaster might be accurate 90 percent of the time but the remaining 10 percent might produce disastrous results. Knowing the degree of uncertainty associated with the forecasts can be as critical a factor as accuracy itself when the objective is to use the forecasts to improve future-oriented decision-making. Many forecasts are as inaccurate and unreliable as those of fortune tellers, but most decisions require forecasts whose accuracy and reliability or uncertainty must be assessed correctly.

3. *Generating Consensus.* The last category of forecasts aims at generating consensus, an important and useful forecasting function little talked about, little understood, and even less exploited. The politicians in ancient Greece used the oracle of Delphi as their main vehicle to achieve consensus. If the god had said something, it was difficult for mortals to argue against it. Obviously no divine power can be called upon today to certify forecasts. Nevertheless, forecasting can play an important role in generating consensus among top management concerning desired ways in which to move the organization. Scenarios and long-range forecasts fall into this category.

Each of the three types of forecasts described above is made using different procedures, aims at satisfying different needs, and requires different criteria for evaluation.

THE SCIENTIFIC BASIS OF FORECASTING

Although some animals (like bees and ants) do possess some concept of the future, humans are unique in their ability to comprehend and plan for a wide range of future events. Humans can predict the future by observing regularities (patterns) in certain phenomena (the daily sunrise or the seasons) or causal relationships (cultivating seeds and growing crops, or intercourse and pregnancy). A prerequisite of any form of forecasting, whether judgmental or statistical, is that a pattern or relationship exists concerning the event of interest. If such a pattern or relationship does exist and can be correctly identified, it can subsequently be projected in order to forecast.

Consider the forecast of how long it takes to get to work after leaving home. Years of experience lend accuracy to such predictions. Some days, or during certain hours, it takes longer. On days when it is raining heavily the commuting time becomes longer, but not as long as it is during snowstorms, when it might take double the usual time. Those patterns (time of daily commuting) or relationships (rain increases commuting time, snow even more) exist in the commuter's head and help him judge approximately how long it will take to get to work on different days of the week, at different times of the day, or in various weather conditions.

Scientific forecasting uses exactly the same principles as those in the commuter's mind, but it does so with more precision and more objectivity. Scientific forecasting uses quantitative data to measure exactly how long it will take to go from home to work. It would require a stopwatch set upon leaving home and stopped on arrival at the office. It would also demand a record of the day of the week, the time of departure, the amount of rainfall, the amount of snowfall, if it is cloudy or sunny, and whatever other factors the commuter himself or an expert might consider important. A statistical (mathematical) model is then employed to identify the important factors influencing daily commuting time and to measure the extent of such influences. Once determined and measured, these factors (variables) can be used to forecast the commuting time for each day of the week, according to the specific time of departure and the weather conditions. The more data (daily observations) included, the more reliable the forecast will usually be.

All forms of scientific forecasting use precisely such a procedure. First, data are found or collected; second, a statistical model is selected; third, the patterns and relationships involved are identified and precisely measured; fourth, forecasts are made by projecting the patterns and relationships identified and measured; finally, the uncertainty of the forecasts can be estimated (for example, an accident blocking the highway can make commuter time longer than average) and used to reduce the negative consequences of unexpected events.

In many areas of the natural sciences or physics, forecasting accuracy is perfect for all practical purposes. Thus, the exact timing of the sunrise tomorrow or a year from now can be predicted to the thousandth of a second. Similarly, one can also predict that water will form if two atoms of hydrogen and one of oxygen are put together. However, such success does not extend to all areas of natural and physical sciences. Predictability in the social sciences, and notably in the economic and business fields, is much more difficult than in the natural sciences.

FACTORS AFFECTING FORECAST ACCURACY

The accuracy of your forecasts will be determined to a large degree by how much patterns and relationships change, and how much people (including the organization itself and its competitors) can influence future events.

Patterns or relationships might change over time. A critical assumption for accurate forecasting is that patterns or relationships, once identified and measured, remain constant. In the commuting example, a new highway or the closing of an existing one for repairs will influence the flow of traffic, causing patterns and relationships to change. Such a change will make forecasting inaccurate until several trips under the new conditions have been made and new estimates drawn.

Despite the fact that satellite photos and huge computer models tracking weather patterns are being used at present, weather forecasts are sometimes wrong. The reason is that certain weather patterns do not always follow the same direction, nor do they move at a uniform speed. Both direction and speed can and do change, and new weather patterns develop that modify or cancel out existing ones. At other times, calm might prevail between two storms blowing in opposite directions. Weather forecasters can predict fairly accurately when weather patterns do not change. However, they do not know when or how they *will* change.[3] Their huge mathematical models, the superfast computers they use, the multimillion-dollar specialized satellites, and their sophisticated weather stations have not increased the accuracy of weather forecasts much over the last thirty years, simply because changes in weather patterns cannot be predicted. Although weather patterns can be better tracked and more accurately predicted if they do not change, inaccuracies inevitably develop when they do change. In the economic and business fields, patterns and relationships change much more, and much more often, than those of the weather.

People can influence future events. In the economic and business environment, predictions can become self-fulfilling or self-defeating prophecies, nullifying the forecasts. Consider, for instance, a forecast of a recession that is going to arrive during an election year. Any party in power that wants to be reelected will take action to avert the predicted recession, thus rendering inaccurate what could otherwise have been a perfect forecast. Similarly, an attractive opportunity for investment might bring big losses if several competitors arrive at the same forecast. The fact that the forecasts themselves can influence future events and in so doing change their course complicates the task of forecasting. It is no longer sufficient to predict accurately what is going to happen—managers must also forecast what competitors will do in response to such predictions. Because people can change the course of future events, the task of forecasting becomes much more difficult. This is different from the natural world, where humans still cannot change future events, such as the weather.

Here are some additional factors affecting forecast accuracy:

1. *The Time Horizon of Forecasting.* The longer the time horizon of the forecasts, the greater the chance that established patterns and relationships will change, invalidating forecasts. Specifically, the more time competitors have to react to predicted events or the predictions themselves, the more able they will be to influence future events for their own

benefit. Thus, all else being equal, forecasting accuracy decreases as the time horizon increases.

2. *Technological Change.* The higher the rate of technological change in a given industry, all other things being equal, the greater the chance that established patterns and relationships will change, and the greater the chance that competitors will be able to influence the industry through technological innovation. An excellent example is high-tech industries, where forecasting is almost impossible as firms strive to create the future according to their own conceptions. By bringing out new technologies, they hope to shape the future in desired directions in order to achieve competitive advantage. Thus, forecasting accuracy decreases as the rate of technological change increases.

3. *Barriers to Entry.* The lighter the barriers to entry, all other things being equal, the more inaccurate the forecasting, as new competitors (both domestic and foreign) can drastically change established patterns and relationships in their quest to gain competitive advantage.

4. *Dissemination of Information.* The faster the dissemination of information, all other things being equal, the less useful the value of forecasting, as everyone will have the same information and can arrive at similar predictions. In such a case it becomes impossible to gain advantages from accurate forecasting, as everyone else will also attempt to do so. This means accurate forecasts are not necessarily useful, a point that is not always understood or accepted, although examples abound. The growth in mainframes and microcomputers was correctly predicted, but few gains resulted, as many companies that used such accurate forecasts went bankrupt.

5. *Elasticity of Demand.* The more elastic the demand, all other things being equal, the less accurate the forecasts. Thus, demand for necessities (for example, food items) can be predicted with a higher degree of accuracy than for nonnecessities (such as vacationing). Obviously, people must eat and acquire necessities, which are given priority over other purchases in case of income reduction, as during periods of recession.

6. *Consumer Versus Industrial Products.* Forecasts for consumer products, all other things being equal, are more accurate than those for industrial products. Industrial products are sold to a few customers. If only one of those customers is lost, the resulting error can represent a substantial proportion of sales, because of the large quantities, or sales value, such customers buy. Those customers are well informed and can receive offers of bargain terms from competitors because of the large quantities or value amounts they buy.

WHAT CAN AND CANNOT BE PREDICTED, AND THE IMPLICATIONS

Over the last thirty years a considerable amount of empirical evidence and experience with forecasting applications has been accumulated. At present it is much easier to decide what can and cannot be predicted and what can be done to benefit from, as well as avoid the dangers of, forecasting. From the study of past forecasts a general observation becomes clear: The vast majority of forecasters underestimate future uncertainty. This bias was discussed in the last chapter and has to be reemphasized here. Uncertainty is underestimated when expected events do not materialize and when unexpected ones occur. In both cases there is surprise, which could have been avoided if decision-makers were willing to recognize that future uncertainty is more extensive than it appears.

SHORT-TERM PREDICTIONS

In the short term, forecasting can benefit by extrapolating the inertia (momentum) that exists in the economic and business phenomena. Seasonality can also be predicted fairly well. Empirical evidence has shown that seasonality does not change much. Thus, once computed it can be projected, together with the momentum of the series being forecast, with a high degree of accuracy. The momentum in series and their seasonality constitute *the two greatest advantages that can be gained by using formal forecasting methods*. Such advantages can be of benefit in production planning and scheduling; equipment, personnel and financial planning; and the ordering of raw and other materials. As seasonal fluctuations can be substantial, accurate prediction can greatly improve short-term scheduling and planning decisions.

The larger the number of customers or items involved, the smaller the effect of random forces and the higher the reliability of forecasting. Thus, firms selling to consumers not only can forecast more accurately but can know that the uncertainty of their forecasts is less than that of firms selling to industrial customers. Estimating uncertainty can be used to determine safety stocks (for finished products and materials), slack in personnel and equipment, and financial reserves, so that possible errors in forecasting can be confronted with a minimum of surprise and unpleasant consequences.

Short-term forecasting and the estimation of uncertainty are technically feasible and can be employed on a routine basis to provide improved customer satisfaction, better production and service scheduling, and so forth. If an organization does not already use a statistical, computerized system to make short-term forecasts and estimates of uncertainty, my advice would be to do so as soon as possible. Overwhelming empirical evidence shows concrete benefits from using simple statistical methods instead of using judgment to make the forecasts and to estimate uncertainty. Human forecasters cost a company a great deal more and are not necessarily more accurate. As a matter of fact, the vast majority of empirical comparisons clearly show the superiority of simple statistical methods over all other alternatives, including judgmental forecasts.

Although few things can happen in the short term to alter established patterns, some changes are occasionally possible, introducing an additional element of uncertainty. For instance, unexpected events (a fire, a major machine breakdown) or special events (a big snowstorm) can take place, or competitors can initiate special actions (advertising campaigns, price decreases, or the like). Such unexpected events or actions can change established patterns, thus invalidating the forecasts and introducing additional uncertainty (for more details and ways of dealing with special events/actions, consult Makridakis and Wheelwright).[4]

MEDIUM-TERM PREDICTIONS

In the medium term, forecasting is relatively easy when patterns and relationships do not change. However, as the time horizon of forecasting increases, so does the chance of a change in established patterns and relationships. Economic cycles, for one thing, can and do change established patterns and relationships. Unfortunately, however, we have not yet been able to predict accurately the timing and depth of recessions or the start and strength of booms. This makes medium-term forecasting hazardous, as recessions and booms can start any time during a planning horizon of up to two years (the usual length of the medium term). In addition, the uncertainty in forecasting becomes greater and less easy to measure or deal with, because the differences between forecasts and actual results can be substantial, especially in cyclical industries.

Medium-term forecasts are needed mostly for budgeting purposes. They require estimates of sales, prices, and costs for the entire company, as well as for divisions, geographical areas, product lines, and so forth, and predictions of economic and industry variables. In the case of a business cycle (a recession or a boom), all variables being predicted will be influenced in the same direction and by similar amounts, thus causing large errors that might necessitate the closing down of factories, the firing of workers, and other unpleasant belt-tightening measures. The deeper the recession, the worse the forecasting errors and the greater the unpleasant surprises and negative consequences. During a boom the opposite type of error normally occurs, giving rise to underestimated demand, personnel needs, and the like.

Medium-term forecasts can therefore become inaccurate. Worse still, their uncertainty is difficult to measure. Although there are forecasting services and newsletters claiming to be able to predict recessions or booms, empirical evidence shows beyond any reasonable doubt that they have not been successful up to now. This means that our inability to forecast recessions and booms must be accepted and taken into account during budgeting processes and when formulating overall strategies. On the other hand, the end of a recession (once it has started) is easier to predict. Recessions last about a year, and their length does not fluctuate widely around the average.

Not all companies are equally affected by cycles. In general, manufacturing firms are more affected than service firms; firms producing or servicing luxury (elastic) goods are more affected than those producing or servicing necessities (inelastic products and services); industrial firms are more affected than consumer firms; and companies in industries where strong competition exists are affected more than those in less competitive ones.

In dealing with business cycles it is important to remember that recessions or booms do not last forever. Past history clearly shows that cycles are temporary and will continue to be so unless some fundamental change in the business and economic environment takes place, which is unlikely at present. Thus, when a company is in a recession, managers must plan for the recovery. If there is a lasting boom, they must be concerned about the coming recession. In forecasting and planning there is one thing that is sure: After a long boom a recession is inevitable. The only thing not known is when it will start and how deep it will be. Thus, contingency planning to face the coming recession becomes necessary. The same is true during periods of recession. A recovery is certain. The only question is when it will start and how strong it will be. Obviously, there is always the possibility that a recession might turn into a depression or even that it might never end. Although such a possibility exists, it is highly unlikely and cannot be seriously considered; a firm trying to provide for it will have to be too conservative in its plans and strategy and will be overtaken by more aggressive competitors. Although we know that a car can hit us when we are crossing a street, no one can seriously consider never walking because of the possibility of being killed by a passing car.

Because recessions and booms cannot be predicted, it becomes necessary, over the medium term, to monitor for possible recessions or booms. This is the second best alternative to forecasting. It is like having a tracking system of radars looking for a possible enemy attack. It cannot tell us when the attack will be launched, but it can warn us once it is on its way. Although monitoring is not forecasting, it helps managers not to be taken completely by surprise by the arrival of a recession or boom. Another way of anticipating recessions is by looking for imbalances in one's own industry, in the economy, or in the international financial system. The bigger and the more widespread such imbalances, the greater the chance of a correction, which usually takes the form of a recession or a boom.

In practical terms, it makes little sense to attempt to forecast recessions or booms. Recessions or booms that are not forecast occur, and others that are predicted do not materialize. Therefore, spending money or resources to predict recessions or booms adds little or no value to future decision-making. It is best to accept that such a task is not possible and to plan budgets by extrapolating established trends and relationships. The company should be capable of adjusting its plans as soon as monitoring has confirmed a recession or boom. This is where contingency planning can be of great help. As recessions or booms are certain to arrive, managers can be prepared to face them by having drawn up detailed contingency plans.

LONG-TERM PREDICTIONS

Long-term forecasts are needed mostly for capital expansion plans, selecting R&D projects, launching new products, and formulating long-term goals and strategies. The critical element in long-term forecasting is prevailing trends. The challenge is to determine when and how such trends might change and how societal and consumer attitudes will differ in the future. The chances that there will be changes in long-term trends caused by new products, new services, new competitive structures, new forms of organization, and other novelties are great, making the task of forecasting difficult but also of critical importance.

I prefer to divide the long term into three types: emerging, distant, and faraway. In the emerging long term (two to five years), most changes requiring consideration have already started. It therefore becomes a question of figuring out their effects on the given organization and what can be done to deal with such changes. A common mistake, repeated over the span of the emerging long term, is to ignore technological and other changes until a crisis point has been reached, in which case organizations often overreact (for instance, AM International or Western Union). An equally common mistake is to be dazzled by the technological wonders of new inventions and to rush into introducing them (the picturephone, robotics). Many new technologies turn out to be uneconomical or to require more time before they can be smoothly implemented (smart credit cards, video text). Besides, new technologies are initially expensive, making it uneconomical and unwise to rush into adopting them (picture phones, smart credit cards, and so on).

When moving to the distant and faraway long term, the accuracy of specific forecasts decreases drastically, as many things can happen to change established patterns and relationships. The purpose of forecasting in such cases is to provide general directions as to where the world economy, or a particular industry, is heading, and to identify the major opportunities as well as the dangers ahead. The foremost challenge is to predict technological innovations and how they will affect the organization. New technologies can drastically change established demand, societal attitudes, costs, distribution channels, and the competitive structure of an industry. The major purpose of such long-term forecasting is to help the organization form a consensus about the future and start considering ways of adapting new technologies once they become economically profitable. Distant and faraway long term forecasts cannot be specific and will always be highly uncertain. Thus, their value lies not in improving decision-making but in helping generate organizational consensuses. (Long-term forecasts will be covered in more detail in the next two chapters.)

The Evaluation of Forecasts

A manager is constantly bombarded with forecasts. How does he or she distinguish the Delphi type from forecasts that are accurate *and* useful? It is not easy. Present-day forecasters have adapted their selling approach to modern times. Computer printouts and fancy mathematical models are often used to legitimize the forecasts and provide them with an aura of scientific objectivity. Here are some guidelines for evaluating the accuracy and usefulness of forecasts:

1. *Use of Benchmarks.* A manager can compare the forecasts given to him with those of simple benchmarks. For instance, are weather forecasts

more accurate than predicting that tomorrow's weather will be the same as today's? Is an exchange rate forecasting model being sold for $30,000 more accurate than using today's actual exchange rate for forecasting next year's? When using simple benchmarks, we often find no difference, or not enough difference to justify the cost of generating or buying the forecasts. Empirical evidence has shown that in a great many cases simple, naïve forecasting models outperform complex or sophisticated methods and judgmental forecasters.

2. *Track Record of Past Forecasts.* Sales of forecasting services or models are often promoted by emphasizing how accurately they have predicted or performed in the past. That does not mean much. Past forecasting successes do not guarantee future dependability. Consider, for instance, a mutual fund that has increased its assets 20 percent. If the S&P 500 index has increased 25 percent (in which case the S&P becomes the benchmark), the fund's record is not impressive. Even if the fund outperforms the S&P 500 for many years, that is not a sure sign that it will do so in the future. Considerable empirical evidence shows that *no* forecaster, forecasting service, or forecasting model *consistently* outperforms the rest. The only accuracy comparisons that count must be made against the future, when conditions will be different from those of the past. Unless a manager can have a look at such future-oriented comparisons (which are impossible to make), he should think carefully before buying forecasting services, newsletters, or models simply because of their superior track record. Other reasons must be offered to prove their worth. Empirical evidence has clearly shown that averaging the predictions of several forecasters or models provides more accurate forecasts than the individual forecasters or the specific models.

3. *Assumptions Used.* Scientific forecasting can accurately predict (and estimate uncertainty) when established patterns and relationships do not change. Any other forecasts are not possible to make except by using analogies (for example, sales of a new product will follow the same pattern as those of a similar existing product), in which case the analogy must be made clear, or by making subjective inferences as to how patterns and relationships might change. Making analogies or subjective inferences, however, requires several assumptions, *which must be made explicit,* as the accuracy of forecasts relates *directly* to the validity of those assumptions. A manager can then judge the appropriateness of the forecasts himself by evaluating the validity of the analogy or the correctness of the assumptions.

4. *The "Don'ts" of Forecasting. Don't* believe any forecasts based on secret formulas or complex computerized models that cannot be explained because they are beyond a manager's comprehension. No such formulas or models have been proved of value in the economic and business fields. *Don't* believe anyone who pretends to possess prophetic powers. Such people are charlatans or, worse, fools who should be treated as such. There is very strong evidence to show that complex or sophisticated forecasting models do not outperform simple ones, and that people do not forecast more accurately than simple statistical methods. Thus, if the accuracy of a forecast is low, *don't* attempt to improve it by introducing more complex or sophisticated approaches or by substituting people for statistical models. It is not likely that they will help increase your forecasting accuracy.

THE PARADOXES

1. The future can be predicted only by extrapolating from the past, yet it is fairly certain that the future will be different from the past.
2. Through forecasting we would expect to reduce future uncertainty, yet as we consider the future more carefully, we realize that unexpected events are possible, thus increasing uncertainty.
3. Although forecasts can and will be inaccurate and the future will always be uncertain, no planning or strategy is possible without forecasting and without estimating uncertainty.

CONCLUSIONS

Forecasting the short term can be done accurately on a mechanical basis in most business situations (although accuracy will vary from one case to another). Uncertainty can be estimated reliably in the short run. As the time horizon increases, so does the difficulty of arriving at accurate forecasts and reliable estimates of uncertainty, as well as the challenge of planning rationally and formulating successful strategies. Can a manager plan and develop effective strategies without accurate forecasts and reliable estimates of uncertainty? There is not much choice. Planning and strategy formulation must be done in spite of inaccurate forecasts and high levels of uncertainty. Success will depend on taking educated risks, being able to forecast changes in established patterns and relationships more accurately than competitors, and taking effective action to anticipate such changes.

EVENTS OR SITUATIONS THAT CAN BE FORECAST AND THE NEED FOR COMBINING

Short Term

- Inertia/momentum
- Seasonality
- Normal uncertainty

Medium Term

- Average growth rates (assuming no recession or boom)
- Expected costs and revenues (assuming average growth rates and average changes in costs and prices)

Long Term

- Established trends
- Existing relationships

Averaging (Combining) of Forecasts

- When in doubt about which forecaster or forecasting model to use, average the predictions of several models or forecasters and employ the average to forecast; empirical evidence has shown beyond doubt that averaging improves forecasting accuracy *and* reduces uncertainty.

FORECASTING CHALLENGES

Short Term

- Special events and actions and their influence on the future
- Dealing with the uncertainty that can be caused by such special events and actions

Medium Term

- Recessions and booms
- Dealing with the uncertainty that can be caused by recessions and booms

Long Term

- Changes from established patterns and relationships, in particular those produced by important technological innovations
- Developing appropriate strategies to anticipate and deal with the uncertainty caused by such changes

4

Identifying Megapatterns: Trends Versus Cycles

I do not forecast apocalypse and disaster. I am doing nothing more than anticipating change. . . . The world as you understand it is about to be turned upside down. You should now be able to profit from the downwave by using it.

ROBERT BECKMAN, *The Downwave: Surviving the Second Great Depression*
(April 1983)

I am an economist, trained in scientific analysis, not a sensationalist or a Jeremiah. Yet all the evidence indicates that another great depression is now in the making, and unless we take immediate remedial action the price we will have to pay in the 1990s is catastrophic.

DR. RAVI BATRA, *The Great Depression of 1990*

Doomsday predictions cannot be supported by long-term historical patterns, which, on the contrary, show surpluses rather than scarcities, and improved standards of living rather than poverty. Doomsday predictions underestimate the human capacity to invent new processes or ways of avoiding scarcities (scarcities cause price increases, which increase supply, as people are motivated to produce more because of higher prices and higher potential profits). Limits-to-growth concerns fail to distinguish between cycles and long-term trends, mistaking the former for the latter. In order to forecast the long term, it is necessary to look at information going as far back as possible and to identify trends, then to study how such trends might change in the future and their effect on society, work, and jobs.

Thomas Malthus, the English economist, wrote in 1798 that poverty and famine were unavoidable because population increases much faster than the means of subsistence. In 1865 another great English economist, W. S. Jevons, predicted that England's industrialization was doomed to halt because of inadequate supplies of coal. After a careful study of alternative solutions, he could see no practical remedy in sight. Jevons concluded that there was no chance that oil would eventually become a viable energy source to fuel English industry. In 1972 the book *Limits to Growth* appeared and sold more than 4 million copies. The conclusion of the book was that the earth's resources were finite. Without taking measures to check growth, we would soon run out of natural resources and pollute our environment beyond the point where it would be physically possible to survive. We had the choice of halting population growth or dying from famine and pollution poisoning.

Famine, energy scarcities, overpopulation, dangerous levels of pollution, and economic depressions are serious concerns that have worried mankind for centuries. Thoughts of mass starvation, deadly pollution, or widespread poverty (think of the Depression in the 1930s) are anxiety-provoking, particularly in our world society, where there is so much interdependence. A problem somewhere in the global system may result in serious repercussions everywhere else. For instance, the New York Stock Exchange's crash on October 19, 1987, had chain effects on all other major stock exchanges. An ability to predict accurately long-term trends and how they might change becomes critical. Two points must be made. First, long-term visions and strategic directions based on the assumption of limits to growth will look altogether different from those based on the assumption that growth patterns that have prevailed until now will continue. Second, if we can see ourselves headed for starvation, overpopulation, pollution, depressions, and so forth, we would be well advised to take measures to contain or even avoid them.

LONG-TERM TREND VERSUS TEMPORARY CYCLES

A trend is a secular increase or decline. By definition the increase or decline must be of long duration to be called a trend; otherwise, it is classified as a temporary increase or decline. Several trends have lasted for many millenniums. The growth in human population has followed an exponential trend. The total population of the earth has been estimated to have been less than half a million people 50,000 years ago. At the time the pyramids were built, it had risen to 60 million; by the golden age of ancient Greece, it had doubled to 120 million; by the time Christ was born, it had reached 250 million. The figure doubled to half a billion a little after 1500 and reached one billion 300 years later. It became two billion in the late 1930s and again doubled to four billion in the late 1970s. At present the world population stands at about 5.5 billion, but its exponential growth has slowed down or even declined in most Western countries and Japan. Increasing trends, even very long ones, do not necessarily last forever; they can slow down or even become declines. As the poet has put it:

> A trend is a trend
> But the question is, when will it bend?
> Will it alter its course
> Through some unforeseen force
> And come to a premature end?

It was pointed out in Chapter 3 that long-term forecasting must not only identify long-term trends but also indicate when and how they will change. In addition, it must distinguish temporary deviations (cycles) from permanent changes in long-term trends.

CYCLICAL CHANGES

The fact that cycles exist can be verified by looking at almost any long-term series (including those of population) in the economic and business fields. Their influence on forecasting should be understood. There are three types of major cycles of various average lengths, as follows:

1. Economic cycles of about four years' duration. The existence of such cycles is well accepted today, as we regularly experience recessions and booms in the level of economic activity.
2. Jugular cycles of an average of nine to eleven years' duration. The consistent existence of such cycles is debatable but some economists argue that they do indeed exist.
3. Kondratieff, or long-wave, cycles of an average of fifty to sixty years' duration. There is also considerable doubt about the consistent existence of Kondratieff cycles. However, long-term cyclical fluctuations do seem to exist, the problem being that they are difficult to classify into specific categories as their duration and depth vary widely.

Although historical data show that shorter cycles exist within longer ones, which in turn are part of long-term cyclical waves, there is no way to apply such knowledge in order to improve predictions of a coming cycle. The length and depth of all cycles vary widely, making any attempt to forecast them accurately impossible. It must therefore be accepted that *cycle forecasting is not within the realm of our present abilities.* This is especially true of long-term cyclical waves, because they vary tremendously from one to another and are too few in number to be able to identify statistically and project into a forecast. At the same time, cyclical effects must be separated from long-term trends so that we can properly identify such trends and use them to decide when and how they might change.

LONG-TERM AVAILABILITY OF ENERGY AND OTHER RESOURCES

To deal with the Malthusian and other limits-to-growth fears, we must consider the long-term availability and price of energy and other resources going as far back as we can. Julius Simon, in an excellent book well worth reading, has done so.[1] He points out, for instance, that at the beginning of our era the price of copper relative to wages was 120 times as great as today (that of iron was 240 times as great). In 800 B.C. it was 360 times as great, and in 1800 B.C. it was 1,620 times as great. This number dropped to eight times as great in A.D. 1800 and has been dropping ever since. Exhibit 4–1 shows the price behavior of copper (in constant 1988 dollars), which is similar to that of all other metals. The overall price of copper is dropping exponentially in the long term, although it is characterized by large cyclical fluctuations.

Exhibit 4–1 shows that prices might be dropping, but what about availability of raw and other materials? Prices are the best measure to determine adequacy of supplies. Scarcity drives prices up (especially today, when information is so efficiently disseminated). Thus, falling prices indicate plentiful supplies. Exhibit 4–1 clearly indicates that the long-term trend is not one of scarcity but rather one of oversupply. There is no reason to believe that such a trend will change in the future. However, if we look at Exhibit 4–2 where copper prices between 1935 and 1973 are graphed, the conclusions reached might be quite different, as this period includes the upswing of a long-term cyclical wave and not the long-term trend. This is why it is imperative that cycles *not* be confused with long-term trends, as can happen when considering relatively short series like that of Exhibit 4–2.

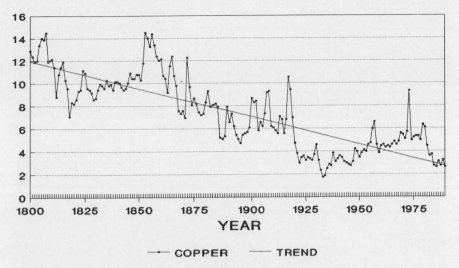

Exhibit 4–1 Copper Prices in Constant Dollars (1800–1988)

What about food? Exhibit 4–3 shows the price of wheat in constant 1988 dollars. It should be remembered that only 2 percent of the U.S. population was working in agriculture at that time. That 2 percent exported more than one-third of its output and could have exported much more had it not been for restrictions on agricultural production in the United States and high import duties or quotas in importing countries. Is mankind in danger of famine? No. The problem today is the opposite:

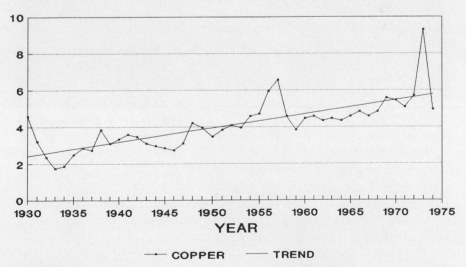

Exhibit 4–2 Copper Prices in Constant Dollars (1930–1974)

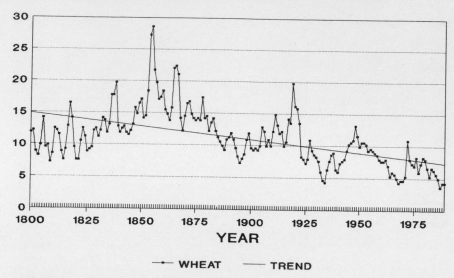

Exhibit 4–3 Wheat Prices in Constant Dollars

overproduction. Agricultural methods have become too efficient, and fertilizers have increased yields considerably. Today farmers are capable of producing almost twice as much food as is needed to maintain current levels of consumption for the entire population of the earth. Governments in the United States and the European Economic Community pay their farmers for not producing food and not raising animals. Certain food prices would have fallen to as low as half their present value had it not been for government restrictions or subsidies limiting food production.

Even the price of energy has not been increasing over time. Exhibit 4–4 shows that the price of oil in 1988 dollars has been constant since late in the last century. Prices did increase tremendously between 1973 and 1980 because of an external event, an action by the OPEC cartel, and that rise was related to the fact that oil prices had been kept artificially low from 1950 to 1973 by a distributors' cartel, the oil companies known as the seven sisters. In 1989 oil prices are very close to the historical trend (a constant value around $10). The same constant trend can be seen in Exhibit 4–5, which shows coal prices since 1900. Although they are characterized by huge cycles (like those of copper, wheat, and oil) their trend is remarkably stable in the long run.

In this chapter and the next, I shall show that there are no obvious reasons why the long-term trends in resources, food production, or energy will change in the future. The challenge, as new technologies are being implemented, will be not scarcities but rather what to do with too much agricultural and industrial production and how to deal with the

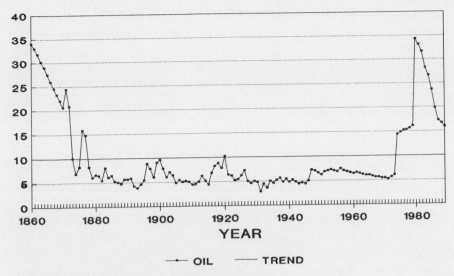

Exhibit 4–4 Oil Prices in Constant Dollars

increased competition because of such overproduction. For instance, automobile executives in United States and Canada estimate that by 1990 there will be four cars for every three buyers. In EEC countries it is estimated there will be five cars for every three customers by 1992. What will happen to the extra supply of cars? Will the automobile (and other manufacturing) companies find themselves in the same position as agricultural producers are today? Will governments pay car manufacturers to

Exhibit 4–5 Coal Prices in Constant Dollars

limit their production? What will existing and new companies do to attract customers? What will happen to the extra car that can be produced but will not be sold? These questions are more relevant than the issue of scarcities, depressions, or other economic catastrophes being predicted.

DEPRESSIONS AND OTHER ECONOMIC CATASTROPHES

Are depressions similar to that of 1929 possible? The upswing in the latest long wave cycle started in 1949 (see Exhibit 4–6) and supposedly lasted thirty-three years, until 1982. However, since 1982 one of the longest economic recoveries has started, and by the end of 1989 there were still no signs of an economic recession, much less a Kondratieff downturn. But if the expansion in economic cycles can be more than twice the average (as was the case in the 1961–69 expansion, which lasted 105 months instead of the average forty-eight), it is also possible that the expansion of long-wave Kondratieff cycles can last more than twice the average, which would mean as long as seventy years. Thus, a depression can take place any time in the next thirty years, *if* no fundamental changes have taken place in the economic environment and *if* we assume that Kondratieff-type cycles exist.

Today there is one piece of evidence suggesting that economic knowledge and governmental action can be combined to avert a depression, diminish its severity, or, if nothing else works, shorten its duration. That evidence is the stock market crash of October 19, 1987, which could have easily led to a depression similar to that which followed the stock market crash of 1929. No depression developed because of effective intervention by the Federal Reserve. As a matter of fact, by the end of 1989 the economy is still on a strong upward swing, and the latest forecasts of the

Exhibit 4–6 Four Alleged Kondratieff Cycles

	Duration in years	*Expansion or Downswing*
1789–1814	25	Expansion
1814–49	35	Downswing
1849–73	24	Expansion
1873–96	23	Downswing
1896–1926	30	Expansion
1926–49	23	Downswing
1949–82	33	Expansion
1983–2005	23	Downswing

Organization for Economic Cooperation and Development (OECD) and the International Monetary Fund (IMF) predict a continuation of growth for another year. Modern technology permits the Federal Reserve to monitor critical economic variables more effectively and therefore to act faster and more efficiently when dangers develop. Thus, excluding major mistakes, great depressions or other economic catastrophes can be avoided. At the same time, I must emphasize that we do not have enough evidence to draw definite conclusions. In 1969, for instance, economists believed that economic cycles were a thing of the past, because no recession had occurred for 105 months. As we know, they were wrong, and there have been four recessions since then.

There is additional evidence pointing to fewer unwanted fluctuations. The length of the expansion of economic cycles has increased, while that of recessions has decreased. The pre–World War II economic expansion (dating back to 1800) lasted, on the average, less than thirty months while the recessions lasted twenty-two months. The prewar U.S. economy was therefore in economic recession more than 40 percent of the time. In contrast, the post–World War II expansion has lasted, on the average, forty-eight months, while the average recession has lasted only eleven. Thus, the economy has been in a recession less than 20 percent of the time, half the pre–World War II average. Furthermore, the depth of the postwar recessions has been much less, on the average, than that of prewar ones. Plagues, worldwide agricultural catastrophes, and other major disasters (excluding Chernobyl and Bhopal) have been avoided. In all, fewer deviations from the long-term trend toward increasing prosperity have occurred. To summarize, the evidence seems positive, although a nuclear disaster, a nuclear war, or a large-scale industrial accident could change the picture entirely.

Can long-term waves and other cycles be predicted with any degree of confidence? If we want specific predictions and exact timing, the answer is a definite no. There is *no way to predict* when a new depression will start (even if we assume that one will occur) or how deep it will be. Since 1930 thousands of forecasters have predicted imminent depressions. Mathematical models, economic analysis, scientific reasoning, large computers, alleged expertise, and insights or prophetic powers have been advanced to persuade readers about forthcoming depressions. Since 1970 a large number of articles and books have been published predicting imminent depressions. None have arrived, but somehow the prophets of doom do not seem to learn. New ones come along to repeat doomsday predictions. Forecasts about depressions and other great catastrophes make news (not to mention money) and are more likely to be published than forecasts predicting that things will continue as usual, which do not make for sensational reading. Believing in doomsday predictions, however, is as accurate as trusting fortune tellers.

A popular book published in 1971 identifies several thousand cycles in such diverse areas as the length of womens' skirts and stock market prices.[2] The book was sponsored by a Cycles Institute, whose purpose was to study and predict cycles. However, its predictions turned out to be disastrous. According to the book (Figure 37 on page 119, for instance), the stock market follows an 9.2-year cycle, which showed a downturn in the 1960s and an upturn in the middle of the 1970s. Well, the downturn and the upturn did happen, except that their timing was exactly the opposite of that predicted. In addition, Beckman (cited at the opening of this chapter)[3] and many similar books and articles have predicted depressions that never arrived.

To make long-term forecasts three tasks must be undertaken. First, established patterns must be identified using information going back, in history, as far as possible. Second, cycles must be separated from trends. Third, a transparent and rational approach must be used to determine when and how long-term trends might change.

LONG-TERM PATTERNS IN HUMAN HISTORY

Established trends in human history are being altered by major innovations or breakthroughs, which bring about revolutions. Revolutions bring about substantial and permanent change, unlike cycles, whose effects are temporary. The tempo of innovations and breakthroughs since the Industrial Revolution has increased phenomenally, and so have standards of living, life expectancy, the speed of transportation, and advances in science and the arts. New trends have emerged, and established ones have accelerated. There is no doubt that the future will bring equally important changes. As the Information Revolution progresses, and as its technologies are combined with those of the Industrial Revolution, more machines will be operated by computers with little or no human interference. Robotics, super-automated factories, new production technologies, superfast modes of transport, and the like are not science fiction fantasies but within the realm of reality by the beginning of the next century. For managers it is becoming important to envision the type and extent of forthcoming change and to take steps, within their organizations, to anticipate them. If we want to determine forthcoming changes in long-term trends, we must study new or forthcoming innovations or breakthroughs, being careful to distinguish cycles from trends, and must try to discern how trends can be modified under the influence of major innovations or breakthroughs to bring about revolutionary change. Exhibit 4–7 lists the major innovations or breakthroughs since the dawn of human history. The exhibit suggests the following conclusions:

1. Humans have tried, since very early in their history, to extend their capabilities, both manual and mental. Physical work has been supplemented (through the use of tools), substituted (using horses or tractors to cultivate the land), or amplified (employing levers or cranes to lift heavy weights). Mental work has also been supplemented, substituted, or amplified by a variety of means, although this occurred much later.

2. Humans have tried to decrease their dependence on the environment. Domestication of animals, agriculture, building of houses, and similar inventions have been conceived for that purpose.

3. Humans have tried to master their environment, sometimes for no practical reason other than the drive for knowledge and personal growth.

4. Humans have tried to conquer disease and in the process to reduce suffering and prolong life expectancy.

5. Humans have demonstrated interests other than those directly related to actual survival. Philosophy, art, socializing, and a drive toward equality can be clearly seen throughout human history.

6. Clusters of innovations or breakthroughs occur concurrently or within a relatively short time span. They are followed by periods, sometimes long, of no new innovations or breakthroughs.

7. The rate of innovations or breakthroughs has increased considerably during the last two hundred years, interrupting established trends that had lasted for millenniums. The reason for the increase was the invention of machines that used mechanical energy to supplement, substitute, or amplify manual work, which gave rise to what is now known as the Industrial Revolution.

8. The late 1940s marked the beginning of another revolution, the Information or Computer Revolution. This revolution is also supplementing, substituting, or amplifying work, but this time mental work, not manual. The Information Revolution so far has produced results similar to those of the Industrial Revolution and has further accelerated the rate of technological change.

Exhibit 4–7 Major Innovations/Breakthroughs That Changed Established Trends in Human History and/or Prevailing Attitudes

I Technology

Epoch	Approximate Time (Years from 1988)	Innovation/Breakthrough	Consequence/Reason
A	1,750,000	• Primitive tools	
B	100,000	• Making and using gear for hunting	
	40,000	• Making and using weapons	• Extending human capabilities
	5,500	• The wheel	
D	4,000	• Bronze and other metals	
	3,500	• Boats and sailboats	
E	800	• The clock, compass and other measurement instruments	• Reducing and/or making manual work easier
	600	• Gunpowder	
	500	• The printed book	
	350	• Mechanical calculators	• Facilitating and/or making mental work easier
F	210	• Engines	
	180	• Railroads	
	150	• Electricity	
	130	• Image and sound reproduction	• Improving comfort and/or speed of transportation
	90	• Telecommunications	
G	85	• Airplanes	
	70	• Automobiles and roads	
	60	• Mass-produced chemical products	• Increasing speed and/or availability of telecommunications

45	• Nuclear weapons	
40	• Computers	
35	• Mass produced home appliances	• Improving quality of arts and entertainment
35	• The transistor	
30	• Extensive use of fertilizers	
30	• Artificial satellites	• Improving material quality of life
25	• Lasers	
20	• Micro technology (Microchips, biochemistry, and genetic engineering)	
20	• The moon landing	

II Exploiting Nature's Resources/Capabilities

400,000	• Hunting	
300,000	• Harnessing of fire	• Decreasing dependence on the environment
150,000	• Shelter	
20,000	• Permanent settlements	
20,000	• Domestication of animals	• Exploiting nature's capabilities
15,000	• Agriculture	
10,000	• Using animals for transportation and labor	

H

A

C

Exhibit 4-7 (*Continued*)

Epoch	Approximate Time (Years from 1988)	Innovation/Breakthrough	Consequence/Reason
D	3,500	Irrigation systems	
	3,000	Harnessing wind power	• Using nature's resources
	2,000	Using horses for transportation and labour	
E	800	Using the energy of falling water	
F	180	Using coal and oil for energy	• Adapting to changes in the environment
H	45	Nuclear energy	

III Social and Intellectual Human Achievements

Epoch	Approximate Time (Years from 1988)	Innovation/Breakthrough	Consequence/Reason
A	1,500,000	Social organization to care for children	
	500,000	Language	• Better mastery of the environment
	400,000	Immigration	
C	20,000	Religion	• Need for socialization
D	7,000	First cities	
	5,500	Alphabet	• Need for knowledge
	5,000	Abacus	
D	3,500	Money for transactions	
	3,000	Number system	
	2,500	Arts, philosophy, sciences	• Drive toward equality
	2,500	Democracy	

IV Medicine

E	500	Scientific experimentation
	500	The discovery of the new worlds
	475	*The Prince* by Machiavelli is written
	400	Large-scale commerce
	300	Scientific astronomy
	300	Mathematical reasoning

• Desire for achievement

F	210	Discovery of oxygen (beginning of chemistry)
	200	French and American revolutions
	150	Babbage's failed computer
	150	Political ideologies (communism, capitalism)
	120	Foundations of genetics

• Appreciation of arts

G	100	Financial, banking, and insurance institutions
	80	The theory of relativity
	50	The concept of the computer is demonstrated mathematically

• Desire to reduce future uncertainty

IV Medicine

D	2,500	The doctor as a healer

• Curing disease

E	500	Therapy based on sound medical reasoning
	300	Drugs with real medical value

• Prolonging life expectancy

	90	X-ray
	55	Antibiotics

• Providing better diagnostics

H	30	Oral contraceptives
	20	Tissues and organ transplants
	10	The CT (CAT or body) Scan

• Preventing unwanted pregnancies

A: The emergence of human domination; B: The first handmade tools to extend human capabilities; C: The beginning of human civilization; D: The foundation of modern civilization; E: The foundations of modern science and society; F: The start of the Industrial Revolution; G: The Industrial Revolution; H: Spin-offs of the Industrial Revolution, the start of the Information Revolution.

The Industrial and Information revolutions have caused some additional changes:

1. There are considerable secondary benefits from the Industrial and Information Revolutions that extend in all areas of our personal and family lives, as well as in entertainment, transportation, and medicine.

2. New inventions combine the technologies of the Industrial and Information Revolutions (e.g., in robotics, or intelligent machines) with far-reaching consequences. The ultimate end of such inventions will be super-automation and the replacement of humans in all repetitive tasks or recurrent problem-solving situations.

3. The importance of technology has increased over time. Consider, for instance, the role of technology in the discovery of America by Christopher Columbus versus its role in the Neil Armstrong moon landing. In such areas as medicine or the harnessing of nature's resources, innovations or breakthroughs depend to a much greater extent on technology now than ever before.

The Industrial Revolution brought about great changes in employment patterns. The manual skills of the farmer, craftsman, and artisan were reproduced by machine designs, which, once operational, could perform the same tasks faster, more cheaply, and with less effort. A skilled shoemaker who could make fewer than one pair of shoes a day was replaced by a machine producing thousands of shoes in the same time. Similarly, a farmer who cultivated a few acres of land by hand and with animals could cultivate hundreds with a tractor. For the first time in the history of civilization, manual skills acquired through many years of apprenticeship and long practical experience became obsolete. Machines were introduced everywhere, bringing unemployment to farmers, craftsmen, and artisans, and creating a new form of employment—that of the factory worker. Except for a few cases, mostly involving works of art, manual expertise lost its economic benefits to machines. The Information Revolution is bringing similar changes in employment patterns that involve supplementing, substituting, or amplifying mental work by computers. The obvious concern, of course, is how fast such changes will come.

Exhibit 4–8 shows some important correspondence between the Industrial and Information revolutions. I believe that the Information Revolution in 1988 was at about the same stage as the Industrial Revolution in the 1930s (derived from such analogies as the penetration of cars in the United States, which in 1935 was 17.7 percent, while the corresponding

Exhibit 4-8 Important Events in Human History: the Industrial and Information (Computer) Revolutions

Industrial Revolution	Steam Engine	Railroad	Electricity	Electricity in Home Use	Motorized Airplane	Ford's T-Car	G.M.'s water-cooled K-Car	Variety of affordable Car Types and Models	Application of technology to all areas where labor could be substituted, aided, or improved. These include home, factory, transportation, entertainment, etc.
1760	1776	1808	1830	1880	1903	1909	1925	1930s	Present 1988

About 175 years   About 50 years

Information Revolution	The Transistor	Computers for Business Application	Micro-chips	Time-shared Computers	Micro-processors	Apple's Personal Computers	Micro-computers	Variety of Affordable Efficient and Fast Computers	Future
1946	1948	1952	1969	1971	1973	1977	1983	Present 1988	Year 2000

42 Years   About 12.5 Years

The Information Revolution is progressing about four times as fast as the Industrial Revolution (i.e., 175 ÷ 42 = 4.17, or about 4).

One can expect that it will take the Information Revolution 12.5 years (i.e., one-fourth of the time) to accomplish what took the Industrial Revolution 50 years.

penetration of computers today is 17 percent, and similar events). This means that during the Industrial Revolution some 175 years were required to achieve what the Information Revolution has achieved in forty-two years, implying that the pace of the latter is about four times greater than that of the former. Thus, the change brought about by the Industrial Revolution between the 1930s and today (a little more than fifty years) is likely to be matched by the Information Revolution in about one-fourth of that time, twelve and a half years, bringing us up to the beginning of the twenty-first century. By then, society and business firms will be as far advanced in the Information Revolution as today's firms are in the Industrial Revolution. Obviously, that will represent a lot of change.

Forecasting by analogies has its dangers. Others might not agree with me about the correspondence and the speed of the Information Revolution vis-à-vis the Industrial. I cannot prove that my interpretation of Figure 4–8 is right. Those disagreeing can construct their own Figure 4–8 and establish their own correspondence between the Industrial and Information revolutions. In forecasting by analogies, value judgments must be made, and that can lead to different forecasts. There is no way, however, to predict the effects of the Information Revolution without some sort of analogy with the Industrial.

LONG-TERM EQUILIBRIA

We live in a stable world. In the biological environment there are many mechanisms that contribute to such stability. Oxygen needed to breathe comes from plants, which consume carbon dioxide, a deadly gas. Animal populations do not grow beyond what their environment can support. Intricate biological mechanisms maintain delicate balances and have allowed life to exist for more than a billion years. Biological life is characterized by natural selection. Darwin's concept of the "survival of the fittest" prevails, bringing improvements in living species and contributing to evolutionary changes to higher, more advanced forms of life. The economic and business world is also stable. Like the biological world, it includes intricate mechanisms that bring stability. Competition is also prevalent and plays a role similar to that among living species.

One difficulty with the economic and business environment, not present in the biological world, is that humans are capable of tampering with the mechanisms that maintain stability. Sometimes they do so in their quest to solve certain problems and do not realize the side effects of their actions. At other times, they attempt to gain personal benefit, thinking they can ignore the stability mechanisms. A good example is oil prices and OPEC (or any other cartels or monopolies). Between the early 1950s and the beginning of the 1970s large multinational oil companies (the so-called seven sisters) were powerful enough to determine oil prices, which they managed to keep artificially low by increasing production. However, low prices elevated demand well above normal levels and discouraged the search for new sources of oil or alternative sources of energy. They also made the use of coal uneconomical. In the final analysis, low prices greatly contributed to excessive dependence on oil, and the major oil producing countries, realizing their potential power, formed OPEC. Thus, one forced deviation from equilibrium brought on another (a cartel), which pushed the pendulum to the other extreme by increasing prices well above normal levels.

Economic stability mechanisms do not work instantaneously. It took time to adjust to exorbitant oil prices. Slowly but surely, however, such mechanisms started to work. Smaller, more efficient cars, conservation measures, increases in supply (through the discovery of new oilfields motivated by high profits), the switch to other sources of energy, and so forth, brought the stabilizing effects: a reduction in demand and an increase in supply. Today oil prices have come back toward their normal level determined by long-term equilibrium mechanisms. Fluctuations have dampened down (see Exhibit 4–4).

Mechanisms contributing to long-term equilibria cannot be ignored. Experience and a lot of empirical evidence tells us they prevail in the long term. Innumerable cartels have failed in the past. Monopolies and oligopolies seem to do no better. IBM and the large automobile companies are an example. Because of their oligopolistic power, they attempted to make excessive gains and impose their will as to products consumers should use and prices they should pay. In Henry Ford II's famous words, small cars make small profits. He and Detroit saw no reason to provide consumers with small cars. The Europeans and the Japanese did just that and captured close to one-third of the U.S. market. Those companies also attempted to stifle competition (IBM, for instance, by not allowing its computers to communicate with those of others) and to bar new entrants. Although they indeed made short-term gains, they attracted competition (in search of their high profits), which managed to break the formidable barriers to entry. Neutralizing barriers to entry was inevitable. It has happened countless times in the past and will continue to happen in the future. Somehow, cartels, oligopolies, monopolies, and the like forget that they cannot keep their power forever. Thus, they become lax, bureaucratic, and less able to stifle competition, which is attracted and intensified by the huge profits made by the firms enjoying oligopolistic or monopolistic advantages.

Long-term equilibria are attained through constant adjustments. For example, economic recessions are necessary temporary deviations from long-term trends. During recessions inefficient firms go bankrupt, costs are streamlined, and organizations are forced to operate more efficiently. The same can be said of longer-term cycles. Inefficient firms go bankrupt and less than average performers must improve their operations or face extinction. Thus, economic hardships become the springboard for entrepreneurship and innovation. An obvious problem arises, however, because recessions and other economic hardships are not desirable in the short term, and governments attempt to avoid them or reduce their impact. Unfortunately, their corrective actions do not always work. The same is true when people act in unison in the hope of avoiding actual or perceived dangers. The result is sometimes worse than if no action had been taken. This creates a dilemma: do nothing and wait for unpleasant moments, or take action whose consequences and side effects cannot be fully predicted. The challenge ahead is to learn to take corrective action to avoid undesirable deviations from long-term trends without causing other damage that will prolong or amplify such deviations.

THE PARADOX

Corrective action is necessary to avoid undesirable economic (or other) hardships, yet we cannot be sure of its negative consequences or side effects (for instance, the huge U.S. budget and trade deficits caused by a series of governmental actions aimed at helping the economy).

Finally, it might even be possible to turn long-term trends in desired directions. This can be done by encouraging basic research, R&D spending, and similar actions. Although, as with cycles, we cannot be sure of the side effects (pollution caused by industrialization aimed at increasing living standards, for example), we humans have the ability to mold our environment, and we shall have to try, attempting to maximize our chances of success and reducing those of failure. These are topics to be covered later on.

THE CHALLENGE AHEAD

Learn (from experience, empirical evidence, and theory) how to avoid unpleasant deviations from long-term trends while avoiding the negative consequences and side effects of action aimed at correcting perceived or actual ills.

CONCLUSIONS

In the long term, material and food prices have been decreasing while those of energy have remained constant. At the same time huge increases (or decreases) can be observed (see, for example, Exhibit 4–2) if shorter series are used. Such increases or decreases can well be part of various cycles, which signify temporary rather than permanent changes. Huge increases or decreases over a few years do not necessarily imply permanent changes in trends, as long-term equilibrium mechanisms bring constant adjustments and force economic and business events toward long-term paths. On the other hand, long-term trends can change in periods of revolutions, which are caused by major, mostly technological, innovations and breakthroughs.

We humans have the capacity to change our environment to fit our needs. We are different from all other animals, which must evolve in order to cope with permanent changes in the environment. Our ability to change our environment is a mixed blessing. We can cause damage as well as reap benefits. In reality we constantly strive to change the environment around us. This makes forecasting difficult. At the same time the basic stability mechanisms cannot be ignored. Thus, we live in a stable chaos (to borrow a term from the physical sciences). Although we can predict certain long-term trends with a fair degree of accuracy (energy and other prices, inability to stifle competition, and so on), we are unable to predict accurately medium- and shorter-term movements. Chaotic shorter-term movements (for example, cycles, deviations from equilibria) cannot be predicted (it is the same in the physical world) no matter how hard we try.[4] In the final analysis, this conclusion introduces a great degree of uncertainty. It must be accepted, and strategies must be developed to deal with it.

5

The Emerging and Long-Term Future

I think it most unlikely that aeronautics will ever be able to exercise a decisive influence in travel. Man is not an albatross.

H. G. WELLS, *The Discovery of the Future (1901)*

This chapter deals with long-term forecasting. It takes the position that computers will greatly affect the way business operates and most other aspects of our everyday lives. Expert systems; robotics; computer-guided tools and machines, and processes; and electronic networking will supplement, substitute, and amplify mental work faster than machines did with manual work. By the middle of the first decade of the twenty-first century, our society will be as far advanced in the Information Revolution as we are today in the Industrial. This implies much change, which will result in fewer jobs in manufacturing, keen competition among firms producing and selling products, and high growth in the service sector. The uses and implications of long-term forecasts are also discussed.

Suppose you were a watchmaker living in France two hundred years ago. At the age of forty, you have managed to open your own workshop. You employ an assistant, twenty-eight, and three apprentices, all under sixteen. You learned your job by first being an apprentice to a master watchmaker for fifteen years and then becoming his chief assistant for twelve. After he died last year, you put together all your savings with money borrowed from relatives and friends, and you started your own workshop. You feel you've accomplished your life's dream, and you look forward to making a comfortable living for yourself and your family. You expect your son to learn to become a watchmaker and take over your business when you become too old to work on your own.

Working with your assistant and apprentices, you can make a watch in about a month. You pay your assistant 1.10 francs a day and your apprentices from 0.40 to 0.60 francs, depending on their age and years of experience. Thus, a watch costs you about 70 francs to produce, plus 10 francs more in material. You sell a watch for about 160 francs, leaving you 80 francs, a nice margin that allows you to live comfortably and to reinvest some of your profits to improve your workshop and eventually hire more helpers to increase the number of watches you can produce.

When we try to envision our future and the changes it will bring, it may be helpful to understand how people in those times conceived of the future. Could our watchmaker, for instance, have imagined in his wildest dreams that a machine would be able to produce a watch in ten minutes, or that a brand new technology would be developed to make digital watches in under a minute at an incredibly low cost? By the same token, can we today contemplate a jet airplane produced in the future automatically, using giant computer-guided machines and robots, in less than half an hour? Can we imagine such a jet costing a few months' salary? Although the possibility of having mass-produced, affordable jets might seem like science fiction, it could become a reality in the future. Again, consider the relative buying power of two hundred years ago (to buy a watch, the assistant watchmaker had to work for more than six months) with that of today (a similarly qualified person could buy a similar watch with a fraction of a day's salary). Then it might not seem too far-fetched, at least on technological grounds, to say that the average person might be able to afford to buy a jet airplane fifty years from now.

Technological innovation can bring huge changes. At the individual level, such changes render obsolete skills attained through many years of education and practical experience. At the societal level, they can alter prevailing attitudes and established trends. At the corporate level, they can greatly affect all aspects of business operations, including the competitive structure of industries. This was particularly true during the last century, when the rate of technological innovations and breakthroughs accelerated.

LONG-TERM FORECASTS

Underestimating or ignoring technological changes is not the only problem to face executives concerned with long-term forecasting. As was mentioned in Chapter 3, an equally serious mistake can occur when, dazzled by technological inventions, managers overestimate the usefulness and applicability of new technologies. Unfortunately, many new technological inventions take years to become economically viable and profitable. Thus, a forecast (or sales talk) about the potential usefulness of some new technology is no guarantee that such a technology can be applied profitably. Exhibit 5–1 shows both sides of the coin. Exhibit 5–1A lists major technological breakthroughs that were *not* predicted, some only a few years before they revolutionized the world. Exhibit 5–1B, on the other hand, lists predictions that have not, as yet, materialized.

The challenge facing a manager concerned with meeting the future in a rational and realistic way is to distinguish accurate from faulty long-term forecasts. The remainder of this chapter provides guidelines on how such a challenge can be met.

The Emerging Long Term

The main task (and challenge) when forecasting the emerging long term is to figure out how existing and newly invented technologies will affect a given industry and firm during the next two to five years. Such a task is of critical importance, particularly today, when we are in the middle of the Information Revolution. The following technologies must be evaluated and their impact considered:

Computers. The cost of computers has been decreasing exponentially while their memory capacity and computational power have been increasing exponentially (see the Appendix at the end of the book, which describes computers and their advantages and limitations). Today a microcomputer selling for less than $10,000 has a larger memory and faster computational capacity than the largest and fastest supercomputer available ten years ago, selling for more than half a million dollars. Most importantly, however, today's microcomputer is much easier to use than its predecessor of ten years ago. A much greater variety of tasks (programs) can be done on the computer today than ten years ago. At that time, computers were geared to serve engineers and other scientists, or were used for data-processing purposes (payrolls, accounting, and so on). Today microcomputers are on the desks of most managers and can be used for a great many tasks. This trend will continue into the future as computer power doubles every two to three years, while at the same time the cost of acquiring the computer decreases.

Exhibit 5–1 Events Not Predicted, and Predictions That Have Not Yet Materialized

---

A. Examples of Events That Happened but Were Not Predicted

The Computer and Information Revolution before 1950 (today the computer industry is approaching $150 billion a year)

The maximum demand for computers in the United States is 100 units (forecast made in the early 1950s).

In 1977 no one thought there was a market for personal computers (twelve years later this market passed $30 billion in sales a year).

Commercial television: In the 1920s no one thought there were commercial possibilities for the newly tested technology.

The airplane: Experts thought it would be impossible to fly.

Airplane travel: The most experts could conceive was airplanes for military purposes.

Wireless communications: Experts did not conceive or believe possible even the idea.

The atomic bomb: Experts thought it was impossible to achieve.

X-rays: Experts did not think it could be done.

Roads for cars: It was thought that it would be impractical and too costly to build roads.

The maximum market for cars in Europe was 1,000 units (it was reasoned that there is, after all, a limit to the number of drivers who will learn to drive cars).

Talking movies: "Who the hell wants to hear actors talk?" (Henry Warner, 1921).

The Walkman: Everyone at Sony, except the president and the chairman, thought there was no market for the Walkman.

The post-it pad: No uses for the post-it pad could be conceived.

Jogging shoes: Existing shoe companies were not willing to produce them when they had the opportunity to do so.

Overnight mail delivery: It was thought to be impossible to compete with the post office and other delivery firms.

High-temperature superconductors: They were considered to be in the realm of science fiction.

Exhibit 5–1 (*continued*)

B. Examples of Predictions That Did Not Materialize or Whose Importance Was Highly Overestimated

Holographic 3-D movies and 3-D television

Widespread utilization of 3-D cameras

Widespread utilization of picturephones

"I am convinced that within a few years every household will have one or several flying machines" (H. Ganswindt, helicopter pioneer, 1891)

The complete substitution of oil and coal by nuclear power

Synthetic and shale oil at a price lower than regular oil

Feasible computer translation

A computer chess program becoming World Champion by 1970

Widespread use of programmed (or computer) learning

Plastic paper

Solar energy

A cheap industrial process for the manufacture of fresh water from sea water

Instant yogurt

The extended use of robotics (being predicted to be much greater than it is today)

Nuclear-powered airplanes

Widespread commercial supersonic flights

Hypersonic planes for commercial travel

Widespread utilization of magnetic levitation trains

Marine cities

Space travel

Artificial intelligence

Room-temperature superconducting material

At present we are on the verge of several technological breakthroughs that will radically change the way computers are used, as well as revolutionizing their value, speed, and cost. First, internal computer memory has grown to the point where the most complicated of managerial tasks can be performed directly by loading all required information (program, data, specific requests) into the main memory of the computer. That will considerably reduce the time required to accomplish a given task. (Computers at present have to search for what to do next—program instructions—and for what data to use each time something is to be done. Then all that must be loaded into the memory, a task that takes time. That is the equivalent of looking through a document the size of a telephone book to find out what you are supposed to do next, and then through another to find the information you need in order to make a certain decision). Second, new computers can perform several tasks at once. Third, as the number of computer users increases exponentially, so do the number of available programs (demand creates its own supply), the ease with which they can be used, and their usefulness. Finally, microcomputers are becoming so cheap that almost everyone can afford them. If present trends continue, a medium-size microcomputer will cost less than $2,500 (in constant dollars) five years from now and will have the memory size and computational power of a big mainframe of today.

Thus, existing computers, or those constructed during the next fifteen years, will become powerful tools supplementing mental tasks in the same way that electric drills, power saws, and other mechanical or electrical tools have supplemented manual work. Just as it is difficult today to conceive doing manual work without the appropriate mechanical or electrical tools, so it will be difficult to perform decision-making tasks in the future without a computer and the appropriate computer programs. As time passes, such programs will be perfected and refined to supplement mental tasks more effectively and efficiently.

Computers will also be used to substitute mental work. As time passes, computers will play a role in replacing people analogous to that played by mechanical automation in replacing semiskilled and skilled manual workers. The first steps in such a process of substitution will be large integrated computer systems, expert systems, and robotics—all three already under way.

Large Integrated Computer Systems. Computers offer the use of huge memories to store information and provide on-line access in a matter of seconds to any detail of this information in any desired form. Consider, for instance, computer reservation systems. They contain information on *all* flights of *all* airlines between *all* origins and destinations. In addition to information about cost, they can also be used to make hotel or car rental reservations, issue tickets, reserve specific seats, order special meals, and do a host of other tasks. Such systems could be accessed through regular telephone lines by all travel agents anywhere in the world. Since the overwhelming majority of passengers book their flights through information found in these computerized reservation systems, they have become of crucial value and have completely changed the face of competition. For instance, if there is more than one flight leaving about the same time and going nonstop to the same destination, the one that is listed first on the terminal screen gets far more customers than the one listed second, which gets more than the one listed third, and so on, as travel agents and individuals stop looking once they have found a flight that satisfies their needs. Similar systems will develop in many other industries, transforming the way business is conducted (consider the implications should all orders for raw or other materials pass automatically between computers, and should a computer program exist that contains and can find the best deal available each time).

Expert Systems. Human decisions are based on knowledge accumulated through years of education and/or experience. A doctor, for instance, reaches his or her diagnosis of a certain disease by examining a patient and matching the observed symptoms and results of medical tests against an array of possible diseases he or she knows to exist. Without such knowledge no diagnosis is possible. An expert system is a set of computer programs aimed at reproducing the doctor's (or any other expert's) knowledge in the form of objective decision rules. Diagnosis in such cases would be done by entering the observed symptoms and results of medical tests and letting the computer come up with the diagnosis of the patient's disease.

A medical expert system aims, by using computers, to replace the knowledge of doctors in the same way that a machine was designed to use mechanical energy in order to substitute the experience of, say, shoemakers. Although still in their infancy, expert systems represent a huge potential for replacing people currently performing mental tasks by extracting their knowledge and putting it into a computer program capable of making similar decisions. In the process, people's mental expertise in the areas in which expert systems can be developed will become obsolete in the same way that the manual expertise of a shoemaker has already become obsolete. At the same time, the expertise of *the same person who can design and improve the expert system* will become extremely valuable. Finally, an expert system can be faster, cheaper, and much more efficient in making decisions, just as machines have become with manual skills.

Robotics. Robots combine computers with conventional machines. The computer provides the flexibility lacking in machines by guiding or controlling their functions. It is the equivalent of putting eyes, ears, and brains into the machines. Although robotics is still in its infancy, the number of robots being used is increasing exponentially because of progress in computers, reduction in their size and cost, increases in their speed, and concern about reducing labor costs. Robots were initially employed to perform very simple, repetitive tasks (mostly unhealthy or dangerous ones); then they were employed in heavy, mass-production activities (e.g., in automobile factories). With time, the range of robots' functions has increased as they have been equipped with sensing devices permitting them to perform a wide range of tasks. In the future, their ability to perform more varied and more complicated tasks will increase further. As time passes, the cost of robots will fall below that of the unskilled and semiskilled workers they will be replacing. After all, robots can work all day and all night, seven days a week. Moreover, they do not disobey orders and do not ask for holidays, sick leave, or wage increases—at least for the time being. Future developments in robotics, coupled with competitive pressures, will provide strong economic incentives to adopt them in manufacturing concerns to replace semiskilled and, eventually, skilled workers.

Computers as Tools. Computers can also be used as tools to improve human work and make it more efficient. For instance, even now there are computer programs that allow car designers to visualize their compositions in three dimensions. The designers can then change parts of the design and immediately see the consequences. In addition, once instructed, the computer can produce a prototype scaled down to the desired size. Already in use are CAD (computer aided designs) and CAM (computer aided manufacturing) systems, which allow for greater flexibility in designing and manufacturing new products and provide considerable reduction in setup times and costs. Along the same lines, computers can be used to guide precision tools and control delicate operations (for example, eye surgery).

Computer Networking. At present, microcomputers can be connected to larger computers, and various types of computers can communicate with each other. Networking will significantly increase in the near future, opening up incredible new opportunities. Computer networking, coupled with advances in telecommunications, will provide the possibility of instantaneous, cheap communication among any number of users anywhere in the world. (To get an idea of the speed of modern laser communication, imagine GTE's technology, which can transmit the equivalent of the content of ten sets of *Encyclopaedia Britannica* every second.) Electronic mail will therefore replace conventional mail for the transfer of text, numbers, images, documents, and the like. Commercial data banks, library services, news reports, stock market transactions, airline or other reservations, and many other tasks will increasingly be done on a wide scale through home and office microcomputers.

Computer networking has not been feasible (technically and economically) until recently. Each computer spoke its own language, and even computers constructed by the same manufacturer were speaking different "dialects." New generations of computers (even of the same make) could not communicate with their "elders"—in other words, Babel. Nobody could understand anyone else without time-consuming and expensive translation services except for computers of the exact same kind and generation. As standards become established, networking is opening huge new vistas and is becoming one of the fastest-growing areas of computer technology.

Noncomputer Technologies. In addition to computers, several other technologies are in the process of becoming economically viable, and extensive applications are being found for them. For instance, fiber optics technology is currently being used to improve the quality of telecommunications while decreasing the costs. Integrated digital service networks (IDSN) have also been developed thanks to fiber optics, permitting transmission of images from regular telephone lines and utilization of computer terminals to access data banks, order books, send mail, send or receive faxes, and so forth. In the area of energy, photovoltaic solar cells, inherently safe nuclear reactors, more efficient engines, lighter construction materials, and more effective lighting are increasing the supply of energy while at the same time decreasing energy demands. Advances in biochemistry and genetic engineering are leading to cheaper products with specifically desired characteristics, while progress in medicine is continuing to bring more effective treatment of disease and longer life expectancy. Such advances could bring huge technological breakthroughs in a short time span. Finally, in the area of transportation, airplanes are becoming more energy-efficient and offer smoother traveling; trains (in which travel resembles flying more and more) are becoming faster (as we head toward magnetic levitation); and cars are getting "smarter" as their functioning is controlled and refined through the use of microchips. These technological innovations will continue the trend toward cheaper and more plentiful products; safer, faster, and less expensive transportation; globalized, higher-quality and lower-cost communications; and plentiful, more reasonably priced energy. They will consequently change many aspects of our daily lives as well as the ways in which business firms operate and compete (see the Appendix and the next chapter).

THE DISTANT LONG TERM

Five to fifteen years from now the trend toward "computerization" of all aspects of office and home will continue accelerating. Toward the end of that period manufacturing will be in about the same position as agriculture is today, as fewer and fewer people will be employed by manufacturing firms. Imagine, less than 1 percent of the population working in agriculture and 2 percent in manufacturing. Mass-produced goods will continue to become cheaper, and there will be overcapacity among manufacturing firms (as there is today among agricultural ones) and therefore strong competition.

As employment in manufacturing declines, opportunities in services will increase. The service industry will continue developing at a rapid pace. Higher incomes, more free time, longer life expectancy, and similar characteristics prevailing between now and the twenty-first century will increase the demand for services and provide opportunities for additional employment to compensate for corresponding losses in manufacturing and farming. The next chapter summarizes those aspects and characteristics and briefly describes their implications for various service industries. Careful strategic thinking will be required to identify opportunities in services, to figure out possible ways of gaining competitive advantages through the changes in the service sector, and to set long-term plans in motion to implement the transition to a full-scale service economy.

In addition to the continuation of trends discussed in the emerging long term concerning the Information Revolution, telecommunications, energy, biochemistry, genetic engineering, medicine, and transportation, brand new technological breakthroughs will inevitably emerge too. Possible candidates for breakthroughs are high-temperature superconductivity, the discovery of new sources of energy, superefficient engines, novel ways of exploiting the capabilities of our minds, new ways of storing and retrieving information in computer memories (including new technologies to construct memories), economical transmission of three-dimensional images, and so forth. We can only speculate as to whether and when such innovations will appear. A number of surprise breakthroughs have occurred in the past, making obsolete certain parts of industries and fundamentally changing others. As managers cannot make contingency plans for unknown breakthroughs, the only alternative is to be vigilant, carefully monitoring the environment for signs of significant changes that might affect the organization. The challenge is to judge correctly the usefulness and applicability of new technologies, so as not to waste valuable resources on ineffectual inventions nor apply them too soon. As no specific plans or actions for the distant long term can be contemplated because of the inherent inaccuracy of forecasts, the role of strategy for the distant long term is to provide a basis of financial strength and organizational flexibility so that unforeseen changes can be dealt with and unforeseen opportunities exploited once they have been judged to be economically profitable.

THE FARAWAY LONG TERM

Forecasts intended for more than fifteen years into the future cannot be used to improve specific decisions. Instead, their purpose is generally to build organizational consensus, which becomes the basis for establishing long-term visions and possibly devising general strategic directions. In addition, faraway long-term forecasts aim at satisfying curiosity about what the future might hold. A few companies, mostly in the field of aerospace, can plan that far ahead, but even in such cases the plans must be general. Too many things can happen to make the best laid plans go wrong, making it futile to plan or formulate specific strategies for such a long period into the future.

Forecasting, in particular for the long term, presents a paradox. To be accurate, forecasts must be general in terms of the events being predicted and the times at which they will occur. However, their usefulness relates directly to how specific, precise, and accurate they are. The paradox can be unraveled only on a case-to-case basis through companywide thinking. Consider our watchmaker, or any other individual living two hundred years ago: Could he or she have imagined global telephone communications, television, airplane travel, two cars to a family, computers, an oversupply of food, less than forty-hour work weeks, or atomic bombs? Most of those inventions were not even in the realm of science fiction at that time. Similarly, today we must be capable of accepting that unimaginable breakthroughs will occur in the future with far-reaching consequences for our way of life, societal attitudes, work habits, business organizations, and governments.

The next stage or breakthrough will come when computers can imitate or surpass the highest of the human intellectual abilities, that is, learning, novel problem-solving, and creativity. However, such computers are not likely to appear soon. When and if they do, it will be interesting to see whether the prediction that at that future time humans will be to computers what pets are to humans today will come true. In the meantime, humans will continue to hold an overwhelming competitive advantage over computers in that they are superb problem-solvers, they can learn if provided with adequate feedback, and they can be creative. Those talents, which must be cultivated as much as possible, will become the critical skills of the next century. Business firms will have to develop those skills to the greatest possible extent if they are to prosper and excel, as they will have few other means to gain competitive advantage.

THE PARADOXES

1. Managers are constantly being bombarded with myriad long-term forecasts (including those in this book), yet a good number of them will be inaccurate or of limited usefulness.
2. Long-term forecasts must be precise and time-specific, yet, to be accurate, they must be general and vague (in terms of time).

THE CHALLENGES AHEAD

We are living at present in a period of considerable change. The Information Revolution is progressing at full pace, bringing fundamental changes that must be dealt with. The challenge is to sort out the various available forecasts of forthcoming change and to decide how they might effect a given organization. However, this will not in itself be enough. Managers must also plan for and take concrete steps to deal with such changes, in particular those of the emerging long term. They must formulate appropriate strategies in order to face the future as intelligently and rationally as possible, knowing quite well that brand new innovations and breakthroughs that nobody can anticipate will inevitably occur. The final objective must be to minimize the organization's chances of failing, while increasing those of succeeding. In so doing, managers will inevitably have to take risks and make mistakes, as the future will not always turn out to be as predicted. The challenge will be not to make fatal, irreparable mistakes and to learn through the mistakes made to anticipate change and to initiate change more effectively within the organization. The executive's ultimate success will certainly depend upon how well he or she can meet such challenges.

THE CHALLENGES AHEAD

1. Being able to sort out useful forecasts from irrelevant ones and correctly predict the impact of the former.

2. Being able to figure out when and how established patterns and/or relationships might change.
3. Being able to make specific plans and take concrete actions in anticipation of the forecasts decided in (1) above without being sure of the reliability of the forecasts.
4. Being able to formulate appropriate strategies to minimize the risk of incorrect forecasts and their negative consequences for the organization.

6

Business Firms and Managers in the 21st Century

*"T*he typical large business 20 years hence will have fewer than half the levels of management of its counterpart of today, and no more than a third of the managers."

PETER DRUCKER, "The Coming of the New Organization," *Harvard Business Review*, January–February 1988.

This chapter discusses the types of business firms and managers most likely to emerge in the twenty-first century. The predictions are made by examining long-term patterns in human history and exploiting the analogy between the Industrial and Information revolutions. The assumptions used to develop such predictions are made explicit. The chapter points out strong similarities (as well as differences) between the Industrial and Information revolutions, which are used to discuss coming changes in business firms and in the role of managers. The importance of flexibility, responsiveness, novel problem-solving, learning, and creativity is explored. It is argued that these will become the critical skills needed to gain or maintain competitive advantages in the twenty-first century.

Suppose you are a businessman living five hundred years ago. Your customers are townspeople who walk to your store to buy groceries and other merchandise. Almost all of the commodities you sell are produced locally and are practically the same as those sold by your father, grandfather, and great-grandfather. Shipments, if made from outside the region, take a long time to arrive, and communications outside the town are slow. In your world change is taking place at a snail's pace, and you do not have to worry much about your future or that of your business, nor about the well-being of your family. You expect your eldest son to carry on running the family business and to take care of his younger brothers and sisters, as you did for your own. But you do worry about epidemics, plagues, and famines, as well as wars, that can affect your family. Five hundred years ago, little forecasting was needed—in comparison to today nothing much changed at that time—and when wars, epidemics, or plagues arrived, there was not much people could do to protect themselves or their families. Transportation and communication barriers minimized competition with other merchants, the tastes of customers were stable, and as long as no major disaster was taking place the buying power of the townspeople did not change much. There was little need for management in those days.

Today, on the other hand, we live in a global village. Products can be shipped worldwide in a matter of days. Communications are instant. Information about new technologies, products, and fashions travels instantaneously. The life cycle of products is short and getting shorter, and competition is intense, because few if any barriers to entry are secure. At the same time, life is much safer, and standards of living are higher than ever before. No major epidemics have occurred (the spread of AIDS is still limited), and plagues and famines have been eradicated throughout most of the industrialized world. We have not had a major war for almost fifty years (a record), although the danger of nuclear holocaust hangs above our heads.

As noted in Chapter 5, we are witnessing an incredible amount of change by all historical standards. Such change will drastically alter business corporations, the way they are being managed, and their managers. The challenge for executives will be to guide their firms in adapting as smoothly as possible to forthcoming change. This chapter provides a rationale for calculating how coming changes will affect business firms and describes the type of manager that will be needed to run them in the twenty-first century. Finally, it explores the challenges of operating in the twenty-first century and the type of organization and structure that will be needed.

COMMERCIAL TRANSACTIONS AND BUSINESS FIRMS OVER TIME

Humans realized early on the value of specialization. Their agricultural production was greater if they cultivated a single crop. Some people could produce more and better-quality goods (swords, shoes, houses, works of art) because of their special talents and experience gained through apprenticeship and years of practice. The exchange of goods, however, was limited to the area of production by the cost and slowness of transportation and the perishability of many products. Venetians in the sixteenth century initiated both the production of goods and commerce on a greater scale than that of the single craftsman or artisan. They established workshops where many people could work and built ships that traveled throughout the Mediterranean and the then known world. But the turning point in the production of nonagricultural goods and their wider distribution came close to 230 years later with the Industrial Revolution, which necessitated the construction of factories and became the springboard to the large, multinational corporations of today.

The Industrial Revolution began in England when peasants (previously working at home) were brought to the factory, where they could be better supervised and could work more efficiently. The output of those workers expanded substantially through the use of manually operated tools available in factories. Increases in productivity encouraged construction of more and larger factories, which began producing greater quantities of goods (by all previous standards). Thus, the arrival of the steam engine, a new invention capable of powering the machines and tools requiring the most manual energy, spurred factory output and brought large gains in productivity.

A turning point in the Industrial Revolution came when production costs, and consequently the prices of goods sold, were reduced to a point where a considerable segment of the population could afford to buy them. That resulted in a surge in demand and the subsequent need for even greater production, necessitating higher employment and bringing about more gains in productivity through additional economies of scale, which permitted even further reduction in prices. In turn, higher employment and lower prices further stimulated demand. Increased demand consequently allowed greater output and resulted in more profits. Moreover, it motivated the development of improved technologies capable of producing the goods faster, more efficiently, and more cheaply.

As the Industrial Revolution progressed, technology became more complicated. Specialized firms to build the machines and tools needed by the manufacturing companies appeared, making technology available to anyone who could afford to pay for it. The competitive advantage of using better machines specially built for a single manufacturer disappeared. Many firms in addition to the large corporations could afford to buy the new machinery through either internal financing or bank borrowing. As a matter of fact, new entrants were often at an advantage, because their machinery was more modern than that of their established competitors. Competitive advantages in production (along with economies of scale) were therefore restricted to manufacturers using the most modern technology bought from specialized engineering firms producing and selling such technology.

Manufacturing technology spread to many areas, including transportation, weaponry, agriculture, housing, domestic comforts, and home entertainment. Service industries proliferated (e.g., banking, insurance, travel, entertainment) to meet the needs of businesses and affluent consumers whose income exceeded their requirements for necessities and durable goods. In addition to the manufacture of goods, chemical production became a growth area during the Industrial Revolution. A wide variety of chemicals were discovered and used to improve agricultural production (e.g., fertilizers), replace raw materials in short supply (e.g., synthetic rubber), mass-produce consumer or industrial goods (e.g., synthetic fibers), and come up with new medicines (e.g., penicillin). The trend toward plentiful and inexpensive goods covering most consumer needs was established.

BUSINESS FIRMS: FROM THE INDUSTRIAL REVOLUTION TO THE TWENTY-FIRST CENTURY

Although progress toward larger firms has been uneven over time, it is indisputable that firms have been increasing in size, first since 1500, and then at an accelerating rate after the Industrial Revolution. Will such a trend continue, or will increased complexity and reduced efficiency limit the benefits accruing to large firms? Will the reduced employee motivation of those working in large firms put the brakes on size? At present, the largest organization in the world is the Catholic Church, whose structure and management have not changed fundamentally for almost twenty centuries. There is no compelling reason why, if necessary, business firms using modern technology and new forms of organization could not surpass the size of the Catholic Church, barring new restrictive legislation in key countries. The trend toward larger firms can be reasonably expected to continue in the next century, resulting in giant and some super-giant corporations. However, the increase in size will not be uniform, nor will it be achieved without some fundamental changes in the organization and structure of corporations, because competitive advantages are not likely to come about solely through larger size and the economies of scale associated with the largeness itself.

ECONOMIES OF SCALE AND SIZE OF BUSINESS FIRMS

Since the beginning of the Industrial Revolution economies of scale have been an important, if not the most important, factor in gaining competitive advantages and have greatly contributed to the creation of large firms. Exhibit 6–1 lists the similarities and differences between the Industrial and Information revolutions. The differences do not suggest a diminution in the importance of economies of scale, as they indicate that information products, once developed, can be reproduced and "shipped" at no cost. Thus, the larger the number of units sold, the faster the recovery of the developmental, sunk costs and the higher the profits. Information firms will therefore be as highly motivated as manufacturing ones to sell as much as possible, to license their products, and to achieve maximum distribution coverage. There are, however, several important differences in the way economies of scale apply to different types of operations or firms that will affect their size and the way they will have to be organized.

Computer Programs. Computer programs will become increasingly important in the future. Such programs can be developed by single individuals or large business firms. Smaller programs require no other equipment than a microcomputer selling for less than $2,000, a desk and a chair, knowledge of programming, and a lot of persistence. As time passes, more firms will start specializing in the development of software. Such firms will be capable of creating libraries of frequently used programs, which could subsequently be combined to produce specific applications (using the same concept as engineering firms that provide "building blocks" for constructing new machinery). Such libraries will facilitate the development of new programs aimed at a wider variety of new applications. Obviously, some new parts will have to be written from scratch, but the entire job of programming will be done more efficiently than before. In the programming field there will always be room for small firms and even single individuals (unless the project involved is large and complex) who can develop their programs using the available building blocks. On the other hand, the marketing and distribution of computer software will require large firms capable of harnessing advantages of scale in the writing of program manuals, printing them, advertising the programs, and providing after-sale advice services. The development of

Exhibit 6–1 Similarities and Differences Between the Industrial and
Information Revolutions

Industrial Revolution	*Information Revolution*
Repetitive manual work is substituted, supplemented, or amplified through the use of tools and/or machines powered by mechanical energy.	Repetitive mental work is substituted, supplemented, or amplified through the use of computer programs (software).

Work done by people is replaced.
Work is made easier and less boring by
eliminating hard or repetitive tasks.
More, less costly material goods
are allowed. The quality of life
is improved.

Energy is required to produce goods. There are possible side effects in terms of pollution and/or waste disposal.	The energy required to produce is zero for all practical purposes. There are no side effects.

The cost of developing new products or
applications is considerable.
The success of the new products or
applications is uncertain.

Once developed and successful, a product must be produced and shipped to consumers. The cost of manufacturing and transport is usually substantial but usually gets reduced as production increases.	Once developed, a product or application can be reproduced and "shipped" at virtually no cost. Reproduction is possible in small batches in decentralized locations.

The sales and marketing costs can be
substantial.

The product is destroyed when used (either at once, or slowly as with durable goods).	The product or application can be used an infinite number of times. As a matter of fact the usefulness of the product or application may improve through repeated use.

The larger the number of units sold,
the bigger the economies of scale
achieved.

Machines cannot operate on their own. They require supervision and/or guidance.	Computers can operate (through appropriate programs) on their own. Moreoever, they can supervise and/or guide machines.

Exhibit 6–1 (*Continued*)

Industrial Revolution	*Information Revolution*
	The techniques of the Industrial (hardware) and Information (software) revolutions can be combined to produce super-automation.
Production facilities can break down because they consist of mechanical components. Similarly, durable products (e.g., cars) do break down through use.	Information facilities and products or applications break down much less often, because they are made of electronic parts (there is no friction, as such parts do not move).

computer programs, as well as their marketing and after-sale servicing, can be completely decentralized using microcomputers and existing communication capabilities.

Manufacturing Technologies. New manufacturing technologies will have to be developed using highly qualified people, incredibly sophisticated equipment, expensive computers, and technologically advanced components. Developing new manufacturing technologies will therefore require huge R&D investments, which can be assumed only by large firms capable of supporting the costs of developing and marketing such technologies. Once developed, manufacturing technologies will provide the highest returns if sold to the largest number of companies. Thus, the larger the number of units sold, the larger the economies of scale. In addition, it seems unlikely that decentralization of production will be possible without losses in economies of scale. The equipment required to produce the machines embodying the new manufacturing technologies will be too sophisticated and too expensive to install at several locations.

Traditional Manufacturing. New production technologies will provide greater flexibility in retooling and switching from one type of production to another. Thus, the minimum production required to achieve economies of scale will certainly be smaller than it is today. At the same time, new manufacturing technologies will be expensive and will have to be bought from specialized high-tech firms. Because of their high cost *they will have to be operated as close to capacity as possible* in order to depreciate such costs. Competitive advantages will therefore be attained by companies that can master the huge capital resources to buy the latest technology as well as utilize the bought technology to the fullest extent (manufacturing a variety of products) in order to achieve economies of scale. Moreover, as consumers become more demanding and as their needs change at a faster rate, it will become just as important to know the consumers' changing tastes as to satisfy them as well as possible (see also "New Products" below). Traditional manufacturing will not have to be centralized, as flexible manufacturing systems can produce small runs economically. Thus, factories could be built to optimize labor cost and availability, legislative concerns, and transportation costs.

Biochemistry and Genetic Engineering. Biochemistry and genetic engineering will play roles that are similar to or more crucial than those played by chemistry and genetics during the Industrial Revolution. Their growth and importance will increase as the biochemical and genetic engineering technologies are linked to computers, lasers, and computer-controlled production. New or improved products for both consumer and industrial uses will appear, and new industrial processes will emerge. R&D costs for biochemistry and genetic engineering will be higher than those required by manufacturing firms since time lags between research and commercialization are long and the personnel required for such R&D is highly specialized and well paid. Moreover, the risk of failure will be significant, necessitating the creation of large or giant firms capable of harnessing economies of scale and spreading the risk of unsuccessful research efforts. As the synergy among biochemical and genetic engineering firms, information technology corporations, and the traditional manufacturing companies becomes more critical, joint firms covering all three areas will eventually emerge. R&D activities for biochemistry and genetic engineering firms will have to be centralized, whereas production, once a product or process is fully developed, can be done at a local level.

Mechanical/Information Technology for Superautomation. The highest demands for R&D resources will arise from the need to combine information technology with conventional mechanical technology. The firms capable of mustering the resources and talents necessary to develop, manufacture, market, and service the new information–mechanical technologies will have to be in the forefront of high-tech and be of giant or super-giant size. Smaller firms will not be able to support the huge cost of R&D and the risk of failure, unless new types of companies (e.g., venture capital ones) specially created to develop specific technologies can be envisaged. The countries or companies that are capable of designing and producing the new superautomated technologies might acquire an important competitive advantage if they limit or delay the selling of such technologies to other firms or countries. Even today Silicon Valley and European high-tech firms complain that Japanese manufacturers hold back exports of new machinery to give Japanese chip producers a head start of up to one year. Chip users in United States and Europe also complain that Japanese firms have an advantage over them even if they get the newest chips at the same time as their Japanese counterparts, because Japanese product designers have access to the blueprints of new chips, while U.S. and European ones must wait until the chip is sold to them to determine its specifications. This delay gives the Japanese a six-month head start and provides them with a big competitive advantage in industries where the life cycle of products is around three years. I believe that in the future, as competition increases, the ability to be first in harnessing the benefits of new technology will become an increasingly important factor in gaining competitive advantages.

Segmentation and Positioning. Product positioning to reach high-income segments has been a successful practice of firms that distinguish their products from those aimed at the mass market (for example, designer clothes, Mercedes-Benz cars). The Information Revolution will further increase disposable income and create even more rich and super-rich. Marketing skills in segmentation and positioning will therefore become critical ingredients in the battle to satisfy the needs of the affluent. The size of the firms in this category could range from the very small, geared to a particular segment, to the super-giants, applying a mixture of high-tech and individualized production to satisfy the needs of specific segments and create new demands.

Services. The service sector will inevitably grow, particularly once the Information Revolution has reached a plateau similar to that of the Industrial Revolution today. New forms of services and new types of service firms will probably emerge in the twenty-first century. Service and marketing practices are likely to change considerably in ways that are hard to predict today. Service industries as well as the types of services they offer will be greatly affected by the Information Revolution, as service differentiation and customer loyalty are usually weak in this sector. Small changes in the conception of the service being offered, its perceived utility, or of the by-products of such services, can drastically affect sales and market shares. Service firms will therefore have constantly to rethink their business, innovate, or keep up with their competitors. The marketing of services will thus become the crucial factor determining success among service firms. Furthermore, since barriers to entry are usually weak, competition will be keen, necessitating constant monitoring of the environment for changes in consumer needs and tastes and a flexible and responsive organization capable of exploiting them as quickly as possible.

Service firms need not be large. Family operations and small firms can operate alongside super-giant multinationals specializing in mass-oriented services (e.g., insurance or banking). Economies of scale, although important for advertising purposes, will not be critical in providing specialized services, which might even be considered of greater value if individualized and custom-tailored. For instance, high-quality restaurants, small high-priced hotels, first-rate universities, high-power research centers, and similar services cannot be mass-produced or mass-marketed. Their value lies in their uniqueness and the limit to the number of customers they can serve. Thus, segmentation and positioning will leave room for small service firms, in particular as there will be a lot of wealthy people willing to pay for individualized services.

New Products. Competitive advantages will be gained or maintained by developing and introducing new products and services and by creating new needs. Thus, identifying new markets, creating new wants, and introducing new fads and fashions will become imperative in order to avoid product saturation or diminished desire for services. In turn, these activities will require large R&D, advertising, and marketing expenditures. Those are areas where economies of scale will become of great importance in providing an impetus for larger firms able to develop the new products or services and to market them effectively. Firms will have to gear themselves more toward the customer and satisfying his or her needs while at the same time operating as close to full capacity as possible in order to depreciate their investments. Computerized technologies will eventually be capable of accomplishing such a task and will contribute toward achieving mass production or servicing aimed at small market segments or even a single customer. Thus the contradictory tasks of customization and mass production and servicing might both be achieved in the future with computer-based manufacturing or information systems. Large firms can therefore compete with smaller ones by successfully exploiting computers and related technologies.

MANAGERS: FROM THE INDUSTRIAL REVOLUTION TO THE TWENTY-FIRST CENTURY

The architects of the Industrial Revolution were engineers. They used their ingenuity to replicate manual skills in a machine design that could produce similar goods at a fraction of the cost and at a much higher speed. At first, a single engineer was capable of learning and applying the technology required to create and repair the new machines or develop variations of existing ones. As technology became more complex, specialized engineers (mechanical, civil, chemical, electrical) were needed. Because engineering expertise could not be instantly acquired, schools specializing in teaching engineering knowledge and skills became essential. As the Industrial Revolution progressed, so did the demand for engineers, who received high salaries and were often promoted to managerial positions, including the top jobs in their firms. The privileged role, the high salaries, and the heavy demand for engineers reached a plateau in the 1960s, when the focus shifted towards MBA education and business graduates. There are still many well-paid engineers today, although their number has diminished and their pay is usually less than that earned by MBAs. Their tasks differ fundamentally from those performed by engineers before the peak of the Industrial Revolution.

In machine engineering, for instance, the role of today's engineers is to develop new machines and production processes or to improve the efficiency of existing ones. Their task is aided by the existence of standardized parts, which can be purchased from specialized firms that design, construct, and produce such parts. Engineers are not obliged to start from scratch; their designs are based on readily available "building blocks." Moreover, few engineers are involved today in machine repair. Machines do not break down as often as before, and when they do, it is often sufficient to identify the problem and change the defective part; an important principle in designing machines today to make them easy to repair by replacing whatever parts are causing problems. Sometimes it is even more economical to replace the inoperative machine with a new one. In either case, engineers are not needed. The repair side of the engineering job has been so simplified and standardized that it can now be delegated to maintenance personnel, who can do the job with tools and procedures developed by engineers. What results is a new type of engineer whose task is to perform creative work or to solve new problems. All repetitive tasks that were previously part of engineering jobs have been simplified, standardized, or delegated.

Managers' jobs have followed, and will continue to follow, a path similar to that of engineers. First, a single manager, usually the owner, managed the entire firm. He was superseded by the specialized functional manager (finance, production, or marketing), whose job, in addition to dealing with people, was mostly to perform repetitive tasks required for the day-to-day operation of the business. Today we are at the point in the Information Revolution where many repetitive managerial tasks will soon be standardized and delegated to support personnel. Such delegation can be carried out in any of several ways. First, routine, repetitive problem-solving can be programmed: A support person can enter the data and let the computer decide. (When the decision cannot be handled by the computer program, an exception message will be given, and the decision will then be referred to a manager). Computerized decisions involving managerial tasks are already being performed by specialized programs. At present the range of problems that can be handled by the computer is narrow and includes only well-defined tasks. As time passes, the computer will be programmed to treat an increasingly broad range of more complex and less well-structured decisions.

Second, consulting and research firms (similar to the engineering firms that design and develop machines) will appear. They will specialize in analyzing repetitive decision-making situations to discover the type of mental skills or knowledge required for performing such tasks. Then they will design and develop computerized decision rules or expert systems to make the same decision more efficiently, faster, and at a small fraction of the cost of having a manager do it.

Third, when managerial decisions cannot be substituted, appropriate decision support tools (in the form of computer programs and relevant information) will become available to facilitate the consideration of alternatives, the analysis of the costs and benefits, and the consequences involved. In that way they will help managers make such decisions in shorter time, more efficiently, and with better results.

Dealing with people has and will always remain a critical management task, but the nature of this task too will change. First, there will not be so many people to manage, especially in manufacturing firms. Second, people will no longer perform routine, boring tasks, which will increase their motivation and decrease the amount of supervision they would require. Third, a great deal of work will be creative (conception of new products or services, research, strategy, advertising, and so on), requiring new types of imaginative managers capable of motivating the creative people who will be needed to perform such work. Finally, computers and information systems will decrease the amount and need of person-to-person interactions (e.g., teleconferencing instead of meetings, computerized search for information instead of seeing the right person possessing such information) and will probably change the current concept that employees and managers must work in a company office.

BUSINESS FIRMS AND MANAGERS
IN THE TWENTY-FIRST CENTURY

Identifying past patterns and recognizing current trends is much safer than making predictions about the future. As the three preceding chapters pointed out, existing trends can change, and unforeseen events or situations can develop. With these reservations in mind, several predictions about twenty-first-century business firms and managers will be provided, based on current thinking, extrapolating established trends, and assuming no major unforeseen events or situations. There is no doubt, however, that new developments will occur and that new forms (unforeseen at present) of business firms will appear in the next century.

Five important trends will influence the twenty-first-century firms. First, there is no reason to assume that the current trend toward more automation will not continue. As a matter of fact, it is likely to accelerate, particularly in the area of office automation, where huge improvements in productivity will result. Second, there is no reason to assume that the current trend toward more powerful computers and information systems will not continue. It is even likely that such a trend will accelerate, as computers become cheaper and more powerful with the accumulation of experience gained from information systems. Third, there is no reason to assume that the trend toward higher personal income and more demanding consumers will not continue. Fourth, there is no reason to assume that the current trend toward globalization of trade and business will stop, although we might see some temporary reversals caused by protectionism. Along with that, the free and almost instantaneous flow of information across the earth will continue, reducing or eliminating market inefficiencies as firms search for opportunities across the world. Finally, it is a fact that population growth in Western countries and Japan is slowing down or is even declining, and that a "graying" of the populations of those countries will inevitably take place, creating a large segment of older people with different needs, income, and aspirations.

Taking the continuation of the five trends to their extremes will have the following consequences:

1. All routine, repetitive work in the factory and the office will be automated. This means that companies large in revenue or production—the size of GM or Philips—will be able to operate with only a few thousand employees. Such companies will specialize in the production of goods or in providing specific services for other firms. Their competitive advantage will be in their low operating costs.

The technology required to achieve the superautomation of the future will be of increasingly high complexity. This would mean specialized and well-trained personnel, sophisticated labs and equipment, and supercomputers. As obvious innovations and improvements will be achieved early, new ones will be harder and will require more effort. Competitive advantages in this area will come from well-trained employees, their ability to be creative, their degree of motivation, and the work environment provided for them by their company, which must have the required resources and be willing to assume the risks of failure.

2. At another extreme, all routine information needed for running a firm will have been determined beforehand (probably by specialized consulting firms) and will be available in a firm's centralized information system. Such information will be available to those permitted access to it through their personal computers. They could interpret the information, make inferences, add their conclusions, and make recommendations, which can be shared by their co-workers and managers. Competitive advantages will come by having more efficient information systems and by the ability to interpret correctly and respond quickly to incoming information, as the majority of competition will have access to the same or similar information.

3. To the extreme, all basic material needs will be satisfied as super-automation will bring cheaper products and less expensive mass services. Higher income will allow people to acquire a wider variety of products and services. Satisfying the next level of affluent consumers will require considerable talents in identifying their remaining, or new, needs and quickly acting to satisfy them so as to gain competitive advantages over other firms.

4. If the extreme of a global environment (village), where information is instantaneously and efficiently disseminated, is reached, any individual or firm with a new and exploitable idea, product, or some form of competitive advantage will get maximum benefits by operating on as close to a worldwide basis as possible. This might involve sublicensing, joint operations, subcontracting, or other special arrangements to produce or distribute the idea or product on a global scale. Competitive advantages will go to firms able to develop and exploit global networks to achieve economies of scale by selling to or servicing the largest number of customers.

5. In a stable environment of zero population growth, where affluent consumers already possess the basic durables they might need while spending a smaller proportion of their income on durable and nondurable products, growth in revenues and profits of firms will have to come from new products, and mostly from new services or novel ways of offering existing services. Otherwise it has to come from targeting the increasing

segment of older people, from providing services in travel and entertainment aimed at the growing free time of the population, or from creating new markets, such as in Third World countries.

If the above trends continue, by the first part of the next century the majority of factories and offices will be superautomated, producing large volumes of customized output. Information will be centralized and will be available at any location, at any time of the day or night, for any authorized person who might need it. Superautomation and easy availability of information will bring the inevitable downfall of hierarchical/ bureaucratic organizations. Growth will be difficult to achieve and will come mostly in the service sector. Products will be cheaper than today and more plentiful, while selling them will be highly competitive. Global firms will exploit opportunities on a worldwide basis, although protectionism and reciprocal agreements between trading blocs might limit the extent of globalization, at least temporarily.

OBTAINING AND MAINTAINING COMPETITIVE ADVANTAGES

Imagine living in 2010. Your personal computer is connected to a network that allows you access to as wide a range of services as the telephone of today. Your color computer screen can also serve as a picture phone and a fax machine, can send and receive electronic mail messages, can have access to your bank and other accounts, and can connect you with libraries of books and music and a host of other services, including reservations and computerized buying. Buying habits will be different, as information about all products and services will be available in computerized data banks (if those offering them want to sell them). Expert systems capable of searching and selecting the best of alternatives among those available, given your own special requirements, will exist. If you want to buy a hi-fi system, say, you can hire an expert system to help you choose one. First it will elicit or measure your musical preferences, your ear for sound quality, the size of your apartment, the potential uses of your hi-fi set, esthetic considerations, your budget, and other facts. With such information, the expert system can determine your "ideal" configuration and can search all around the world for the system that best fits your specific needs at the lowest cost.

If your computer can search databases of hi-fi equipment of firms from all over the world, your choice will be extremely large. The competition among those selling such equipment will be fierce. Computerized consumer protection data banks will reduce or eliminate your risk of being cheated; your computer will be able to consult them in order to verify the information provided by the seller. If your computer zeroes in on a few sets, you could examine them by yourself by looking at their three-dimensional photographs and designs and listening to their sound. The set you decide to buy can be ordered through your computer, debiting your bank account. The set will be delivered to you overnight. If you decide instead to order a customized set geared to your specific wants, it can be manufactured and shipped to you within a couple of days.

In the twenty-first century few intermediaries between the consumer and the producer or the provider of services will be needed. Computerized access to products and services will change distribution channels in a fundamental way and will bring about some completely different forms of organizations. Will you need a travel agent if your computer can find the most appropriate routes and the best bargains for you? Will you need a car dealer (and the cost he adds to your car) when your computer can search out the best bargain from all over the world for you? You could test-drive the car in a computerized simulation model. Finally, think of being able to make the final decision when you want to, without the pressure of the car salesman telling you what to buy, and able to custom-order exactly the configuration you have in mind. In such an environment, where will competitive advantages come from, and how will they be maintained? They will have to come by providing some real benefits to the consumer.

To provide real advantages, companies in the next century will have to be superspecialized and capable of quick and constant innovation based on the correct recognition of existing or emerging consumer needs. In order to be innovative, flexible, and responsive while achieving economies of scale, organizations might have to be structured in such a way as to minimize the negative consequences of larger size. Economies of scale might then be achieved in ways other than larger and larger size. For instance, existing corporations might be willing to act as mother companies, financing spinoff businesses, which they would support until maturity. Such new businesses would consequently be part of the "family," operating in unison with the mother firm, or they would break off for reasons of efficiency. (In such a case the mother company could have a percentage of the shares.) Alternatively, decentralized, semi-autonomous firms or new types of organizations (e.g., manufacturing–distribution companies similar to the fast-food chains like McDonald's or R&D–dealer symbiosis, where the dealer is a part-owner of the R&D organization) might emerge in order to reduce the disadvantages of increased size. Already many companies are experimenting with alternative forms to the bureaucratic, hierarchical organization so prevalent in our day.

THE PARADOX

Although it is safer to identify and extrapolate current trends in business firms and management, it is not clear how and when changes in such trends will occur or when new, unforeseen events or situations will develop. Moreover, it is not always obvious when such changes will begin, how they will specifically affect different organizations and industries, and what can be done in anticipation.

CONCLUSIONS

In this chapter, I have predicted the types of business firms and managers most likely to exist in the twenty-first century. When established patterns in human history are analyzed, a trend showing that technology has been playing an increasingly important role becomes obvious. Furthermore, such a trend does not seem likely to change, but will instead probably accelerate through the influence of the Information Revolution. The critical assumption of the predictions made in this chapter has been that there is an analogy between the Industrial and Information revolutions. Moreover, five well-established trends in the business environment were identified and their consequences and influence for the firms of the twenty-first century explored.

Although it is not possible to predict the exact timing or the specific extent of coming changes in management, it is clear that gaining and maintaining competitive advantages in the twenty-first century will not require the same skills as those of the past. Hierarchical corporations concerned about controls and the maintenance of the status quo will not be able to do well in the future, when identifying new needs and quickly responding to exploit them will be of paramount importance. Instead of following orders from the top, employees will have to show initiative, use the right information in making correct decisions, and be creative. Thus, flexible, responsive, and creative organizations will replace the hierarchical, bureaucratic ones of today. Moreover, competitive advantages will come not from buildings, machinery, or capital, but rather from people and their creative talents. Finally, management and business firms are likely to experience some major changes in the way they operate and are organized, as automation (in the factory, the office and in managerial decision-making) will be increasing and competition will be moving from the tangibles (products and services) to the intangibles (ideas, gimmicks).

7

Planning for the Future

*M*an has a set of gifts which make him unique among the animals: so that, unlike them, he is not a figure in the landscape—he is a shaper of the landscape.

JACOB BRONOWSKI, *The Ascent of Man*

This chapter describes planning, its several purposes, and its elements. Various analytical planning models are presented, with a discussion of when they can be used and also the different situations where planning defies analytical treatment and has to be based on intuitive and creative thinking. In addition, the challenge of planning under uncertain conditions is presented, and techniques for facilitating management's ability to deal with uncertainty are described. The chapter ends by looking at planning effectiveness and the factors that might influence it.

Russia's 1957 launching of Sputnik, the first artificial earth satellite, caught almost everyone by surprise. The U.S. administration responded to the challenge by setting in motion an extraordinary program that culminated, twelve years later, in the landing of Neil Armstrong on the moon on July 21, 1969. The multibillion-dollar project of sending a man to the moon was a remarkable achievement. It necessitated many technological breakthroughs, required the solution of innumerable problems, and brought about many new scientific discoveries. In addition, it demanded the cooperation and coordination of thousands of people, hundreds of companies, and many federal agencies. The planning effort required to accomplish all those tasks was enormous. The fulfillment of the initial goal, the moon landing, meant a giant step for mankind not only because it opened the ultimate frontier—space—but also because it was one of the greatest planning achievements of all time. It also repre-

121

sented a big psychological victory in the battle for technological prestige between the United States and the Soviet Union.

Large-scale tasks such as the moon landing, the Manhattan project, the crash programs to produce equipment and weapons during World War II, the building of the huge cathedrals of Christian Europe, and the construction of the pyramids exemplify the necessity and importance of planning, without which they could not have been accomplished. But beyond grand-scale projects planning is necessary for most aspects of human endeavor and most business activities.

The unique human ability to foresee the future allows us to plan ahead in order to accomplish desired goals or meet future needs. Planning for the future has been a widely practiced human activity for many thousands of years. The domestication of animals, agriculture, the building of houses, saving for old age, the storing of food, preparing meals well ahead of getting hungry, and myriad other activities are motivated by anticipation of future needs. Business firms, the military, and governmental agencies must and do plan for the future. Their planning is usually more complex and more elaborate than that done by individuals, but the motivation and the intended purpose are the same. This chapter concentrates on planning in business firms, although the ideas presented are applicable to nonprofit organizations as well.

THE PURPOSES OF BUSINESS PLANNING

Business planning encompasses a wide variety of tasks and can have any or all of the following purposes:

1. *Dealing with Lead Time Requirements.* Many human needs cannot be satisfied instantaneously. Forecasting is required to predict them and to decide what actions must be taken ahead of time to fulfill them; forecasting is useless (apart from its academic interest) unless concrete steps are taken to benefit from it. This usually means *doing* something ahead of time so that future needs can be satisfied at the time and place they appear. The demand for a specific make and model of car in Kansas City must be predicted ahead of time, so the right car will be ready at the dealer's waiting for the customer; otherwise, the customer will have to be without a car for several months while the car companies take his or her order and then produce the car according to his or her specifications. Planning for potential demand improves service and permits quick or instantaneous satisfaction of consumer needs.

2. *Achieving Desired Goals.* Through careful thinking, concentration of efforts, and coordination of action, it is possible to achieve results that otherwise would have been impossible, like the moon landing. In the business world there are many uses for this type of planning, for instance, designing and producing cars, trains, airplanes, or most other products. Similarly, attempts to shape the environment in desired directions or gain competitive advantages, as the Japanese did in their quest to achieve superiority in the microchip market, are also part of plans aimed at achieving some desired goal through careful thinking, concentration of efforts, and coordination of action. Such plans often aim at implementing a busincss strategy or some long-term vision.

3. *Commitment and Control Tool.* Top management often uses planning as a tool aimed at communicating its objectives to operating managers and in turn assuring their commitment to implementing the plans agreed upon between them. Rewards (bonuses, promotions) and punishments are often tied to how well the agreed-upon targets are being reached, thus making planning a control tool against which the achievement of objectives is being measured.

4. *Coping with Uncertainty.* Inevitably the forecasts on which the plans are based go wrong, or events that were not predicted and planned for occur. In such cases organizations must be able to minimize or avoid the negative consequences of the wrongly predicted or unforeseen events and the financial and other implications of the inappropriate plans. A common approach among manufacturing and distribution firms is to plan for extra stock in case demand is higher than predicted. Similarly, extra cash or marketable securities are held to avoid financial problems when expenses exceed receipts. Another way of coping with uncertainty is by buying insurance to minimize the negative effects of a fire that destroys, say, one of the factories. An important and interesting question is the extent and cost of planning to deal with various types of uncertainty. For practical reasons, the ability of firms to plan for a wide variety of rare and unforeseen events is limited and means other specific planning actions must be employed. (This topic, a major ingredient of strategy, is dealt with in Chapter 9.) For normal, repetitive events and the uncertainty associated with them, much can be done in an intelligent, rational manner that balances the costs and benefits involved. A major purpose of planning is to deal practically with such routine uncertainty.

5. *Combinations of Purposes.* Often planning includes dealing with lead time needs *and* achieving desired goals, while at the same time facing an uncertain future. An airplane must be conceived and designed

fifteen years ahead of the time the first plane will be delivered. But the goal of designing the right type of plane at as low a cost as possible depends upon estimating future demand, consumer preferences for the most comfortable plane, technological innovations, competition, and many other factors that are by no means certain. Human and financial capacity, as well as other constraints, further complicate the task of planning and eventually building airplanes. Nevertheless, the difficulties must be overcome, as it is practically impossible to avoid planning, particularly for large, complex projects. Thus, management must devise practical procedures for gaining the highest benefits from planning, while being aware of the problems, uncertainties and costs associated with any attempt to plan ahead and the games being played when growth and other objectives are being agreed upon by top and operating managers.

THE ELEMENTS AND STEPS OF PLANNING

There are six elements or steps needed in order to plan for future events. Planning is not likely to succeed when one of them is omitted or when it is not carried out properly. On the other hand, completion of all six planning steps does not guarantee planning success, as failure can be caused by a variety of other factors (faulty forecasting, environmental changes, competitive actions or reactions, accidents, and so on). A good example of the inability of elaborating planning to bring success is the Ford Motor Company's Edsel car introduced in 1957. The thinking, rationale, market research, design characteristics, testing, and competitive analysis that went into that car were impressive. Market research studies started as far back as ten years before the car was introduced; extensive interviews were made to discover consumer preferences; the best designers were selected to bring a distinctive style to a size considered perfect for what the consumers of the time wanted. Lavish resources were put into building the car, and huge sums were spent to promote and advertise it. Yet all those efforts were in vain. Consumers did not like or buy Edsels, which were considered one of the biggest planning blunders of all time, costing Ford an estimated $200 million in losses, the equivalent of close to a billion of today's dollars.

The six planning steps are as follows:

1. *Seeing the Need for Planning.* The first step in any planning attempt is to realize that something needs to be done ahead of time and that action is required in order to attain some desired future goal. Understanding the

situation at hand, considering the problems that might arise if nothing is done, exploring the uncertainties, examining the constraints (human, financial, capacity, material) and the possible benefits involved, as well as studying the various possibilities for planning and which is the best way to go about doing it are critical tasks that must be carefully thought through before any decision is made.

Studying potential planning situations is a task usually engaged in at the level of top management, especially when important planning projects are being considered and great amounts are at stake.

2. *Formulating Alternatives.* Once the need for planning has been established, a careful study is required to bring out all salient aspects of the task being considered and at the same time to determine various planning alternatives. The generation of alternatives is of critical importance and requires (a) knowledge about the planning situation being considered, (b) creativity in order to generate novel and potentially successful alternatives, and, (c) realism—the alternatives found must be pragmatic and feasible given the actual organizational, human, financial, and other constraints.

The end result of this stage of planning, which usually involves a fair amount of deliberation, is the formulation of a number of planning alternatives, which are presented to management for further consideration. The study of the most appropriate way of approaching planning and the formulation of alternatives is usually a job delegated to a committee made up of managers assisted by staff people. Knowledge, creativity, and realism are the three critical ingredients necessary to come up with clever and practical alternatives.

3. *Selecting the "Best" Alternative.* Available alternatives have to be evaluated by senior management so the "best" among them can be selected. In a world characterized by certainty selecting the best alternative might be trivial, but that rarely happens in business and economics, where uncertainty in forecasting, changing environmental conditions, competitive actions and reactions, and unforeseen events can affect the best of plans and bring unexpected results or even failure (such as the Edsel). Selecting the "best" of alternatives becomes a subjective process in which benefits and costs must be weighted in relation to future uncertainty and the potential risks involved. In such an evaluation a great deal depends upon managers' subjective preferences, their vision of the future, and their willingness to take risks. In deliberating on the "best" of alternatives management must be aware that the greater the dollar value of the plans being envisaged and the longer the planning horizon, the

larger the potential benefits but also the bigger the possible risks if something goes wrong. Planning requires commitments and can result in losses if the future turns out to be different from what was expected.

Planning for short-term, repetitive situations is usually more straightforward than planning for the medium term (budgeting) or the long term (capital expansion, new product introduction), particularly when short-term situations can be quantified and a single measurable objective specified and subsequently optimized in the search for the best solution. For the medium and long term, evaluation becomes much harder, as tradeoffs between short- and long-term benefits are not possible, uncertainty cannot be quantified, and consumer preferences might change. In such cases, determining the essential features of planning, deciding on the main problems confronting the planners, and coming up with appropriate objectives are critical aspects that inevitably influence perception of available alternatives and selection of the best among them. If the essential features, the problems, and the objectives cannot be correctly identified, planning might degenerate into an analytical exercise in correctly dealing with the wrong alternatives or in evaluating unimportant alternatives with a lot of numbers and computer models. In such cases the analytic selection process might be perfectly applied, but its value ends up being nought.

4. *Implementing the "Best" Alternative.* Planning requires concrete action that includes commitment of resources, overcoming people's resistance to change, and specific tasks to be accomplished within certain time constraints. A great deal of coordination and considerable human relations skills are usually needed to implement the selected planning alternative successfully.

The person in charge of implementation has to be able to get things done and to solve a wide array of problems that inevitably arise in any implementation effort, in particular when large or complex tasks are involved or when implementation is carried out for the first time.

For repetitive planning tasks, implementation can be formalized so that it can be applied on a routine basis each time planning is required. Moreover, for the first few times extra effort can be concentrated on refining the plans and making the process of implementation more efficient. It might even be possible to implement both the new planning procedure involving the "best" alternative and another alternative (if one had been considered as a rival to the best one selected) so as to compare the results and confirm the value of the best alternative. Similarly, the new planning procedure can be compared with the ongoing approach to planning, if one exists, in order to smooth out problems of transition.

5. *Monitoring and Controlling Results*. It is rare that actual outcomes are the same as those predicted when plans were being made. Inaccurate forecasts, competitive moves, unforeseen events, unanticipated difficulties, lack of adequate resources, changing environmental conditions, new or underestimated constraints, unpredicted resistance to implementing the plans, and many other factors can affect implementation and cause deviations between plans and reality. Such deviations must be discovered as soon as possible through effective monitoring. The reasons causing them must be established so that corrective action can be taken. Monitoring actual results, establishing causes, and taking corrective action are indispensable planning/implementation activities, more difficult in practice than academic books on the subject of planning seem to imply. In many planning situations feedback is neither frequent nor precise (consider, for instance, the evaluation of long-term investments, or entering new markets). Moreover, the causes of deviations are not obvious, as results below expectations can be attributed to many factors.

6. *Pursuing Versus Abandoning Plans and Planning*. Many plans never come to fruition no matter how much effort is expended or how many adjustments or modifications are made. Similarly, planning processes (e.g., budgeting, production scheduling) can become inappropriate, ineffective, or even obsolete. Fundamental changes in the environment or the market place, serious errors in implementation, unrealistic assumptions about the future, or ill-conceived plans or planning procedures can necessitate abandoning existing plans or planning processes. A correct assessment of the situation at hand and timely and effective action are not always easy, as management may feel that investing additional effort and resources and continuing a little while longer might change the situation and bring the long-expected benefits.

Examples of human optimism (see Chapter 2), of seeing "the light at the end of the tunnel" and not wanting to give up after large amounts of money and effort have been expended, abound. On the other side of the coin, premature abandonment can bring huge opportunity losses when persistence and some additional effort could have brought success and profits. For instance, several companies abandoned their entry into the computer market because of mounting losses and strong competition. They found out later that microchips and microprocessors were required for their basic manufacturing activities and that they had to pay much higher prices to acquire new companies capable of providing the needed expertise than if they had kept their initial computer operations. The example of Xerox is the most prominent. In 1968 Xerox bought Scientific

Data Systems (SDS), a computer company, for $900 million. It also created a research center in Palo Alto, which built the first personal computer (Alto) in 1973. In 1975 Xerox abandoned its computer operations and took a writeoff of $1.3 billion. Worse, it never capitalized on the development of the personal computer constructed by its Palo Alto center. Such a computer was further developed by Steve Wozniak and Steve Jobs, who started Apple Computers. Had Xerox continued devoting resources for a few more years, it would have had an unbeatable lead over IBM and other microcomputer manufacturers. If Apple, with little financial support, no marketing organization, and little engineering expertise, did so well, Xerox could have wrapped up the microcomputer market had it not given up prematurely just before microcomputers became a multibillion-dollar market. But Xerox did give up, and with that decision lost the opportunity to be a major (if not the most important) player in the fast-growing microcomputer market. New efforts by Xerox to reenter the microcomputer market in the 1970s brought no results as the opportunity had passed. Worse, suggestions that the new personal computer be used to develop a word processor were not followed, further aggravating Xerox's opportunity losses.

PLANNING TASKS AND
ANALYTICAL PLANNING TECHNIQUES

Business organizations are faced with a large number of planning tasks that cover all functional areas and extend over the short, medium, and long term. Some of the tasks are repetitive; others are unique. Some are simple and quantifiable; others are complex and defy analytical treatment. Exhibit 7–1 describes many planning tasks, provides a brief description of them, and lists possible techniques for accomplishing or facilitating them. A prominent analytical technique widely used in planning applications is mathematical programming (linear, nonlinear, integer, and dynamic). The purpose of such a technique is to optimize some objective (e.g., minimize costs or maximize profit) by taking people, material, equipment, or capacity constraints into account. The optimization is achieved by examining all possible solutions in a systematic way that allows computational shortcuts and guarantees optimal solutions. The applications listed in Exhibit 7–1 (transportation, assignment and allocation tasks) are the principal ones covered by mathematical programming. In addition, other analytical techniques that can aid planning are described in Exhibit 7–1.

Quantitative models can be and are being used for planning purposes, but they are not a panacea that will solve all problems. Their advantages and limitations must be understood before such models are applied to real-life planning situations and tasks.

Model assumptions. Analytical (quantitative) planning models require several assumptions. For instance, they assume that everything is quantifiable, that measurement errors do not exist, that there is a single and known objective to optimize, and that things do not change over time. Moreover, they assume a perfect degree of predictability or that the degree of uncertainty is known and will remain constant. Obviously those are a lot of assumptions and are not always borne out. If one or more of the assumptions are incorrect, the potential negative effects must be explored, as there is little room for avoiding the negative consequences when using the planning techniques listed in Exhibit 7–1.

Model advantages. Planning models provide objectivity, consistency, and optimal computational solutions. Their biggest advantage is that they can include hundreds of factors and select from many millions or even billions of alternatives. Besides, they impose on managers careful study of the planning task at hand so that a formalized, well-thought-out solution can be selected. Finally, their cost is considerably lower than having humans do the same tasks, in the vast majority of cases.

For repetitive, well-defined tasks where quantification is possible, planning models are of great value, especially for the immediate and short terms, where predictability can be realistically assumed. Distribution, scheduling, and production tasks can be readily quantified in a way that optimal solutions can be found. For instance, today it is not considered a viable alternative to dispense with a scheduling model, based on linear programming, when assigning pilots and flight attendants to various routes and airplanes. For big airlines this planning task cannot be performed manually without serious actual and opportunity losses. Determining the best product mix in producing various grades and quantities of gasoline is not considered within the realm of possibility without some form of linear programming. Large supermarkets, telephone companies, airports, and highway tollbooth agencies could not conceive of determining their staffing and amount of equipment necessary without using queuing models.

As time passes, as more experience with planning models is gained and better and faster computer programs are developed, a wider range of planning tasks are being delegated to models and performed automatically on a routine basis using computers. The challenge when using these models is in formulating them realistically, specifying objectives accu-

Exhibit 7-1 Planning Tasks and Techniques

Type of Task	Description	Major Planning Technique
Distribution Transportation	Amount of goods (items) to be transported from a number of origins (factories/warehouses) to a number of destinations so as to minimize transportation costs or ensure availability of goods	Linear or integer programming
Scheduling/ assignment of machines/equipment	Determining the most efficient way of assigning people to jobs, machines or equipment to tasks, salesmen to territories, etc.	Linear or integer programming
Production scheduling/ planning	Determining the optimal schedule/planning of labor, machines or equipment, raw and other materials, taking into account personnel, capacity, space, and other constraints as well as estimates of potential demand and costs	Linear and/or dynamic programming
Production mix	Determining the optimal production mix of products given available raw and other materials and taking into account existing constraints	Linear programming
Production blending	Determining the optimal blending of two or more resources to produce one or more products in order to minimize costs or maximize profits	Linear programming
Inventory	Determining inventory policies (when and how much to order) to balance inventory costs and the actual or opportunity losses of being out of stock	Inventory models

Queuing	Determining slack in personnel or equipment so as to balance the inconvenience of waiting to be served and the cost of having extra personnel or equipment	Queuing models
Resource allocation	Determining the optimal allocation of resources to more than one activity in order to maximize benefits while taking into account existing constraints	Linear or nonlinear programming, decision theory models
R&D planning, capital investment	Select R&D projects and capital investment opportunities in order to maximize net present value or internal rate of return	Decision theory models
Large-scale or complex projects/tasks	Plan over time, assign tasks, coordinate their execution, avoid bottlenecks, monitor subtasks, monitor progress, control outcome	Program evaluation and review technique (PERT) or critical path method (CPM)
New products and markets	Determining when and what products to introduce and when and what markets to enter	New products planning models, strategic planning models, decision theory

rately, and measuring the various parameters correctly. Once those tasks have been accomplished, it suffices to monitor the outcome of the planning models to know when it is necessary to modify the way they are formulated, the objectives being optimized, or the values of their parameters. If monitoring does not point out changes or potential problems, management can concentrate its efforts on less quantifiable planning tasks or other nonplanning activities.

PLANNING TASKS DEFYING
ANALYTICAL TECHNIQUES

In many planning tasks the critical element is not the planning technique used but the estimates made and assumptions employed. For instance, in order to compare several investment alternatives and select the best among them, the net present value (NPV) technique can be used. NPV computes the value of each investment in today's dollars by discounting future costs and benefits and translating them into present-day dollars. In order to compute such a value, however, the NPV technique requires predicting the yearly stream of all future costs and returns of each of the alternatives being considered, which are then converted (discounted), assuming some specific interest rate, to come up with their equivalent present value. Once such NPVs have been computed, the investment alternative corresponding to the highest value is chosen. In this selection process the critical task is not the technique of NPV itself, but predicting the future costs and returns for each investment alternative and assuming (forecasting) specific interest rates for future years. Also, the investment alternatives being considered are of paramount importance, as some useful ones might not be included. Similarly, selecting R&D projects, deciding upon new products, identifying opportunities, and entering new markets require forecasting and planning considerations that usually defy analytical treatment. In such cases intuition, gut feelings, and creativity become the important elements of success in planning, while the role of planning models is restricted to providing an analytical framework for formalizing the planning process (possibly aided by decision theory models). Planning models oblige planners to systematize the process of making decisions, force them to quantify their subjective opinions for each alternative being considered, and then allow them to use a framework that facilitates the choice of the ''best'' alternative.

In the past many mistakes have been made by attributing more usefulness to analytical planning models than was justified, in cases where the real value of planning was in the intuitive thinking and creativity process required to formulate alternative plans. Overreliance on analytical techniques can bring disastrous results and swing the pendulum in the other direction, where it is thought that *no* analytical planning can be useful. Such an attitude is equally wrong as far as repetitive, operational planning tasks are concerned. Operational planning applied to repetitive situations can greatly improve efficiency, if the right analytical technique is chosen and properly implemented.

PLANNING UNDER UNCERTAINTY

Dealing with uncertainty is a crucial planning and strategic concern that must be dealt with explicitly by studying the various types of uncertainty under different environmental conditions.

1. NORMAL, QUANTIFIABLE UNCERTAINTY

In the short term uncertainty can be dealt with by carrying extra stock, when materials or products are involved, or by introducing slack in cases of demand for services. However, it must be clearly understood that carrying stock and having slack in equipment or personnel increase costs. Planners must therefore balance the extra costs against the benefits of greater customer satisfaction. Inventory and queuing models offer the possibility of dealing analytically with short-term uncertainty. However, several points must be clarified concerning the assumptions and use of such models. First, inventory and queuing models require that uncertainty be quantified, and it must be assumed at the same time that its magnitude will not change in the future. In the reality of the business world, uncertainty can be quantified and assumed constant when large numbers of items or customers are involved. But with few customers and unusual or unexpected events occurring, uncertainty cannot be adequately measured or introduced effectively for planning purposes. The extra inventory and additional slack required would be too large to be practically incorporated into the planning model.

2. UNUSUAL AND LESS QUANTIFIABLE UNCERTAINTY

Unusual situations (such as a major machine breakdown), and less quantifiable events (fluctuation in the demand of a few large industrial customers), and unpredictable but repetitive happenings (the start of a recession) require making contingency plans in cases where such events can influence operations. Contingency planning is required because the events are almost sure to occur, but no one can predict their exact timing or the extent of their influence. For instance, predicting the start and depth of the next recession is not realistically possible (see Chapter 3), but it is almost certain that a recession will start. Having contingency plans ready (what to do when recessions of various intensities begin) is the only realistic solution in that case. Similarly, a recovery is also a near certainty once a recession has started, which warrants contingency planning for recoveries of different strengths.

There are no quantitative models enabling us to plan for various contingencies, although the implications of contingencies can be considered in various circumstances by performing a "what if" type of analysis (see below). The success of contingency planning lies in the identification of the most critical contingencies (it is impossible to plan for all eventualities) and the realism and effectiveness of the proposed plans when a certain event occurs and the plan has to be put in motion.

A common practice in dealing with inevitable but unusual events whose timing cannot be predicted is buying appropriate insurance policies (e.g., fire insurance), or setting up funds to deal with recurrent but unpredictable contingencies (e.g., bad debts). Bank credits can be negotiated to deal with cash shortfalls during periods of recession or financial reserves built to cope with unexpected declines in cash flows.

As the costs of extra inventory and slack must be balanced against the benefits of improved service, the costs of being prepared must be weighed against the benefits of being ready to face a certain contingency. The obvious challenge for planners is to be realistic in their assessment of both costs and benefits. For instance, planners will have to decide whether the extra cost of buying foreign exchange in the futures market to hedge for decreases in the value of foreign currencies compensates the risk of devaluation of such currencies or the opportunity losses of reevaluation. Moreover, keeping cash reserves to deal with unexpected shortfalls in receipts must be weighed against the opportunity losses resulting from not using such cash for productive investments.

3. HIGHLY UNLIKELY EVENTS AND THE UNCERTAINTY THEY INTRODUCE

Highly unlikely events with low probabilities of occurrence require the drawing up of scenarios. Scenarios involve unusual or rare events that might never happen, or whose likelihood of occurrence is rather small. The difference, therefore, between contingencies and scenarios is that the former refer to repetitive events almost certain to occur while the latter involve nonrepetitive, highly unlikely situations.

Scenario planning has been proposed as a way of dealing with today's turbulent environment.[1] Scenarios aim at increasing sensitivity to unlikely events and forcing planners to study dangers or opportunities they would not have considered otherwise. Unlike contingencies, which are well defined and easily identifiable, scenarios can cover a wide range of situations whose likelihood of occurrence is very small. There are many unexpected events (for example, the energy crisis for planners before 1970) that cannot even be conceived so that scenarios for them can be developed. Nevertheless the scenario approach is popular at present because it allows planners to think carefully about threats or opportunities in the environment and to focus their attention on scenarios that seem more likely than others.[2]

As with all forms of planning, preparing for unlikely scenarios can be costly and can divert efforts and resources from other planning activities. Thus, a balance has to be achieved between actual or opportunity costs and the perceived benefits of scenarios. By their very nature scenarios are more appropriate for long-term planning, usually to explore various environmental possibilities and consider their impact on the organization. They allow management to study threatening or beneficial possibilities and to assess their likelihood of occurrence as well as the planning and resources required in case such a threat or opportunity does indeed occur.

ANALYTICAL TECHNIQUE FOR CONSIDERING THE EFFECTS OF UNCERTAINTY

Several analytical techniques allow for the evaluation of uncertainty in planning and the consideration of its possible impact. Such methods can be classified in the following categories:

Monte Carlo Simulation

Monte Carlo simulation is a mathematical technique that attempts to represent the features, characteristics, and relationships of real business situations. It also introduces the idea of chance by experimenting with different values (inputs) and observing their influence on the outcome.

The representation and experimentation are two distinct aspects of the Monte Carlo technique. The former provides the mathematical relationships of the reality being studied, while the latter relies on the probabilistic (chance) aspects that might exist in reality and thus govern the uncertainty. The chance element is replicated by generating random numbers, which become the equivalent of uncertainty. If a sufficiently large number of random numbers are generated, they can be used to study their own influence on the system represented by the simulation and the variability, and therefore uncertainty, they might bring. Planners can consequently observe the impact of such variability and consider appropriate planning strategies to deal with it.

Monte Carlo simulation can be used for a broad range of applications and is one of the most widely used analytical planning techniques in business. It covers such areas as the effect of fluctuations in demand or lead times, financial risks, the influence of machine breakdowns on operations, variability in the time it takes to complete large projects, the effect of various external events on budgets, and so on.

The advantage of Monte Carlo simulation in comparison with other analytical techniques is its simplicity. Others are much more complex and difficult to understand. Once developed, the Monte Carlo simulation can be applied on a routine basis to study variability and therefore uncertainty and risks. Using only desk-top computers, the method can be applied easily on an automated basis any time a user desires to do so.

The disadvantage of Monte Carlo (and other forms of simulation) is that it is only as good as its representation of reality and its realism of uncertainty. Since reality is complex, a simulation model makes many assumptions and simplifications in the mathematical relationships it uses. If such assumptions and simplifications are realistic, so will the Monte Carlo simulation and its study of uncertainty be. Otherwise its value will be limited or its use even harmful, as it can provide misleading results that can suggest the wrong alternatives to follow. Besides, business relationships, even if adequately captured, do not remain constant for long, which poses a serious problem unless changes can be promptly identified and adequately incorporated.

"WHAT IF" MODELS

The "what if" type of analysis is another way of using simulation models to study uncertainty. For instance, if future prices or interest rates cannot be predicted, the financial implications can be considered using different prices and interest rates and observing their influence on profits. "What if" simulations are similar to Monte Carlo ones except that the various inputs are not generated randomly. Instead, the user specifies what he or she considers to be the most likely range of values these inputs can take so that their implications for financial results can be studied.

SENSITIVITY ANALYSIS

Sensitivity analysis also requires a simulation model. However, it goes a step further than the Monte Carlo and "what if" models by examining the influence of not only randomly selected inputs (as in Monte Carlo) or a discrete number of values and their influence (as in "what if" models), but *all* possibilities. The main advantage of sensitivity analysis (as the name implies) is that it allows managers to study the sensitivity of output (e.g., profits) under all possible values of input (say, prices of raw materials and prices of finished products). Such sensitivity allows planners to visualize the extent of uncertainty, as prices of raw materials (in this case) cannot be predicted; they can subsequently consider appropriate pricing policies for finished products. A difficulty with sensitivity analysis is that it must be restricted to a few important variables, which must be identified subjectively by the user; otherwise, the number of factors and sensitivities involved is too large to consider (reality is too complex) in any intelligent manner.

Desk computers permit fast and efficient construction of planning models. With a little extra effort they permit users to perform Monte Carlo, "what if," and sensitivity analysis. Today, many managers use those models regularly to explore various planning possibilities and to consider the effects of uncertainty. Although a definite step in the right direction, such models can provide a false sense of security, since the relationships used might not represent reality accurately. If that is so, neither the simulation nor the study of uncertainty will be of any value. In the final analysis, the most important aspect of planning models is not the analytical manipulations but the realism and accuracy of the relationships used in constructing the model. Thus, a challenge for management is to continue using analytical planning models as a point of departure, but then to expand the study by considering additional, more creative alternatives and thus go beyond the simplicity of planning models and their rather limited representation of future uncertainty.

PLANNING EFFECTIVENESS

The effectiveness of planning depends upon many factors, most of which are outside the control of planners and business organizations. In order to improve planning effectiveness, serious efforts have been made in the last decade to reduce the number of factors that cannot be controlled. One example is the just-in-time (JIT) production system, which emphasizes coordinating production in a way that eliminates in-process inventories. The work done in many departments and by suppliers must be coordinated so that their output can arrive at just the moment when it is needed. In addition to coordination, just-in-time also requires accurate forecasting and detailed planning so that the right materials, parts, and semifinished items have been ordered and can arrive at the right time and in the appropriate quantity needed. Uncertainty is reduced or eliminated, together with production costs, as material and in-process inventory are gone.

New marketing techniques coupled with computers might make it possible to reduce or eventually eliminate uncertainty not only in production but also in short-term demand. Potential clients could directly connect their home computers to those of a given manufacturer and custom-order the exact products they want. With computerized, flexible manufacturing systems, such individualized demand could be automatically registered, needed materials ordered, and the product constructed and shipped to the client the same day it was ordered. Although customized ordering and manufacturing on a mass scale might still be some years away, once used on a wide basis it will reduce uncertainty in planning and lower production costs while at the same time increasing customer satisfaction.

Along the same lines, raw or other materials and additional items required for manufacturing can be ordered automatically through computers, thus shortening lead times and reducing uncertainty in receiving the orders. Planning for services can be similarly improved if the computer of the client can directly communicate with that of the service firm so that reservations are made automatically and the computer of the service firm directly uses the information to assign the right number of personnel and the right equipment to satisfy forthcoming demand. I believe that in the next ten years planning effectiveness for the vast majority of short-term events involving repetitive situations will be greatly increased by computerization and automation. The Tandy Corporation's use of computers to facilitate planning and reduce inventories is a good example. Each of the close to nine thousand Radio Shack stores that are part of the Tandy chain are connected by computer to corporate headquarters in Texas. That lets management know what is selling and what is not, the remaining stocks of each item in each store, and the orders received from each store at the end of each day. With such detailed knowledge at its disposal, management is able to monitor actual results as well as make plans and take actions for the future before the day is over. The possibilities are limitless, as results can be achieved at a small cost, quickly, and without bureaucratic obstacles.

In the final analysis, planning effectiveness can be made to mirror that of living systems, in which all operational tasks (planning and otherwise) are performed automatically and routinely (e.g., the circulation of the blood, digestion) without depending much on forecasting (such as knowing when food will be available or how long it will take to cook it) or external information. Instead, effective monitoring and automatic corrective action control any deviations from objectives (homeostasis). If operational, repetitive planning tasks in business organizations can also be delegated and automated, giving management more free time to monitor possible changes in the environment and to consider their influence on planning. Management can then concentrate more of its efforts on strategy, on coming up with creative solutions, or on cultivating the intuitive aspects of planning.

I doubt that uncertainty will ever decrease for medium- and long-term planning. In such cases planning effectiveness will depend greatly upon the firm's ability to predict future events accurately and to monitor planned versus actual results in a timely manner. It will be important to take corrective action if necessary, or even abandon or greatly modify established plans if reality turns out different from what was planned for. As the time horizon of planning becomes longer and feedback less precise, it will become exceedingly difficult to forecast accurately and to monitor planning results precisely in order to evaluate their effectiveness. Intuitive thinking will be necessary to decide on the need for corrections, the possibility of abandoning the plans, and the value of planning in general. In such cases the versatility and flexibility of living systems can be considered an ideal to imitate. Living systems learn and adapt to changes in the environment precisely because they know that such changes will inevitably occur. They do not try to predict them or be prepared to face them on a case-by-case basis—such tasks are not practically possible. Instead, they are able to recognize permanent changes in the environment and either change internally or master the environment in order to deal effectively with the changes.

In turbulent environments there is a need for organizational versatility and flexibility. Irreversible commitments must be made as late as possible. Flexibility and late commitment allow the organization to modify to a large extent or even drop plans when later information shows the need to do so. Alternatively, plans can be implemented incrementally or designed in such a way as to leave maximum freedom of action for cases where the future turns out to be other than what was expected. But flexible, incremental plans that allow for maximum freedom of action are not always possible, as firms must sometimes commit themselves well in advance, particularly when substantial benefits are sought. In such cases there is not much to do except understand the choices involved and the possible risks and consequences if the reality turns out different from the predictions. Taking calculated risks or even gambling large amounts of money on long-term projects that sometimes take years to complete are facts of business life and an indispensable element of success (see Chapter 12).

THE PARADOXES OF PLANNING

1. To be prepared for future uncertainty, planners must allow for extra stock, slack, and/or insurance policies, yet these cost additional money, which has to be balanced against the benefits of improved consumer satisfaction.
2. The longer the time horizon of planning and the greater the commitment of financial and other resources, the larger the possible benefits when the planning is effective and reality turns out as planned, yet the greater the risks and the bigger the losses when planning is not effective or when forecasting is wrong.

THE CHALLENGES AHEAD

The cost of inventory and of slack in equipment or personnel is a substantial part of overall cost (usually estimated to be close to one-fifth). Lowering such costs therefore becomes a big challenge for management. Advances in computer technology coupled with clever, creative thinking can reduce uncertainty in demand or lead times for receiving materials or semifinished goods once they have been ordered, especially in short-term planning situations where forecasting is more accurate and controlling supply is more feasible. Obviously, if uncertainty is reduced the production or service costs can also be reduced without affecting customer satisfaction.

Another managerial challenge is to identify those planning tasks that *can* be dealt with efficiently using one of the planning models listed in Exhibit 7–1. Since the majority of planning tasks that can be dealt with analytically belong to the short term, it might be possible to combine the advantages and challenges of lowering uncertainty in demand or lead times *and* increasing the number of planning tasks that can be efficiently treated analytically.

In the final analysis, any planning task involves real out-of-pocket costs in order to be prepared to face future uncertainty and potential risks if the plan turns out to be wrong or ineffective. One of the biggest planning challenges facing management is to balance such costs against actual benefits or opportunity losses. Balancing planning costs versus actual benefits or opportunity losses cannot be reduced to an analytical treatment, as many of the costs and benefits may be hidden, and most of the opportunity losses might not be obvious. For instance, French and British planners saw benefits in building the Concorde plane other than operational profits from passengers crossing the Atlantic. They were willing to gamble more than $2 billion to develop the airplane. Air France and British Airways operated the plane at a loss for close to ten years. Today the Concorde provides a healthy operating profit and has given Europeans a competitive lead in the high technology needed to design and build regular passenger airplanes. Had the planners only considered the direct benefits, they would never have decided to build Concorde.

As computers become more powerful and their use more extensive, all forms of planning will be affected, providing management with a constant stream of opportunities to reduce costs and stay ahead in the game of achieving or maintaining competitive advantages. If taken successfully, they will provide operational benefits by improving planning efficiency and lowering costs. They will also free managerial time, which can be concentrated on the more intuitive parts of planning as well as the strategic and creative aspects of running the organization.

8

Competitive Strategy

*I*n war everything is simple but simple is difficult.

KARL VON CLAUSEWITZ, *On War*

In a utopian world characterized by certainty and lack of competition, no strategy would be necessary. Deterministic planning would suffice to deal in an optimal way with all future needs, which could be forecast with a perfect degree of accuracy. However, uncertainty and competition are integral parts of our world. Competition necessitates the formulation and implementation of appropriate strategies in order to gain competitive advantages and maintain them as long as possible. Strategy is concerned with defense against efforts by existing or new competitors to attack a firm's position directly or indirectly, in order to gain advantages of their own. This chapter discusses competitive strategy and the problems and opportunities it involves by drawing heavily on military strategy.

In the spring of 1978 Pepsi won an important battle in its ten-year war against Coca-Cola by achieving a higher market share over an entire year (30.8 percent for Pepsi, 29.2 percent for Coke). In a race where every percentage point of share was worth $100 million, Pepsi's success was astonishing, given its starting position as a distant second, the strong competitive advantages enjoyed by Coke, and Coke's huge financial resources. Yet slowly and consistently Pepsi dethroned Coke as the undisputed leader in the soft drinks market. Through a combination of moves aimed at changing the ground rules of competition and nullifying Coke's accrued advantages, Pepsi managed to compete on a more equal footing. It first achieved superiority in a few products and regions, which it then used to broaden its beachhead and win the battle. It did so while Coke fought back at each step with all its might. Pepsi's management knew that it could not fight Coke head on, so it used a variety of indirect approaches to make inroads and eventually was able to compete more directly. Its efforts were helped by the attitude of Coke's managers, who could not conceive of anyone's dethroning them. Exhibit 8–1 is a summary of the main elements of Pepsi's strategy in its efforts to spot weaknesses in Coke's market position and strategy and to exploit them.[1]

Success in business rarely comes without serious challenges from established competitors. Successful firms can never rest on their laurels. Existing competitors and new entrants will constantly attempt to undermine their advantages. Thus, firms are in constant need of a strategy in order to gain competitive advantages or defend accrued ones. An important element of this book's approach is to examine the question of what we can learn from military strategy and apply to business strategy or, conversely, of what strategic mistakes can be avoided in the area of competitive business strategy by studying military strategy. Years of military experience can teach us something useful, particularly as the field of business strategy is still in its infancy. Although there are differences between military and competitive business strategies, there are also important similarities that can help us to understand competitive business strategies and to formulate and implement them more successfully.

WHAT IS STRATEGY?

Strategy is a commonly used word that means different things to different people. To avoid misunderstandings, the term "Strategy" is defined and the way it will be used in this and the next chapter clarified. Strategy and stratagem are defined by *Webster's New World Dictionary* as follows:

Strategy: 1 (a) The science of planning and directing large-scale military operations, specifically (as distinguished from tactics) of manoeuvering forces into the most advantageous position prior to actual engagement with the enemy. (b) A plan or action based on this.

2 (a) Skill in managing or planning, especially by using stratagem. (b) A stratagem or artful means to some end.

Stratagem: 1 A trick, scheme, or plan for deceiving an enemy in war.

2 Any trick or scheme for achieving some purpose.

Exhibit 8–1 Major Elements of Pepsi's Strategy in Winning Its Battle Against Coke

In 1970 a plan was conceived for dethroning Coke and a basic strategy for doing so was formulated. The strategy consisted of two overlapping ideas or principles. First, do not fight head-on on Coke's terms; instead change the ground rules of competition. Second, identify and neutralize Coke's competitive advantages.

An efficient system for measuring market share was devised and used to monitor results on a national scale. A panel of 350 families was used to determine consumer preferences and buying habits.

In analyzing the panel data, an opportunity was spotted: No matter how much Pepsi the 350 families ordered each week, they always consumed it.

The opportunity to create bottles and packages easy to carry was seized (thus allowing people to buy and bring home larger quantities of Pepsi). This was done by replacing the standard 6.5-ounce glass bottle with bigger (in ounces) plastic bottles and by allowing pack sizes containing more bottles than before but at the same time easier to carry.

Bigger bottles and larger pack sizes provided Pepsi with an advantage for those who wanted to buy larger quantities of soft drinks. It also nullified one of Coke's competitive strengths: its sleek, distinctive, and familiar 6.5-ounce glass bottle. As a matter of fact such bottles became a disadvantage, as they were heavy to carry.

As larger bottles and varied pack sizes became the industry norm, Pepsi's competitive advantage disappeared, but Coke's lead had been reduced. Pepsi had to come up with new strategies in its continuing battle.

Pepsi developed a new strategy of attacking Coke's image. "Pepsi Generation" commercials portrayed Pepsi as the drink of the young generation, while Coke, by inference, was for older people. Such a positioning strategy was very successful, for Coke could not be marketed as both a classic and the drink of the younger generation.

Pepsi focused its attack on Coke by going after specific local markets and distinctive distribution channels (discount stores, supermarkets, restaurants, etc.). Such a strategy allowed Pepsi to concentrate its attacks against the dispersed resources of Coke, which had to defend all its territories (markets, products, distribution channels) while Pepsi was specializing and making gains on specific, well-selected targets (by gearing to their needs while at the same time providing big discounts).

Comparative advertising was introduced by Pepsi (another change in the ground rules, which had prohibited such advertising until then) showing people drinking colas without knowing the brand involved (blind tests). In such tests it was found out that the majority of people preferred Pepsi to Coke when the brand name was not shown, while when the name was known they preferred Coke.

Comparative advertising and the slow but consistent improvement in Pepsi's

Exhibit 8–1 (*Continued*)

market share angered Coke's management, which overreacted by threatening Pepsi's bottlers with retaliation and by bringing out commercials ridiculing comparative ads. Such overreaction solidified Pepsi's momentum and strengthened its determination to win.

Pepsi created brand managers for various market segments and product sizes. They were directly responsible for sales and were more highly motivated and more capable of exploiting opportunities and increasing their sales than the previous sales structure.

A major mistake by Coke was exploited as Coke continued to monitor market share according to the number of bottles being sold. Coke failed to register Pepsi's substantial improvement (selling fewer but larger bottles) and did nothing about it until it was too late.

These definitions of strategy, particularly 2 (a) "skill in managing or planning," are very general, making strategy equivalent to "management." Such terms as "strategic planning," "strategic visions," "strategic actions," "strategic environment," "strategic marketing," "strategic finance," "global strategies," and the like are, if anything, even less specific. Hence it is necessary to find a more restricted meaning for the term when applied to business organizations by looking at its origins.

MILITARY STRATEGY

The term "strategy" originates in the military. As wars became more global, costlier, more complex, and more frequent, it became obvious that victory depended on factors other than a big army, bravery, and straightforward fighting prowess. An army had to be trained, equipped, and supplied, then had to be at the right place in order to face the enemy. Delays and other mistakes during wars were becoming costly and had to be avoided at all costs. The role of leader of the army grew in importance as the outcome of wars began to be determined to a great extent by his intelligence, experience, and personality.

Generals had to motivate their troops, conceive of ways of outsmarting the enemy, formulate a battle plan for each engagement, and carry it out successfully. The outcome of the war was of the utmost importance to those doing the fighting (most would end up dead or in slavery if defeated) and for the state itself (which faced the loss of sovereignty), both sides were motivated to strive their hardest to win. Both sides prepared as much as they could and did everything in their power to outwit each other through tricks, schemes, or plans (that is, stratagems). Winning the war became an end to justify all means.

To improve their chances of winning wars, experienced generals had to formulate, as well as implement, effective strategies. However, strategy has always been and always will be an elusive art. Victory in a single battle, or even a war, could not guarantee success in another, as winning generals in one battle could perform less well in the next. Learning from past battles and past mistakes, better preparation, new alliances, larger armies, new military technologies, and different fighting conditions made each battle unique, so past experience and wisdom, although important, were not the only factors contributing to victory. The ability of a general to judge correctly the uniqueness of each situation and to come up with the most appropriate strategy, given his own and his opponent's relative strengths and weaknesses and the battle conditions, became an important determinant of success, outdistancing the contribution of other factors. Because both opponents had the same objective, they both tried to come up with the winning formula. Military strategy came to resemble closely the quest for competitive advantages, real or psychological, over the opponent before and during hostilities. Such advantages had to be attained by outsmarting one's opponent by any means that could produce victory. The preferable way to victory was to force the opponent to surrender rather than through bloody warfare. It is only lately that strategy has become a buzzword used beyond its original meaning in wars.

THE ESSENCE OF MILITARY STRATEGY

Liddell Hart, in the best scholarly treatment on the topic, concludes after studying wars and strategy throughout history that "the true aim of strategy is not to battle but rather to achieve a situation so advantageous which, if it does not of itself bring the enemy to surrender, would produce a sure victory in the battlefield."[2] Such an advantageous position, he adds, can be achieved by physical action or psychological means. Physical advantages are gained by concentrating one's forces, psychological ones by surprising the enemy and making him believe that such concentration has taken place and he can do nothing to avoid it. But Liddell Hart points out that in war every problem and every principle represents a duality. Thus, "in order to hit with effect, the enemy must be taken off his guard. Effective concentration can only be obtained when the opposing forces are dispersed; and, usually, in order to ensure this, one's own forces must be widely distributed. Thus, by an outward paradox, true concentration is the product of dispersion.''

The effective concentration of one's forces, either real or perceived, produces a psychological advantage for oneself and a disadvantage for the enemy once he realizes that he has been trapped. His reaction is amplified if the realization that he is at a disadvantage is sudden; it turns to panic when he realizes that his freedom of action is limited or nonexistent. An important aspect of strategy is, therefore, to play upon the fears of the opposing general, who must be made to believe that he has lost his ability to avoid entrapment and defeat. Such fears have their greatest effect when they spread to his troops and lead to eventual surrender or defeat without a bloody battle.

Liddell Hart emphasizes the ''fallacy and shallowness of attempting to analyze and theorize about strategy in quantitative terms.'' Specifically, he writes that ''even more remote from truth—because in practice it usually leads to a dead end—is the tendency of text-books to treat war as mainly a matter of concentrating superior force.'' He re-emphasizes the constant need for doing the unexpected and using the indirect approach to ensure the opponent's unpreparedness. He points out that in military strategy the longest way around might be the shortest way home.

In summarizing his study, he concludes that *the* principle of war can be condensed into a single word, ''concentration,'' which can be elaborated as ''concentration of strength against weakness.'' In order to be effective such concentration requires the dispersion of the opponent's forces, which must be done by deceiving the enemy into believing that one's own forces are also being dispersed. Then, before the opponent has time to concentrate, the strike must come, and with it victory.

Liddell Hart provides eight principles for the successful formulation and implementation of military strategy. The first six are positive, the last two negative.

1. *Adjust your end to your means.* Do not try to accomplish more than you can achieve. In other words, you must set realistic objectives. Being overconfident is dangerous, because the men upon whom you depend might not share your optimism.
2. *Keep your object always in mind.* Although it might be necessary to change your plan and objective if the battle conditions turn out not to be as expected, do not do so easily. Keep in mind that there is more than one way of achieving your goal.

3. *Choose the line (course) of least expectation.* Put yourself in the enemy's position and do the last thing he would expect you to do.

4. *Exploit the line of least resistance.* Identify and attack where your enemy is weakest. Then exploit your initial success to achieve final victory.

5. *Take a line of operations that offers alternative objectives.* Attempting to achieve more than one objective at the same time obliges the enemy to disperse his forces. At the same time it allows you to accomplish the objective he is least prepared to defend by attacking and winning in some specific geographical region. Then, it might be easier to gain further objectives and victories through the real or psychological advantages that come from the initial victory.

6. *Ensure that both plans and dispositions are flexible.* Your plan should include contingencies in case of success, failure, or partial success (the most common case in war). You should be able to redeploy your forces in the shortest time and maintain freedom of action even in the worst-case scenario.

7. *Do not throw your weight into a stroke while your opponent is on guard.* Unless you face a much inferior enemy, do not launch a direct attack when one is expected. History has shown that no effective assault is possible until your opponent's power of resistance has been neutralized.

8. *Do not renew an attack along the same line (or in the same form) after it has once failed.* Once the enemy has repulsed you, he will be more confident and have time to strengthen his defenses. Thus, the chances for success of a similar attack are small, even if you employ additional forces.

FAMOUS MILITARY STRATEGISTS

Although wars have been fought for many millenniums, there have been few great strategic thinkers. Most of the renowned strategists have used ideas that already existed, modifying and molding them to fit their specific needs. Below, four well-known strategists are singled out and the essence of their contribution described.

Sun Tsu. Sun Tsu produced the earliest known treatise on strategy.[3] According to Collins,[4] no other book has surpassed *The Art of War* in comprehensiveness and depth of understanding concerning military strategy or how to use it. Sun Tsu cautioned commanders and rulers against reliance on sheer military power. "Numbers alone could confer no advantage," he said. Instead he advocated moral, intellectual, and psychological factors as means of winning victories in war. He did not believe in slaughter and destruction. For him the proper aim of strategy was to "subdue the enemy's army, without engaging it, and taking it intact, or as nearly intact as possible." According to Sun Tsu, the army was the instrument used to deliver the final, fatal stroke to an enemy previously made vulnerable. He also believed in careful planning, based on sound information, and a speedy conclusion of the war. "No country," he wrote "has ever benefited from a protracted war." Sun Tsu points out that it is bad practice to underestimate the complexities of war, the strength of the enemy, or the dangers inherent in battles. Finally, he emphasizes the importance of the indirect approach and the need for deception as a means of winning wars. Many of the conclusions of Liddell Hart described seem to come from Sun Tsu's writings almost 2,500 years ago.

Alexander the Great. Alexander (356–323 B.C.) was a virtual contemporary of Sun Tsu. Like Sun Tsu, he recognized that war always operates at two levels—one physical, the other psychological. Alexander was competent at the physical aspect of war, but he was also a master of the psychological. He always fought along with his troops, usually stood toward the front of his regiments, and chose the most dangerous part of the battle for himself. He fought as much and as bravely as any of the soldiers he led. His example obviously did not go unnoticed—he motivated his troops to do their utmost by daring them with his own heroic example. At the same time he was a skillful tactician, never letting his role as a soldier interfere with his duty as a general.

Alexander was a great leader who, in a period of ten years, created a vast empire covering what is today Greece, Turkey, Syria, Lebanon, Israel, Egypt, Jordan, part of Saudi Arabia, Iraq, Iran, Pakistan, Afghanistan, and part of India. Such an achievement, realized with fewer than 50,000 soldiers and at a time when the speed of transportation was that of walking, proves the genius of Alexander as a grand strategist, a perfect tactician, and far-sighted visionary. His goal was to civilize the known world. His death from fever, at the age of thirty-three, put a premature end to his undertaking. Had Alexander lived longer he might have left us with a different world.

A battle that proved Alexander's genius was that of Gangamela (331 B.C.), where he fought against Darius III, the Persian king. Darius had an army more than twenty times the size of Alexander's. It included a strong cavalry, 200 horse-drawn chariots with knifed wheels, and elephants, as well as superbly equipped soldiers. Alexander counted on his meticulously trained, highly disciplined, well-organized army. The battle was won by his correct assessment of the enemy's position and the redeployment of his troops in order to open one of the enemy's flanks. When the Persians saw that they were in danger of being encircled, they abandoned their position and ran to safety behind their king, who was already fleeing on his horse. Had Alexander not spotted the weakness of Darius's formation and maneuvered his army to exploit it, fighting as hard as he could, he never would have won. Alexander's strength lay in the fact that he was a superb general, an able tactician, and a charismatic leader and that he could be sure his troops would follow him until death or victory. And victories he won, one after another, without a single defeat, until his death from illness (or poisoning).

Karl von Clausewitz. Clausewitz (1780–1831) is still considered the most influential, but also the most controversial, of all theorists on military strategy. His book *On War*[5] is a classic. Clausewitz viewed war as a rational instrument of national policy. He argued that the decision to wage a war ought to be based on estimated costs and gains. A war should never be started unless the gains exceed the costs and some goal related to national interest can be accomplished. "War is an act of violence intended to compel our opponent to fulfill our will," Clausewitz wrote. Thus, according to him, moderation in war is an absurdity. A nation at war should mobilize all its resources and direct all its energies toward one end: victory.

Clausewitz distinguished between abstract war (studied in military academies) and real war, and between theory and practice. He accepted the constraints imposed on generals during battles and the role of chance. He wrote that "war is the province of uncertainty: three-fourths of those things upon which action in war must be calculated, are hidden more or less in the clouds of great uncertainty." Clausewitz, like all great military strategists, stressed the importance of psychological factors and cautioned against dogmatism, outdated principles, and obsolete assumptions. His image of a military genius was someone who could learn from the situation and use to his advantage any means that could help him succeed. He did not believe in "rules of the game" or the other preconceptions about war that existed at his time. Clausewitz postulated "absolute wars" and "decisive victories" in which the end justified the means (he hailed Napoleon as a military genius when he broke the "rules of civilized warfare" that prevailed at the time, and in so doing crushed his enemies). Clausewitz was a proponent of the concept of "grand strategy," aimed at achieving long-term national policy objectives determined by political leaders. Military strategy, related to battles and war, was, on the other hand, the province of generals and had to be determined by them.

Clausewitz exercised a profound influence on European military thinking. Some theoreticians forcefully argue that his theories were mainly responsible for the murderous, excessively destructive World Wars I and II. Clausewitz's philosophy of war (and competition)—or the way people interpreted it—is the opposite of that of Sun Tsu, who believed in moderation, subduing the enemy rather than fighting, and ending a war as quickly as possible.

Clausewitz's greatest contribution to competitive business strategy is his concept of "grand strategy" and his rational approach of weighing costs and benefits before starting a war. His idea of a total war, where everything is done to win as quickly as possible, might also have merit in business if the company involved is large and strong and is being attacked by small competitors. Finally, his maxim that in war everything is permitted (one does not have to abide by the rules of the game) is also pertinent.

André Beaufre. Beaufre is a contemporary student of strategy. His small book on strategy contains an up-to-date compilation of the latest strategic military thinking and some unique, perceptive interpretations of strategy.[6] Beaufre does not believe that universal principles or theories of strategy exist unless they are of such generality that they provide little practical value (efficient and effective utilization of forces, maintaining freedom of action). He holds that successful strategy is based on the correct and timely interpretation of the constantly changing battle conditions when information obtained is used to take decisive action, outsmarting the opponent. Beaufre envisions strategy as a way of thinking that allows generals to develop realistic alternatives and choose the one that best corresponds to the *unique* situation with which they are faced. But since both generals in a conflict are aware of the same strategic principles and thinking (in particular when they are familiar with each other), strategy becomes a game of wills in which each general tries to outwit the other by interpreting incoming information and taking strategic action based on such information. In the final analysis, the winner is the general who better judges the changing situation on the battlefield and is capable of using information to concentrate his forces against the weak points of his opponent. Finally, Beaufre, like earlier writers, emphasizes the importance of the indirect approach, especially when one is militarily weaker. He forcefully argues against too much reliance on superior force alone.

Beaufre's integration of strategy as a game of wills between generals has, I believe, definite applications for business corporations, where CEOs know each other and try to outmaneuver their opponents. Also, his idea that no general strategic principles of value can be formulated deserves further consideration. Successful business strategists are those who can interpret incoming information correctly and act faster than their competitors to exploit opportunities or avoid threats. The strategy required in each situation is unique, and success depends to a great deal upon the ability of the CEO to comprehend that uniqueness, formulate a workable strategy, and implement it forcefully.

Decisive Battles

Over the centuries there have been many important battles, some of which have had a decisive influence on the course of human history. A study of these battles[7] confirms Sun Tsu's principles and Liddell Hart's and André Beaufre's conclusions on military strategy. Wars are not won with superior power or larger armies alone; psychological factors are just as important. From the battle of Marathon (500 B.C.) all the way to the Iran–Iraq war, larger armies have not necessarily been victorious. In war strategy is crucial, as battles cannot be won decisively without a great general who finds some way to deceive the enemy, usually by doing the unexpected. Besides that, novel concepts of strategy and new military technology have been instrumental in winning battles and wars. However, as Napoleon found, others are quick to discover and imitate successful technology, new strategic principles or tactics, or novel concepts of waging warfare. Thus, advantages gained in one battle cannot be assumed to last for long unless new technologies, methods, plans, or tactics are constantly invented and applied. In war, opponents cannot be underestimated. If they are stronger, they can use their might to crush their enemy. If they are weak, they know they cannot win by direct attack, so they have to come up with indirect means of confrontation. Guerrilla warfare and protracted wars of attrition are ways of overcoming powerful enemies. The will of the opponent to wage warfare and withstand punishment must not be underestimated. The defeat of the French and Americans in Vietnam and the forced withdrawal of the Soviets from Afghanistan clearly illustrate how difficult it is to subdue the combative spirit of a guerrilla army fighting for the liberation of its homeland. The high morale of an army when its country is being invaded must not be underrated either. The repelling of more than forty Russian divisions by fewer than ten Finnish ones in 1939–40 and the crushing of the superior Italian army when it attacked Greece in 1940 are examples of what the superior fighting spirit of officers and soldiers can do when they know that losing would mean occupation of their homeland.

Finally, the importance of surprise—doing the unexpected—cannot be disregarded. Surprise provides psychological as well as concrete gains and allows one side to take the initiative and control the battle or the war. The destruction of the air forces of Syria, Jordan, Egypt, and Iraq by Israel in less than half an hour just as the Six-Day War of 1967 was starting is an example of the value of surprise (catching and destroying all the planes on the ground) and its contribution to quickly winning a war.

The study of military strategy brings out some firm and widely accepted conclusions that provide fertile ground on which to build the field of competitive business strategy. Although there are obvious differences between warfare and competition among businesses, there are also important similarities to be exploited. In the next section such similarities and differences are explored, and recommendations are made about ways in which competitive business strategy can profit by studying and better understanding military strategy.

COMPETITIVE BUSINESS STRATEGY

During the early and middle 1970s, in the face of increasing antagonism among business firms, strategic thinkers started focusing on competition. In the first place, some general principles about what yields competitive advantages were proposed. They included the experience curve (postulating that economies of scale are achieved through increased production volume) and the portfolio planning approach, first introduced by the Boston Consulting Group. That emphasis on competition, although it moved the field of strategy in the direction of military strategy, created more problems than it solved.

The first attempts to associate strategy directly with competition were made in the late 1970s. Michael Porter's book on competitive strategy published in 1980 formalized the approach and popularized it within the business community.[8] Competitive business strategy stresses understanding one's industry and competitors. It counts on competitive signaling in order to anticipate and counteract competitive actions. Although knowledge of existing competitors is important, new competitors can also enter the market, and new technologies can fundamentally change the competitive structure of an industry, while existing competitors can create alliances or merge with others. Competition, moreover, involves the use of deception, which includes the dissemination of false or misleading information. Competitors are not required to follow established rules or procedures that will aid an opponent in the formulation and implementation of its competitive strategy. On the contrary, they will attempt to figure out and attack the very core of such a strategy, as their purpose is to nullify the competitive advantages of their opponents (see Exhibit 8–1 for an example). In such circumstances, the field of competitive strategy will be of better use if it is amplified with a better understanding of the similarities and differences between military and competitive business strategy.

SIMILARITIES BETWEEN COMPETITIVE BUSINESS AND MILITARY STRATEGIES

In competitive business strategy, deception cannot be ruled out. Advantages also can be sought and gained through the indirect approach, which means that competitive actions can be launched when and where they are least expected. They can be concentrated by focusing the attack on some specific target, or geographical area while the opponent's forces are unprepared or dispersed, and they can be successful before the opponent has time to concentrate his own forces and counterattack. Direct frontal attacks, when expected, are of little value, as they rarely work and at the same time are costly for both sides. Finally, changing the rules of the game is a fact of business life. It cannot be ruled out while formulating one's own strategy or attempting to neutralize that of an opponent.

In business as well as in the military, psychological factors (morale, confidence, sense of entrapment) are as important as physical ones (size, technology). Excellent executives, like great generals, are those who can take the initiative and subdue their opponents psychologically. In doing so they do not have to abide by outdated assumptions. They must be capable of recognizing changes in the environment and using such changes to their advantage. Objective evaluation of one's own strengths and weaknesses, as well as those of the opponent (competitor), is crucial. Stratagems before and during the competition are crucial elements for gaining psychological victories and achieving perceived or real benefits.

Technology influences strategy and must be exploited to gain competitive advantage before and during competitive fights. With the passage of time, the cost of technology has been rising, putting at a disadvantage those who cannot afford or at not willing to adopt new technologies.

Finally, as the size and complexity of firms (or armies) increases, the importance of an appropriate structure to implement a given strategy becomes greater.

The "glamour" of strategy must not lead to overlooking tactics (operations). Many wars have been lost because of errors in tactics.[9] Likewise, strategy must be correctly implemented in business, as mistakes in execution can ruin the best of strategies. Miscalculations, faulty judgment,[10] unexpected developments, and other operational difficulties might require modifying or completely abandoning espoused strategies. It is not enough just to have a strategy—it is necessary to monitor its effectiveness constantly in order to ensure that it is properly implemented and that it can produce the desired results.

Given the above similarities, the conclusions of Liddell Hart and André Beaufre concerning military strategy are of great relevance to competitive business strategy. Price wars (direct attacks), for instance, rarely produce the intended results. A&P's strategy to cut prices in its food store chain produced quick imitation by other major food chains and resulted in other competitive reactions (keeping stores open longer, deep discounting of certain items, spending more on advertising).

The effect of such imitation and counteraction was to nullify A&P's expected large increases in volume of the sales, which were supposed to compensate for the smaller margins caused by reduced prices. In addition to attempting a direct attack, A&P ignored another basic principle of military strategy, namely, adjusting your end to your means. A&P was not strong enough to fight its stronger competitors (Safeway, Kroger) head on. Its management was too conservative, the organization too inflexible, and the majority of its stores too old and inefficient to be able to capitalize on the advantages presented by the lowering of prices. Furthermore, A&P threw all its weight into a "stroke" (see Liddell Hart's principle 7) while its opponents were on guard (having seen the extensive advertising campaigns promoting cuts in prices). In such a case, it is highly unlikely that the opponent will not react, especially when they are so openly provoked and are strong enough to fight back. A&P's strategy did not succeed. The more than $50 million loss resulting from the price cuts was not recovered. As a matter of fact, losses increased as Safeway's market share became higher than that of A&P. The overall losses of A&P over a two-year period exceeded $200 million and brought about the fall of A&P's CEO, William J. Kane. The new CEO, Jonathan Scott, had to close 1,700 stores, fire 10,000 employees, and, of course, raise prices. Those actions could not stop Kroger from also surpassing A&P in market share, so A&P fell to third position.

The idea of an attack by the indirect approach is to ensure that the opponent does not recognize the threat and thus does not fight back, or else the attack must be so concentrated that the competition is unable to respond. Pepsi's strategy, for example, was to attack local markets and concentrate on items that were not measured by Nielsen's surveys. Coke did not feel threatened and did not respond until Pepsi's attack had gained momentum. By that time it was difficult to stop Pepsi's advances, which continued by expanding the attacks to additional markets and products, changing the rules of the game when possible and thus nullifying Coke's superior advantages.

Superior size seems to be no guarantee of a successful defense in the case of IBM, as its opponents concentrate their forces against particular areas. The victories of DEC in the minicomputer market, CRAY in the supercomputer market, and Apple and Compaq in the microcomputer market show the importance of the indirect approach and the value of flexibility when competing against a bureaucratic, conservative opponent like IBM (see Liddell Hart's principles 3, 4, and 6).

Finally, competitive battles, like military ones, cannot be waged for personal reasons, to settle old accounts or to satisfy the ego of top executives. They must be rational. Thus, expected gains must outweigh costs and possible damage or potential unexpected losses. Further, succeeding in a competitive duel should not whet the appetite for a succession of future ones.

DIFFERENCES BETWEEN COMPETITIVE BUSINESS AND MILITARY STRATEGIES

Along with the similarities in military and management strategies, there are also differences. Competition among businesses does not include murderous and destructive acts, although it might result in hardships and financial difficulties (such as loss of jobs). Competition among firms improves efficiency and effectiveness (survival of the fittest), making competition acceptable or even desirable. Business opponents can rarely deliver fatal blows to each other, so the prospect of long-term competition with the aim of slowly gaining and keeping competitive advantages by capitalizing on actual or psychological factors or the mistakes of one's opponent becomes essential. It is unlikely that firms will develop the equivalent of long-range bombers and nuclear weapons of immense destructive power, which means competitive business strategy is not likely to evolve beyond the point where military strategy was before the start of

World War II. Firms might find it advantageous to cooperate as both sides can benefit from such cooperation. Thus, alliances, joint ventures, and cross-licensing agreements are alternatives to direct fighting.

Segmentation and positioning constitute another critical difference between business and the military. Segmentation raises the importance of the indirect approach (concentration of one's forces against a point where the opponent is dispersed) to new heights, as it is always possible to find and target a specific segment of the total market. Positioning to increase one's appeal to specific audiences by specializing to satisfy their needs better is another available and often used strategic alternative.

Segmentation and positioning make defense difficult; a firm can never know where it will be attacked, so it has to disperse its forces in order to protect many fronts at the same time. Meanwhile, the competitor can concentrate his or her own forces to attack a specific segment. If a company does concentrate its forces to defend one segment, that will make the firm more vulnerable to attack in others, in particular when more than one competitor can attack at the same time. Defense in such cases is extremely difficult unless creative new approaches can be imagined and implemented.

Segmentation and positioning might become the nightmare of defense in the future, requiring brand new ways of dealing with the problems they will be posing to large, well-established corporations. They will also necessitate the development of creative new approaches to competitive strategy. Consider, for instance, the situation of IBM, which is being attacked simultaneously on all fronts by competitors (DEC's minicomputers, CRAY's supercomputers, and Apple's and Compaq's microcomputers, the low end of this market). As minicomputers and personal computers become faster and larger, they expand their range of capabilities into what previously belonged to larger mainframes—IBM's main competitive strength. How can IBM defend itself?

USING MILITARY STRATEGY IN BUSINESS FIRMS

Several books have been written on the topic of how military strategy has been applied by various firms as a basis for their own business strategy.[11] They provide many examples of specific business situations and how they can be classified or explained in terms of military strategy (attack, defense, tactics, concentration of one's forces against opponent's weaknesses, strategic principles). Although examples and concrete illustrations are important, my belief is that the greatest benefits coming from military strategy lie in the help it can provide CEOs and top management in cultivating their strategic thinking and understanding the power and limitations or dangers of strategy. Managers must accept the fact that there are no universal rules or specific recipes enabling them to formulate successful strategies. Moreover, implementing a strategy goes far beyond advice found in textbooks or offered by consultants. Strategy can never be formulated in a vacuum. Competitors must be taken into account and organizational strengths and weaknesses must be correctly assessed, together with constraints. The changing environmental conditions of tomorrow must be predicted and incorporated into the strategy being formulated. That is what makes the strategy required for each situation unique (which military strategists discovered many centuries ago) and therefore makes formulas and recipes useless.

Strategy implementation confronts competitors who are most likely to respond to outside threats and challenges with a strategy of their own. In competition there is always a duality (or even plurality) that leads to a clash of wills and necessitates changes and modifications in both the original strategy and the subsequent tactics. Those unable to be flexible, without giving up too easily, are not successful strategists; neither are those who cannot lead and motivate their people to compete with all their might and stay on until victory. Business strategists must be aware that psychological factors as well as their own leadership are as important in winning as physical advantages such as large size or huge resources.

Finally, CEOs and other students of strategy must recognize the futility of chasing fads and the "benefits" to be gained by following the "newest" of strategic theories. Great strategists (Alexander the Great, Hannibal, Frederick the Great, Napoleon) did not achieve their victories by imitation but by their abilities to innovate, to see and exploit opportunities, their fearlessness, incredible energy, and clear vision. Great business strategists must have similar qualities and must realize the inherent dangers as well as the opportunities in strategy and their own critical role in formulating and implementing such strategy.

As time passes, the importance of competitive business strategy will increase, as has been the case with the military. Business strategy will be globalized. Collusions, alliances, and similar relationships will develop in order to balance unequal forces and reduce or check the competitive advantages of some firms[12] or even nations.[13] Finally, the indirect approach will become more important, as markets stabilize and existing competitors accumulate advantages over newcomers, making it difficult to displace them by direct means.

COMPETITION AMONG NATIONS

In wars and other forms of competition (import and trade practices, industrial policies, and so forth), nations aim at protecting their interests at home and abroad. That is what Clausewitz and later Liddell Hart called "grand strategy," which goes beyond conflicts, battles, and wars. Grand strategy is based on long-term goals and is the outcome of policy considerations whose objective is to gain or maintain competitive advantages for a specific country over the long term. Although most nations possess a grand strategy (explicit or implicit), great powers constantly rise and fall.

In a book on this topic, Paul Kennedy analyzes the factors that have contributed to that cycle over the past five hundred years. His conclusion is that "wealth is usually needed to underpin military power, and military power is usually needed to acquire and protect wealth." He also concludes that history "shows a very significant correlation *over the long term* between productive and revenue-raising capacities on the one hand and military strength on the other."[14]

National wealth is a relative concept; it depends not only on how rich a nation is in absolute terms but also on the richness of other nations. The balance of power and consequently of wealth changes because nations grow unevenly from an economic standpoint with the arrival of technological organizational breakthroughs. As relative economic power changes over time, so does the ability of nations to finance military expenditures. Less military spending tilts eventually the balance of power to those who can spend more, who then grow stronger and more confident and are eventually able to surpass their formerly stronger opponents.

In addition to technological breakthroughs and organizational factors, national wealth can also diminish in comparison with that of other nations if a much higher percentage of such wealth is devoted to military expenditures, which are nonproductive. More military spending in the long run will diminish national wealth relative to that of nations that devote a smaller amount of their income to military spending, and will trigger a decline. The recent economic rise of Japan and Germany, with their small military budgets, confirms Kennedy's hypothesis.

Kennedy found that an important reason for overspending on the military has been that great powers tend to overextend themselves in terms of objectives. That tendency forces them to spend more than they can afford on military budgets, which become relatively larger than those of their competitors. More unproductive military spending contributes to the weakening of their economies (the example of the Soviet Union is striking). Countries in relative decline, in order to "feel more secure" vis-à-vis the emerging, wealthier competitors, also make larger military expenditures than they can afford. Such disproportionate military spending accelerates their decline. Countries not directly involved in conflicts and those far away from theaters of war find themselves with a competitive advantage, as they can concentrate their energies on productive, wealth-generating activities while spending a lower percentage of their GNP on the military (consider again the examples of Japan and West Germany in relation to the United States and the Soviet Union after World War II).

Nations have constantly shifted alliances to maintain a balance of power so that no nation or bloc of nations can achieve overwhelming military or other advantages.[15] Nations that believe they are militarily stronger than their opponents tend to go to war for territorial and other gains. Peaceful coexistence seems to work only when a balance of power exists or when, as in the last forty years, given the destructive power of nuclear weapons, war promises to bring about mutually assured destruction.

Although business organizations cannot fight wars, they do compete using other means. They also become part of national policy and are therefore instruments or objects of competition among nations. Interestingly, Kennedy's conclusions are both true and inapplicable in our day. The miracles of Japan and Germany have been partly due to their small military budgets in comparison with those of other industrialized countries. Yet more wealth has not resulted in increased military strength, as both countries are not allowed to augment their military power. At the same time, they benefit from U.S. and NATO military might, which protects their wealth against external threats. On the other hand, the Soviet Union is economically weak as it spends a disproportionately high percentage of its wealth on unproductive military expenditures.

CONCLUSIONS

In competition, and therefore strategy, there is perfect duality. For someone to win, his or her competitor must lose, and vise versa. But competitors will learn from each other's successes and mistakes, as well as their own. Both sides will imitate successes and attempt to avoid mistakes. Both will have access to similar information, and both will be prepared to deceive the other while trying to avoid being deceived. Finally, successful competitive practices that worked in the past cannot guarantee equally successful results in the future. New ideas and practical alternatives will constantly be required. Strategy will have to be creative and more effective in relative terms than that of competitors. There are no generic principles or magic formulas. Even if they existed they would not be useful for long, as competitors would learn about and apply them too. Thus, the big challenge ahead is to formulate and implement a successful competitive strategy without exactly knowing what such a strategy should contain, what the opponents will do, or how the environment will change—no small task. It requires overcoming the paradoxes of competitive strategy.

Liddell Hart's conclusion about the "fallacy and shallowness of attempting to analyze and theorize about [military] strategy in quantitative terms" is definitely applicable to business strategy. The observation that superior forces alone cannot secure victory is equally relevant to business situations. Competitive strategy must be accepted as an intuitive process where intellect, creativity, and outsmarting the opponent are as important as size, material resources, or previous experience.

THE PARADOXES OF COMPETITIVE STRATEGY

1. Competitive strategy is a necessity for business firms, yet few general rules or principles guiding its formation or implementation exist.
2. Although your company might have an excellent competitive strategy, you can never be sure that your opponent does not have a more effective one.
3. A competitive attack on your company might take place at any time. Yet you cannot be constantly prepared to face such an attack, as preparation will take resources and attention away from other activities.

Exhibit 8–2 presents a summary of the principal concepts of competitive strategy coming from wars and competition among nations. Business executives can benefit from understanding these concepts by exploiting the possible benefits they can gain if they use them while avoiding the pitfalls involved. Although it is clear that businesses do not have to be in constant competition, at the same time the possibility of battles and wars cannot be ruled out, which necessitates learning as much as possible from military strategy and competition among nations.

Exhibit 8–2 Major Ideas/Concepts of Competitive Strategy Coming from Military Wars and Competition Among Nations

I. Military Wars

1. Avoid undue reliance on mere size or other superior characteristics
2. Exploit any relative strengths to gain as much competitive advantage over opponents as possible
3. Importance of the indirect approach:

   a. Concentration (real or apparent) of forces against weakness of the competitor
   b. Surprise
   c. Doing the unexpected
   d. Deception
   e. Changing the rules of the game
   f. Upsetting the key factors for success on which competitor has built significant advantages

4. Importance of psychological factors
5. Avoid falling behind in technology, as well as underestimating the ability of competitors to catch up
6. Avoid mixing personal (or personality) issues with the formulation of the organization's competitive strategy
7. Importance of accurately interpreting incoming information and acting decisively
8. Vary competitive strategies depending on the intended action and the expected outcome

II. Competition Among Nations

1. Avoid overextending one's resources
2. In case of a relative decline vis-à-vis competitors, consolidate before attempting to catch up
3. Avoid getting involved in competitive battles that drain resources and energy
4. Use financial strength to gain real advantages (larger market share, high profits, reducing your opponents competitive strengths) instead of advantages of prestige

Noncompetitive Strategies

Winning, to me, was an obsession. I was driven not only by
the competition but by the force of powerful ideas. I demanded
the best of myself.

JOHN SCULLEY, Odyssey: Pepsi to Apple

*Unlike countries in war, where winning is the only acceptable out-
come, business organizations are faced with additional tasks.
Those also require strategies, which demand motivation and impose choices beyond those imposed by competition. In this chapter, the need for and types of noncompetitive strategies are
discussed, the alternatives available to achieve such strategies
are mentioned, and the challenges they present are outlined.*

The Merck Corporation has a simple and highly successful strategy that
blends scientific excellence with commercial success. It implements this
strategy by outspending its competitors on R&D, by fostering a university
campus atmosphere in its research labs, and at the same time by letting
hard-nosed product managers get the most out of the work conducted in
the labs. Although it acknowledges its competitors and races to be first
with new drugs, Merck is mostly interested in research excellence and
outstanding quality. It spends huge sums on products that will not be
commercial for more than ten years and cares little about short-term
performance and the price of its stock. "The only thing I worry about,"
says Merck's CEO, Roy Vagelos, "is our own performance." Yet Merck
consistently outperforms other leading pharmaceutical companies and
almost all other companies in the United States. Its stock is a darling of
Wall Street, which values Merck more than GM, a company with revenues more than eighteen times as high ($100 billion for GM, $5.5 billion

for Merck in 1988). In a survey of CEOs, Merck was named as the best-run and most successful U.S. company.

Merck's strategy of scientific excellence requires well-paid researchers, expensive research labs, large libraries, and considerable travel and lodging money for conference attendance. Scientific personnel cannot be "managed" effectively. Their research work will produce returns, if any, in the long term, so evaluating the short-term performance of scientists or research projects is practically impossible. One can say that Merck has a single strategic objective of achieving scientific excellence, and all the rest of its strategy for success follows naturally. Its drugs are highly profitable because they come from the best researchers in the field, who have the best equipment and other support at their disposal. Everything seems simple and obvious in Merck's strategy, yet many other companies have failed miserably when trying to achieve the exact same objective. Others produce important scientific innovations (AT&T's Bell Labs, IBM's research centers) but do not manage to exploit them for profit, and still others see the burden of their R&D department as a significant drain on their resources because their scientific personnel cannot be well motivated, well managed, or effectively directed to produce commercially profitable products.

How do strategists know when decisions are important, when to delegate, what objectives to focus on, and how to concentrate on the long term? After all, CEOs and other top management in charge of conceiving, formulating, and implementing strategy are humans with limited time and a plethora of other tasks besides the strategic ones. They must be selective and make hard choices about where to concentrate their attention and what to delegate, postpone for later on, or ignore altogether. Unfortunately, the decision-making process involved in such choices is highly intuitive, so I doubt it can ever become part of an analytical procedure or be computerized. A good part of being an excellent strategist is the ability to decide what to do, what to delegate, and how to choose between narrow and short-term objectives and holistic, long-term ones. Ohmae, in a book describing the mind of the strategist and attempting to explain the success of Japanese companies, writes:

> The answer is easy. They [Japanese companies] may not have a strategic planning staff, but they do have a strategist of great talent: usually the founder or chief executive. . . . They have had little or no formal business education. . . . They may never have taken a course or read a book on strategy. But they have an intuitive grasp of the basic elements of strategy.[1]

Successful business strategists process insights and are capable of formulating realistic objectives and strategic plans that will steer their organizations toward several types of noncompetitive strategic options. Those, in conjunction with competitive strategies, in the final analysis determine the long-term success of their firms.

TYPES OF NONCOMPETITIVE STRATEGIC OPTIONS

Strategy is not monolithic. It can take several forms, each of which provides different opportunities and challenges for management.

STRATEGY AS A DRIVE TOWARD EXCELLENCE

Overemphasizing competition might divert time and energy that could be spent more successfully on other tasks. Paradoxical as it may seem, competitive advantages cannot be gained or maintained in the long run through competition alone. In wars between nations, both parties end up weaker and in relative terms worse off than before the conflict started. Similarly, waging battles with other companies requires spending a disproportionate amount of resources on advertising, promotions, cutting prices, and so on. This causes the ''belligerent'' firms to spend relatively less on productive investments than companies not directly involved in the fighting. In the end the ''neutrals'' can make large gains on the ''belligerent'' companies or overtake them.

The same can be seen in competitive sports. Although athletes compete with each other, they are mostly motivated by an internal drive for excellence. They see competition as a challenge against themselves rather than a fight against their competitors. Great athletes excel and maintain their dominance for long periods because they care little about winning the next race. They constantly strive to improve their performances even when they can easily beat their opponents. Their goal is not to win the next game or to be the best during the current season, but to reach new heights of excellence because of the challenge of doing so.

Top tennis players, for instance, do not play to win but to enjoy the game as much as possible and to give the opponent as great a challenge as they can. Winning or losing becomes secondary, a side effect. That attitude removes the strains of competition and the fear of defeat, which in turn improves one's game as well as one's chances of winning.[2] Similarly, great artists, scientists, and inventors are not prompted by competition. Even when they are far ahead of the nearest competitor and have no reason to worry, they constantly strive to achieve more and to raise their level of excellence. Competition and war might at times become necessary for survival, but progress usually comes through humans who are self-motivated and self-driven toward excellence and perfection. This is an aspect of strategy that gets lost when excessive reliance is placed on competition. One of the most important things business people can learn from great individuals or teams is how to facilitate in their organizations the development of similar internal drives toward excellence so that high achievement can become a challenge rather than an imperative dictated by the fear of competitors.

STRATEGY AS A MEANS FOR SPECIALIZATION AND ADAPTATION

The evolution of living species indicates that ultimate survival depends on two simultaneous and seemingly contradictory types of behavior: (1) the ability to compete successfully, which is attained through specialization, and (2) the ability to deal with environmental changes.[3] In a dynamic, constantly changing environment, however, specialization may become a double-edged sword. If a drastic change takes place in the environment, the living system runs the risk of not being able to adapt to the change. To counteract the risk of specialization, living systems have acquired a host of evolutionary abilities enabling them to deal more effectively with environmental changes. These include the mechanism of homeostasis (maintaining a position of equilibrium through effective monitoring and instantaneous control if something causes a disturbance in the equilibrium), developing better senses, reacting quickly and effectively to dangers, increasing their ability to move more freely, acquiring a safer shelter, and diversifying their sources of food. Such abilities are not part of specialization; on the contrary, they are purposeful efforts to decrease dependence on single aspects of the environment.

Shelter, the domestication of animals, and agriculture were early manifestations of the human strategy to reduce dependence on the environment and minimize the negative consequences of unwanted change. Recent expedients include life, health, fire, and other types of insurance, as well as bank savings and investments. Governments encourage or even compel people to insure themselves against the negative consequences of unwanted events.

Business organizations face similar hazards. The more they specialize in order to reap competitive advantages, the more they expose themselves to the risk of becoming obsolete in case of environmental changes. An obvious challenge for business strategists involves solving the paradox of being both specialized *and* capable of coping with environmental changes. This challenge never ends. The distinctive advantages brought about by specialization and the acquisition of unique skills cannot last for long—unique skills will inevitably be imitated or become obsolete through technological and other changes. Strategists must constantly strive to refine and improve unique skills so that they retain their value.

Diversifying into different industries is not a viable strategy, as it reduces the ability to develop or maintain unique skills. In fact, diversification inevitably produces *average* performance, thus decreasing the relative advantages vis-à-vis more specialized organizations. Diversification can therefore be considered an avoidance of strategic choices rather than a creative effort to resolve the specialization–adaptation paradox.

STRATEGY AS A CREATIVE PROCESS

Creativity is not restricted to the arts, advertising agencies, or R&D departments. It is equally important in strategy as a means of gaining competitive advantage. Creativity in strategy can be used to achieve one or combinations of the following:

1. Conception of original ideas for new business opportunities or new ways to capitalize on present opportunities that lead to superior results
2. Creation of new products and new services that lead to increases in sales and greater profitability
3. Discovery of a niche leading to successful specialization and development of unique skills
4. Elaboration of tricks, schemes, or plans that succeed in outsmarting competitors by deceiving them
5. Identification of commercially profitable needs nobody has recognized or exploited before
6. Anticipation of forthcoming changes that can bring economic benefits and exploiting them before others do
7. Detection of existing or forthcoming dangers and devising means of avoiding them in a more ingenious manner than competitors
8. Identification and solving of important problems in new, imaginative ways

For the reasons I outlined in Chapters 5 and 6 (mostly as a result of computers, superautomation, and the efficient dissemination of information), the value of creativity as a strategic tool will increase in the future as the importance of competitive advantages coming from other areas decrease. That will mean a greater demand for creativity at the strategic level and a greater emphasis on creative thinking and output to gain competitive advantages (see also Chapter 10).

STRATEGY AS A CUSHION FOR UNCERTAINTY

It is obvious that there are definite limits to the human ability to predict the future. To increase its chances of long-term survival, an organization should always be ready to face unanticipated change. However, even if we could identify and list all possible changes, it would be impossible for practical purposes to prepare for all of them. The cost of preparedness in such a case would be prohibitively high. A critical strategic issue is the extent to which an organization should prepare itself for unanticipated events and unwanted change, and what kind of events it should take into consideration.

The extent of uncertainty depends on four factors: (1) the intensity of unanticipated change; (2) its type—normal, unusual, unexpected, inconceivable; (3) its duration; and (4) the extent of its predictability. The more intense and unexpected the change, the greater the uncertainty and risk involved. As already noted, it is likely to be prohibitively expensive to prepare for all possible types of change (for example, by buying insurance covering *all* possible future risks). It might even be useless (for example, in the case of a full-scale nuclear war).

One way of attempting to assess environmental change and the uncertainties and risks involved is by categorizing change as normal, unusual, unexpected, and inconceivable. How much of that range of change can be dealt with by strategists? Top executives must consider how much uncertainty they are willing to live with and then assess its implications for business strategy. First, they must accept that anything is possible; then they must decide how much of what is possible they can do something about, in practical terms. The choices made will have to consider the tradeoffs inherent in various alternatives. Do they stop with unusual events, or are they willing to consider even unexpected changes in some key areas of critical importance? How much will it cost for a plan to be prepared, and how much for an attempt to control change? How much financial flexibility should be available to deal with economic downturns?

Should contingency plans be available in the event of drastic changes in technology? How many scenarios of unlikely events should be considered? Should companies spend R&D money to search for unlikely technological breakthroughs in case competitors stumble upon one? Should firms attempt at all costs to discourage competition? These are the types of questions that have to be answered.

STRATEGIC ALTERNATIVES

Business strategies can be carried out in one of three ways, depending on the specific firm and the philosophy of its management, although in reality firms will follow some combination of the responsive or preventive, planning, and proactive strategies described below.[4]

RESPONSIVE OR PREVENTIVE STRATEGY

In a responsive or preventive mode of strategy, the emphasis is on reacting to environmental changes. Uncertainty is accepted, and sufficient flexible or idle resources are made available to cope with unforeseen change. It is a *modus operandi* essentially geared to taking advantage of opportunities and reacting quickly and efficiently to environmental change.

The strategic variables for responsive or preventive strategies are the amount of slack, the degree of flexibility, and the extent of specialization. For instance, a random breakdown of machinery, forcing a halt in production, can be dealt with by having extra inventory (slack). A cash shortfall during a recession can be met by selling marketable securities (financial flexibility). A permanent environmental change can be weathered if the organization is not overspecialized, so that it can change its structure and eventually adapt to the change. Such a robust strategy allows the organization to redeploy its resources to cope with a wide range of occurrences. What is important to accept, however, is that having slack costs money, flexibility requires unused resources that usually will yield little return, and less specialization might mean reduced efficiency and higher costs in the short term, which might in turn reduce the competitive position of the organization in the long term. Strategists must study these tradeoffs before they decide to what extent they are willing to use responsive or preventive strategies.

PLANNING-ORIENTED STRATEGY

Planning-oriented strategies are based on the belief that some environmental changes can be predicted. On that assumption, strategists do not have to wait and react but can make specific decisions and take specific action in anticipation of forthcoming changes. The decision to follow a planning strategy or not must consider several factors related to the accuracy of forecasting, the willingness and ability to act, and the strategies of competitors.

The ability to forecast accurately is central to effective planning strategies. If the forecasts turn out to be wrong, the real costs and opportunity costs (costs that could have been avoided had something been done) can be considerable. On the other hand, if they are correct they can provide a great deal of benefit—if the competitors have not followed similar planning strategies.

Successful planning strategies imply not only accurate forecasts but also the ability to act on them efficiently. Does the organization have the necessary resources? Is the lead time sufficient to plan adequately? Can the organizational resistance to change be overcome? This last point is particularly crucial when permanent changes are expected, because such changes force the organization to alter its structure and mode of operations significantly.

A last element to be considered is the competitors' success with planning strategies. How good is their forecasting ability? To what extent do they have the advantage of proprietary information? Given their own resources and skills, how likely is it that their plans will be more efficient? In fact, there is no advantage in correctly predicting a change and developing planning-based strategies if the same predictions can be made by competitors who are better equipped to plan for and exploit forthcoming change.

PROACTIVE STRATEGY

The third strategic option is proactive. Its premises are accepting that a wide range of environmental changes are unpredictable, but attempting nevertheless to anticipate events and to do things ahead of time to exploit their arrival. That is done by shaping the environment in some desired direction so that unwanted changes will be less likely to occur or their undesirable consequences for the organization less likely to harm it. Alternatively, purposeful action can be taken by the organization to bring about desired change that would not have occurred otherwise or would have happened later. The strategic variables that can be manipulated to bring about desired change are market demand, reduced dependence, R&D expenditures, barriers to entry, and financial strength.

Market Demand. An important proactive strategic variable concerns the firm's attitude toward the market. Traditionally, market demand has been considered beyond the control of a firm but it does not have to be if creative new ways are found to market or price existing products or to outsmart competitors. Market conditions can thus be partly determined by self-fulfilling or self-defeating prophecies related to the firm's attitudes (and strategies) in comparison with those of competitors.

Reducing Dependence. Heavy dependence on a single feature of the environment is a danger. That feature could go sour or vanish, or those in control of it might decide to take advantage of their powerful position (the 1973–74 oil embargo worked because of the West's excessive dependence on OPEC oil). To avoid such dependency and discourage such an event, a firm can diversify its sources of supply, customers, and so forth. It might decide instead to integrate vertically, if possible, to secure stable sources of supplies or captive customers. The disadvantage of reducing one's dependence on a single aspect of the environment may be inefficiencies and higher costs. Vertical integration also increases specialization and decreases the chance of adaptation to a permanent environmental change, which could render obsolete the material or process on which such integration is based.

Research and Development. R&D inventories require implementation by investment in new projects or ventures aimed at providing new products or services. The obvious tradeoffs are related to the payoffs from R&D expenditures and the success of the new projects or ventures. The degree of commitment to new projects or ventures can often make a big difference between success and failure, particularly when long lead times are involved and large amounts of capital are needed. In such cases, the heavier the initial commitment, the bigger the risk, but also the greater the chance of success through shaping the future in the desired direction. IBM's pioneering introduction of third-generation computers has been referred to as the "five-billion-dollar gamble." Proactive strategy proved successful in that case, as it changed the computer field in the direction envisioned by IBM and brought huge competitive advantages. Other "gambles" involving billions of dollars have not paid off, however (Exxon's attempts to enter the office equipment market; RCA's, GE's, and Xerox's attempt to diversify into computers). Some firms with responsive strategies and flexible organizations can quickly imitate or even improve on new inventions without having to spend huge amounts on R&D.

Barriers to Entry. Strategies must carefully consider their ability to build and maintain effective barriers to entry. It is important to distinguish between short-term and long-term barriers, since experience has shown that in the long run few barriers hold. No matter how clever the people who build barriers are, there is no guarantee against someone's finding a more ingenious way to break them down. The tradeoff here is between devoting organizational resources and energy to building barriers versus attempting to improve the organization and making it competitive in the marketplace in a way that can directly meet competition. An interesting case is AT&T and the airline companies before and after deregulation. It is not obvious that AT&T and the airline companies and their consumers were better off after deregulation than before.

Financial Strength. Retained earnings can be used by corporations to reduce their dependence on shareholders and increase their financial flexibility. The disadvantage of high retained earnings is that shareholders might not be getting sufficient return on their investments in the short term; also, borrowing might be a more desirable form of improving profits. Still, less borrowing and more retained earnings (capital) provide a strong financial position for organizations, which are thus better equipped to weather unexpected changes.

THE CHALLENGE AHEAD: FORMULATING AND IMPLEMENTING SUCCESSFUL STRATEGIES

Empirical studies of how top executives of large companies spend their time have shown that a full-fledged strategy rarely exists at the outset.[5] Important decisions and actions are seldom the result of a planned sequence of moves or explicit strategies. Instead, the process of strategy formulation evolves slowly, step by step, by trial and error. This incrementalism allows executives to pursue successful strategies further while modifying or avoiding unsuccessful ones. The outcome is a stream of resource allocation decisions committing the firm to a certain course, which eventually becomes its *de facto* strategy. The resource allocation commitment reflects not only competitive factors but also the aspirations, goals, and long-term visions of those who have the power to commit the firm's scarce resources to specific areas or projects.

Another question is whether strategists can formulate and execute more successful strategies by being more proactive and less incremental. The answer is that there are obvious advantages *and* dangers involved. The tradeoffs provide multifaceted challenges for top executives.

First and foremost, strategies are ideas. Their greatness lies in their simplicity and originality; competitors have not thought of them too, or else are in no position to implement them. Their power derives from their capacity to yield realistic visions and effective direction. Strategies cannot be reduced to recipes or analytic tools; they must be intuitive and creative. But the value of intuitive and creative ideas cannot be checked in any rational way beforehand, so the consequences are uncertain. Applying such strategies presents risks, but so does choosing not to.

The more drastic the change and the greater the commitment of resources to achieve a strategic objective, the higher the potential returns. On the other hand, conservatism will counsel an incremental approach, where ideas are tested slowly by waiting to see their consequences. The risk inherent in incrementalism is small, but so are the potential returns, because competitors will be able to formulate plans and adapt their strategies, if necessary, whenever the evidence turns out favorable. If strategy is not bold and is not implemented well ahead of other firms', competitors will be able to catch up easily and reduce the value of the competitive advantage. On the other hand, if something goes wrong when huge resources have been committed, the losses can be very great.

Strategy must be forward-looking, but at the same time it must take account of uncertain events, including the unknown strategies and reactions of competitors. The choice is between waiting to reduce uncertainty and committing oneself well in advance to decisions and action based on anticipating and exploiting forthcoming changes. Both waiting and acting involve risks. Doing nothing might give an edge to competitors who correctly anticipated and acted in order to exploit future changes, while committing resources too early might mean a disadvantage if the future does not turn out as expected. Thus, strategy cannot be formulated too early or too late. Neither should it commit more resources than necessary, yet still enough to be effective vis-à-vis competitors.

Strategy must be consistent but not rigid. That means it should not change at the first sign of difficulty. A fair amount of persistence will be required to get beyond difficulties and problems. On the other hand, if substantial environmental changes are occurring, if competitors' reactions have been misjudged, or if the future is turning out contrary to expectations, strategy must be modified to take such changes into account. In other words, strategy must adapt: It is better to follow a side alley that leads somewhere than to finish at a dead end.

Finally, strategy cannot be formulated in a vacuum. It must be concerned with competitors and their strategies, the correct assessment of internal strengths and weaknesses, and the actual situations in which the firm finds itself. Strategists cannot be so timid as to fail to exploit fully their organization's competitive strengths, while at the same time they must be realistic and not try to achieve more than is practically possible. They must adjust their strategy to the specific time and place, for rarely will they find themselves in the exact same situation twice.

Znosko-Borovsky provides an excellent description of strategy and its formulation as applied to chess:

> It must not be thought that a plan will occur to us fully worked out in detail. . . . Step by step it takes shape in our mind, at first in vague outlines, gaining gradually in definition and character. . . . Even the most general strategic plan cannot embrace all the varied phases of a game. . . . But usually, more or less clear-cut plans follow one another, covering a series of moves, more or less extended. . . . It is impossible to play a satisfactory game without following a strategic plan, which sooner or later will have to be evolved. To settle on a plan too late means an advantage to the opponent . . . to have no plan at all would render our play inconsistent—without logic and therefore without strength.

Znosko-Borovsky continues, discussing the danger of blind reliance on strategy:

> It is quite easy to become the slave to a preconceived idea, and, whilst following it up methodically, to overlook a clandestine mate, subtly engineered by the opponent . . . sad would be the fate of the strategist who, having formulated his plan, thought that he could go to sleep, nothing more being required of him.[6]

Thus, formulating and implementing strategy is not the straightforward matter some attempt to portray. It involves tradeoffs and requires dealing with a series of paradoxes. The paradoxes pose the challenge and determine the ultimate success of such strategies.

THE PARADOXES OF STRATEGY

1. Strategies must aim at achieving unique advantages gained through specialization, yet they must permit the organization to adapt successfully to permanent environmental changes.

2. Strategies must be cautious and incremental in order to minimize risks, yet only bold and powerful strategies bring great advantage.
3. Strategies must anticipate and exploit forthcoming changes, yet it is well known that predictions of the future (and of competitive actions or reactions) can be wrong.
4. Strategies must be daring but not overly optimistic.
5. Strategies must be consistent, but at the same time they cannot be rigid.

THE STRATEGIST

In order to be effective, the strategist must satisfactorily solve the above paradoxes while at the same time adequately dealing with many personal and organizational conflicts that provide additional paradoxes and challenges.

THE PARADOXES OF STRATEGISTS

1. Be a specialist in your own business, but also be capable of visualizing the whole picture.
2. Be creative, but also practical.
3. Be visionary, but also pragmatic.
4. Be concerned with the long term, but also deal with the day-to-day operations and with crises.
5. Be flexible, but also persistent.
6. Be conservative, but also take risks.
7. Be intuitive, but also understand judgmental biases such as being overly optimistic or the search for supporting evidence.
8. Set demanding strategic goals, but not so hard and unrealistic that they will discourage those who attempt to achieve them.

The job of the strategist is not easy. It requires a good understanding of established trends and present conditions, as well as future changes. He or she must be able to motivate people but also be practical in his or her demands. A strategist must be persistent in achieving goals, but not to the point where he or she becomes rigid, ignoring signs of fundamental change. Finally, a strategist must have ambitious goals, believing that success can always be achieved, but without becoming too arrogant. All this is why successful strategists are rare birds. They must be able to recognize the difficulty of their task and must spend the time and effort required to formulate and implement successful strategies, while at the same time making sure that day-to-day operations are carried out smoothly and efficiently.

THE CHALLENGE AHEAD

1. Create a climate of excellence where success comes naturally without necessarily competing directly.
2. Accept and successfully deal with the paradoxes of strategy and strategists.
3. Formulate and implement a successful strategy, knowing quite well that no rules or magic formulas exist and that constant innovation and new ideas are needed to continue being successful.

CONCLUSIONS

The purpose of strategy is to gain and maintain long-term competitive advantages. That goal can be achieved in different forms (successful competition, self-motivation, specialization, creativity, a cushion for uncertainty) and in several modes (responsive or preventive, planning, proactive). There are no recipes or analytic rules for formulating and implementing successful strategies. Instead, strategy requires a great deal of ingenuity, the assuming of risks, and the capacity to resolve many paradoxes as well as personal and organizational conflicts. Strategists must be aware of the difficulties involved in their jobs and must attempt to deal with them by increasing their understanding of the environment, of the strengths and weaknesses of their organizations, and of their competitors' strengths and weaknesses.

10

Creativity

*O*ften when one works at a hard question, nothing good is accomplished at the first attack. Then one takes a rest, longer or shorter, and sits down anew to the work. During the first half-hour, as before, nothing is found, and then all of a sudden the decisive idea presents itself to the mind.

HENRI POINCARÉ (1913) in Hadamard, *The Psychology of Invention in the Mathematical Field*

New ideas, new strategies, new needs and effective solutions to new problems, as well as more imaginative ways of dealing with old ones, are critical elements for achieving success and avoiding failure in business organizations. Yet we know little about creativity or how to stimulate it, while myths and misconceptions about creative geniuses and unblocking the creative part of our minds abound. This chapter describes creativity and provides an objective evaluation of what we know and what we don't. It looks at creative companies and creative breakthroughs and discusses the common factors that contributed to creative success.

Nikola Tesla was born in 1856 in a small village in what is now Yugoslavia. Tesla showed signs of creative genius in his childhood. He became a brilliant mathematician who could solve complex problems in his head without using a pencil. In 1884 Tesla arrived in New York, where in a little more than ten years he came up with a dozen highly creative inventions. Two of them changed the world as we know it today. The first allowed electricity to travel long distances cheaply and efficiently, while the second became the basis of radio and other forms of broadcasting. For his alternating current invention alone he received some $220,000—a huge sum at that time.

Tesla was not satisfied with his successes. He kept looking for bigger, more powerful inventions. He wanted to transmit electric power with no wires, construct bladeless motors, send low-frequency energy through the earth's core, and carry out other far-fetched projects. His efforts failed, as did his expensive experiments, which left him penniless. He died in New York City poor and frustrated, sixty years after he had arrived there.

Thomas Edison, a contemporary of Tesla, was another creative genius. He produced more than a thousand patented inventions in his lifetime. Edison was the opposite of Tesla. He had left school at the age of twelve and had no formal mathematical or scientific training, but he was immensely curious and had a practical mind. Edison's method was to come up with an idea and then turn it into a commercially viable invention. His approach was trial and error coupled with extremely hard work until he succeeded. He died in 1931, very rich, after an astonishingly long and productive career.

Creativity has fascinated mankind for millenniums. The Greeks thought it was a gift of Zeus transmitted through his nine daughters, the muses, who provided the inspiration for creative work. We immensely admire creative geniuses, such as Michelangelo, Mozart, Edison, and Einstein. As for someone like Tesla, we are not sure. We might call him a failed genius, a man who had flashes of brilliance, or an eccentric.

Creativity is of critical importance both for our everyday lives and for business organizations. In management, creativity is an important factor contributing to success and a key element in at least these areas:

1. Competitive strategies—finding creative ways of outsmarting opponents without, at the same time, being outwitted by them
2. New products and services—inventing new, economically profitable products or services (or improving existing ones)
3. Advertising and promotional campaigns—coming up with creative ideas to improve the effectiveness of advertising and promotions

THE LITERATURE ON CREATIVITY

Much of the current thinking about creativity has its origins in the work of Poincaré, who first reported on his own process of coming up with novel solutions to mathematical problems. Poincaré believed that one should let a problem settle in his or her mind and then come back to it after some time, during which the unconscious has gone to work. The problem would then be reexamined. According to Poincaré, it was likely that the solution would come at that point in a flash of imagination.

BISOCIATION

Arthur Koestler originated the bisociation theory by attempting to combine Poincaré's ideas with those of Freud.[1] Koestler viewed creativity as the marriage of what were originally considered unrelated ideas. The creative process was at work when connections were made in the mind where none had existed before (this is what made bisociation different from association, which refers to connections already established). Koestler illustrated his ideas by examining many important inventions and showing how they could be explained in the light of bisociation. Like Poincaré, he emphasized the importance of the unconscious mind. In addition, he took into consideration the role of sleeping and dreams, which, he maintained, freed the thinking process and allowed sudden creative illuminations.

Both Poincaré and Koestler argued that creativity originates deep in the unconscious mind and involves the novel combination of ideas that have formed and are waiting there. Both held that creative ideas come to the conscious mind in flashes of imagination, much like the "Eureka" of Archimedes.

THE FOUR STAGES OF CREATIVITY

As far back as the 1920s, Walles proposed the following four stages of creativity:

1. *Preparation.* The gathering of material and information about the task or problem at hand and a period (sometimes long) of conscious thinking

2. *Incubation.* After the period of preparation, putting the task or problem aside for a while—perhaps taking a rest, a long walk, or a brief vacation—so the unconscious mind can go to work and come up with novel connections

3. *Actual birth of the idea.* If incubation is successful, the passage of the creative idea into the conscious mind, experienced as a sudden flash, attended by the feeling of "Eureka!" and the thrill of discovery

4. *Refinement and testing of the idea.* Creative ideas might come in a crude form, hence their details have to be worked out. In business applications, it might be necessary to test them and make sure they are appropriate. Their feasibility and practical (or economic) usefulness has to be checked.[2]

Theories based on the four stages of creative thinking have not changed much since Poincaré and Walles. An excellent description of the creative stages was later provided by Young, an advertising executive, in a little book first published in 1940.[3] Drawing on his own experience of inducing creativity in advertising, Young provided useful hints on facilitating creative thinking by following the four stages of creativity described above. Young was a strong believer in a liberal arts education and advocated searching and accumulating a lot of general knowledge. Such knowledge and information could be used eventually during periods of incubation when the unconscious mind is considering possible creative solutions.

UNBLOCKING THE CREATIVE PROCESS

An alternative to following the four stages to facilitate creativity is to unblock it. According to more recent authors, creative thinking can be improved if the various blocks that inhibit creativity can be removed. In a book entitled *Conceptual Blockbusting,* J. L. Adams discussed four blocks to creativity: perceptual, emotional, cultural, and environmental. He argued that these four blocks had to be understood and then overcome by using a variety of means. The means included adopting a questioning attitude during which nothing is taken for granted, making lists of ideas, freeing "unconscious" thought, undergoing psychoanalysis, practicing yoga, or whatever other method works best for each person.[4]

E. De Bono wrote that creativity could be improved if separated from logical thinking. He coined the term "lateral thinking," by which he meant thinking that generates new ideas or novel approaches to solving problems.[5] According to De Bono, lateral thinking should be separated from analytical or logical thinking, which is best suited for evaluating ideas, further developing them, or implementing them. De Bono compared logical thinking to an attempt to make an old hole bigger, while lateral thinking represented digging a new hole. He said that by concentrating on lateral thinking creative output could be improved. De Bono's approach advocated breaking away from old habits; looking for fresh approaches that move sideways; reformulating a problem; and looking for new patterns and novel combinations. He also proposed different modes of thinking (objective, emotional, negative, optimistic, creative, deliberate) that fit various situations being considered and preferable ways of combining all of them to avoid the disadvantages of the conventional way of thinking, which emphasizes one type at the time (see his book *Six Thinking Hats,* where he proposes six types of thinking).

It is commonly held among writers on creativity that formal education encourages analytical thinking rather than creative thinking and that it induces a structured approach to problem-solving that discourages new ideas. Creativity requires intuitive thinking, flexibility, and lack of structure. According to the literature, creativity can be taught by bringing people to accept the fact that it requires a new way of thinking and helping them to understand inhibitions on creative thinking. In business, creative thinking can be encouraged by the following:

1. *Challenging Assumptions* by not taking anything for granted and daring to question what most people accept as indisputable truths
2. *Withholding Criticism* of new ideas, no matter how outrageous they might seem, while reserving judgment until later on when all ideas have been collected
3. *Making Connections* by looking for patterns to seemingly unrelated ideas or events in order to come up with new concepts and original approaches
4. *Combining and Improving* ideas read or expressed by others in order to end up with novel variations
5. *Perceiving Things in New Ways* by seeing the same things as others but recognizing potential that others have not been able to identify
6. *Turning Problems and Dangers into Opportunities* by being able to see them in a new light
7. *Taking Risks* by being willing to work in new directions, or by exploring outrageous ideas
8. *Exploiting Chance* by recognizing lucky accidents and being willing to pursue them in order to discover why they occurred
9. *Having Confidence in One's Creativity* by believing that one can succeed in coming up with original solutions to what might seem like unsolvable problems

BRAINSTORMING

Brainstorming has been proposed as a way of improving creativity by combining the creative potential of several people in a group. Osborn, one of the original proponents of brainstorming, maintained that all people are endowed with creativity.[6] However, *because of education and experience* the analytical (what he called judicial) part of our mind, rather than the intuitive, is emphasized. Furthermore, generally speaking, people tend to use intuition much less than they do logical reasoning. Thus brainstorming techniques were aimed at reducing the inhibiting effects of education and experience and making it possible to produce as many new ideas as possible. Such ideas could subsequently be evaluated using a logico-analytic approach.

The brainstorming procedure can be summarized as follows:

1. Gaining agreement from all group members to use brainstorming.
2. Selecting a facilitator, who fosters a warm, supportive atmosphere among the group members and who:

   a. does not introduce his or her own ideas
   b. emphasizes quantity of ideas (as opposed to ''quality'')
   c. reminds the group that criticism is not allowed
   d. stimulates the generation of new, far-fetched ideas
   e. suggests that ideas expressed by members of the group be further pursued and/or improved by others
   f. encourages all group members to participate and discourages one or a few individuals from dominating the brainstorming session

3. Evaluating the ideas generated using logical thinking and specific criteria to determine their appropriateness and usefulness

EVALUATING THE LITERATURE ON CREATIVITY

After having read a large number of books and articles on creativity, one is left with the feeling that they lack the very creativity they seek to describe. Ideas that can be traced back to Poincaré are reformulated, using new buzzwords and the same trite examples. Poincaré's concept of incubation becomes bisociation, making connections, or seeing things in a new light. Intuitive thinking becomes nonjudicial thinking, freeing the unconscious, lateral thinking, or divergent thinking. The theory of the various stages leading to creativity has not changed much since Walles, except that the description has become longer, more involved, and more dogmatic.

Writers on creativity expect the reader to accept the ''gospel'' in good faith. This attitude can be seen in the following quotes from *Creativity in Business:*

Probably the most important aspect of our course and this book is that we go directly to what helps people bring out useful creativity in business. We don't try to solve the basic mystery of the physiological, cognitive, and social processes that underlie a creative act.

and later,

Who knows why our course works? But work it does. We—Myers and Ray—through teaching the course have gained the individual conviction that an ever-present creative source (in this book we call it Essence) is available to each one of us.[7]

If we are not willing to accept the merits and benefits of creativity-stimulating methods on blind faith, there is not much evidence to support the various claims being made. As a matter of fact, experimental studies refute those claims:

1. Creativity comes, via the unconscious mind, in a flash of imagination.
2. There are four stages in creativity (or some other number).
3. There are ways of unblocking the creative process that work all the time.
4. Brainstorming increases creativity.

Analysis of the results of empirical experiments shows clearly that these are myths with little or no scientific basis.

More than a dozen studies have demolished that favorite tool for improving creativity, brainstorming. They have shown beyond any reasonable doubt that brainstorming does not produce more or better-quality ideas than do regular groups or individuals spending similar amounts of time generating original ideas. Weisberg concludes: "The fact that many institutions enthusiastically adopted brainstorming means nothing more than that Osborn was able to convince people of brainstorming's effectiveness."[8]

Today brainstorming is rarely used by organizations and has also fallen out of fashion in books on creativity.[9] What can convince us that the new proposals for improving creativity being advanced today will not meet the same fate? Although creativity can be stimulated and organizations can create an environment that encourages creativity, many authors and approaches make exaggerated claims about their ability to bring about organizational creativity.

A PRAGMATIC VIEW OF CREATIVITY

Can creativity be taught? Can all people be creative? Are there techniques that can stimulate creative thinking? Can creativity within organizations be encouraged? Can organizations become more creative? Those important questions must be answered in an objective manner based on scientific reasoning and empirical evidence rather than on wishful thinking, dogmatism, or salesmanship.

Exhibit 10–1 summarizes what we know about creativity and what we assume we know. To avoid following up on unproven claims, it is necessary to adopt a more sober view toward creativity, a type of view being advanced by a growing number of researchers.

CREATIVITY VERSUS INTELLIGENCE

Creativity is defined by many writers as the ability to produce *novel and useful* ideas, while creative problem-solving means finding new responses to problems at hand. Some authors distinguish creativity from innovation by defining the latter as the ability to *implement* creative ideas or solutions. I do not believe such a distinction is necessary, for we can always use the words "applying or implementing creative ideas or solutions" instead of introducing a new buzzword that does not necessarily mean the same thing to all people.

The definition of creativity just cited does not always capture the essence of creative acts. For instance, was Charles Babbage (see Chapter 11), who in 1822 built a full-scale computer that never worked, less creative than Howard Aiken of Harvard, who built an early computer in 1942? Although Babbage's invention could not be called useful (as the definition requires) and has been of no value to the designers of modern computers, no one can seriously argue that Babbage was not a creative genius. Indeed, his idea of building a computer was so far ahead of his time that technology was too primitive for him to make it actually work. The fact that he succeeded in building a crude computer attests to his creative genius. The fact that the computer did not work is a detail that changes nothing if one understands the circumstances under which his computer was built. Aiken, on the other hand, was instrumental in building a computer for IBM. His creative contribution was in finding technical solutions to myriad design and construction problems. Thomas Watson, Sr. (see Chapter 12), a different type of creative genius, saw a need for the computer as a business tool and was willing to take the risk of financing Aiken so he could build the computer. Watson's creative vision made IBM a formidable company, one of the most successful ever built. Of Babbage, Aiken, and Watson, who was the most creative? What about Tesla and Edison? Obviously, answering such questions is not

Exhibit 10–1 Creativity: What We Know and What We Assume We Know

What We Know About Creativity

1. There are a number of myths about creativity.
2. Some people are more creative than others.
3. There are some geniuses and supergeniuses who can consistently produce extremely creative output over long periods of time.
4. A prerequisite of creativity is a considerable amount of information or knowledge gained through education, training, and experience.
5. Some very creative people were not thought to be so for a long period, or even during their entire lives.
6. Many creative ideas were not recognized as such until long after they were proposed.
7. Some organizations have managed consistently to produce above-average creative ideas by developing a supportive environment or by encouraging the right people and beliefs.

What We Assume We Know About Creativity

1. The following four (or some other number) stages in creativity:

   a. The gathering of raw material about the problem/idea that requires a creative solution
   b. The incubation, where one lets his or her unconscious do the work
   c. The "eureka," when all of a sudden the bright idea is born in the unconscious
   d. The refinement, possible improvement, and testing of the creative idea

2. Creativity can be taught by telling people how to cultivate the various stages of creativity, by breaking the barriers inhibiting creative thought, or by encouraging nonrational, nonanalytical thinking.
3. Brainstorming or other types of group work enhance the generation of creative ideas.
4. Creative individuals can be identified.
5. Creative ideas can be recognized and pursued to advantage.
6. There are set procedures, which, if properly carried out, can increase creative output.

easy. Each of the five was a creative genius in his own way. Although simple creative ideas are very different from technological breakthroughs, there is little doubt that commercial success can as easily come from one as from the other. For instance, improving the absorption capacity of its disposable diapers enabled Procter & Gamble to increase its market share by more than 10 percent.

Creative geniuses are an object of human fascination, but creativity is a common phenomenon we can observe thousands of times each day, as with a baby learning to play with toys. His or her play is highly creative, for it has never been done before. Learning to talk also involves the creative process, as young children construct new sentences and put words together in novel combinations nobody taught them. All of us solve problems in novel ways and come up with new ideas many times a day. A driver who suddenly sees a deer in front of his car slams on the brakes and turns the wheel to avoid the deer. He may never have tried not to hit a deer in front of his car before, but he still tries and probably avoids hitting it. As an experiment Herbert Simon, over lunch, asked eight of his colleagues (all good applied mathematicians) to help him solve a mathematical problem, which he described in detail. Five of the eight came up with the right answer—nothing unusual in that. However, the problem Simon provided his colleagues was Planck's quantum-theoretic law of black-body radiation, which had earned Planck the Nobel Prize in 1918. None of Simon's colleagues recognized the problem as Planck's while they searched for the solution that won Planck a Nobel prize. Were the solutions of Simon's five colleagues creative? Within the strict definition of creativity the problem was not new, but they did not know that when they came up with their solutions. For them the solution was new and, therefore, creative.

Most ideas we have and problems we deal with are new to us, because we rarely face the exact same situation twice. An activity like playing chess involves creativity almost all of the time since very rarely does a game resemble one already played. Similarly, hardly ever are two business situations or problems exactly the same. What counts here is not whether or not an idea or solution is creative, but the *degree of creativity involved and its perceived usefulness,* since most ideas are more or less new. Separating creativity from normal, everyday thinking might be artificial, and talking about creative geniuses might be the same as talking about intellectual geniuses. Simon contends that creativity is an ordinary human process:

> It is not necessary to surround creativity with mystery and obfuscation. No sparks of genius need be postulated to account for human invention, discovery, creation. These acts are acts of the human brain, the same brain that helps us dress in the morning, arrive at our office, and go through our daily chores, however uncreative most of these chores may be.[10]

Simon consequently proposes that we need not separate creativity from the general processes that people use to solve problems, an area about which we know much more than we do about creativity. Minsky, the father of artificial intelligence, goes a step further when he writes: "I don't believe there is much difference between normal and 'creative' thought. Right now, if asked which seems the more mysterious, I'd have to say the ordinary kind."[11]

If creativity is part of everyday general thinking, how is it that some people are more creative than others. This question is much the same as asking why some people are "smarter" than others. Just as there are many factors that determine intelligence, so there are many factors that contribute to creativity. Just as we attempt to understand the factors that make people "smarter" (or more successful) so also do we try to understand those which make people more creative—although it might not be easy to recognize such factors.

Are we coming up against another paradox? What is the point of singling out creativity and treating it in a special way if we cannot identify creative people or ways of enhancing creativity?

The key word in creativity is "novel," in reference to either ideas or problem-solving. The critical distinction, however, is how new is "novel." Small, incremental novelty is very different from a big creative breakthrough. The former is easy to achieve, the latter much more difficult. This does not mean that the process of creativity in producing small, incremental ideas is any different from that of creative breakthroughs. The same is true with intelligence: The mind works the same way to deal with small or complex problems. However, the mental state it takes to generate novel ideas is different from that needed to deal with repetitive situations. Novel ideas require much more thinking, the kind of reflection that only a mind that is calm and free from busy, mundane tasks can do. Isaac Asimov superbly describes the ability to be creative:

> I think almost everybody has it in his or her capacity to do something creative, without necessarily being able to explain how it's done. Society just doesn't give most people the chance to do this. . . . What we have to do, generally (for a living), is not the sort of thing that utilizes our brain function to the fullest.

Asimov adds that until very recently, by historical standards, at least 95 percent of the people had to do "unskilled" work that did not require using their intellect.[12] Well, the same applies to executives. If they are busy all the time dealing with day-to-day problems, attending meetings, and solving crises, they have no time to think, much less to be creative.

Thus, if only they recognize the need to be creative and free some of their time to try to do so, that in itself will amount to a giant step in coming up with creative ideas and producing creative output.

The need for creativity will never be satisfied. If large numbers of people could suddenly become creative, creativity would become mundane—what was previously novel and creative would not be so any more. True creativity would then be pushed to new heights, incremental novelty (high by previous standards) would not be easy to achieve, and new creative breakthroughs still harder. Thus, creativity will always be a relative concept. A breakthrough will remain an unusual achievement, occurring only when someone invents what the vast majority cannot recognize as practical or feasible. Similarly, profiting from creative ideas or solutions will always be restricted to a few cases. If it were otherwise, many people would have recognized and exploited the opportunity beforehand.

PREREQUISITES OF CREATIVITY

Preparation is a necessary prerequisite for becoming more creative, but not a sufficient condition—it cannot, by any means, guarantee creativity.

The Acquisition of a Knowledge Base and Substantial Experience. Simon and other researchers suggest that a prerequisite for substantial creative output is the acquisition of considerable knowledge and experience. Simon cites studies estimating that at least ten years are required to acquire such knowledge or experience and to develop appropriate skills that increase one's chances of producing high-level creative output. For instance, Simon writes, no world-class expert has reached his or her level without at least ten years of intensive effort.

High Motivation and Persistence. Knowledge and expertise are not enough. In addition, creative breakthroughs require considerable motivation in the form of hard work and complete immersion in the task or problem at hand. James Gleick describes the work habits of a scientist who discovered a major theory in physics: "He worked for two months without pause. His functional day was twenty-two hours. He would try to go to sleep in a kind of buzz, and awaken two hours later with his thoughts exactly where he had left them."[13] Similarly Levy describes how a computer terminal was completed "that took six weeks of fourteen- to seventeen-hour days, seven days a week."[14]

The same is true of great artists. Great art is rarely produced in flashes of imagination. A detailed monograph on Van Gogh or Picasso will bring to light a multitude of drawings, studies, and unfinished paintings done in preparation for the final version of a great work. Moreover, great scientists, artists, or creative thinkers must be self-motivated, because money, competition, or fame alone can never adequately explain their hard work and desire to excel.

Taking Risks. It might be possible to systematize incremental creativity by designing procedures contributing to small increases in creative output. Marginal improvements in products or production processes or slight variations in existing services can be achieved through R&D, engineering, or "creative" departments. However, breakthroughs can rarely be systematized or planned for. As our previous examples show, moreover, not all creative ideas succeed. The more far-fetched the idea, the greater its chance of failure will be.

Thinking Differently from the Crowd. It is possible that people who do not like to follow tradition, have no taste for formal education, or take little interest in the work of others can come up with new ideas. Their thinking is virginal and not influenced by conventional wisdom, so they can follow paths no one else has discovered and hit upon new solutions. Although the chances of failure might be higher among rebels or unconventional thinkers, so is their chance of coming up with new creative ideas.

Adopting an "Open-minded" Attitude. Important creative ideas or solutions and creative breakthroughs require adopting an open-minded attitude whereby assumptions are questioned, unusual or even improbable solutions are considered, stereotypes are avoided, and reverse thinking is used. An open-minded attitude also encourages learning about how similar problems are dealt with outside the area of one's expertise, and in general being capable of thinking in different ways from the majority of people. That is a key element of novelty; ideas are regarded as new and original because the majority of people have not been able to discover them through conventional thinking.

Creative Accidents. A great deal is made of the occasional creative ideas or discoveries made by accident. However, recognizing accidents and exploiting their significance also requires an open mind and the ability to accept that conventional wisdom does not always hold. Even accidents favor the prepared and the open-minded, who can recognize their implications and use them to come up with original ideas or discover novel solutions.

Exhibit 10–2 summarizes the above prerequisites. However, it must be emphasized that these are necessary but not sufficient conditions for creativity.

Exhibit 10–2 Prerequisites for More than Incremental Creativity

1. The acquisition of a knowledge base and substantial experience before high-level creative output can be produced.

2. High motivation and persistence in surpassing the difficulties involved and bringing the task at hand to successful conclusion.

3. Being willing to be "different" or take pleasure in being a "rebel."

4. Adoption of an "open-minded" attitude that questions assumptions and "conventional wisdom" in order to come up with new ideas or solutions others have not recognized.

5. Recognition and exploitation of accidents whose creative contribution would otherwise have been lost.

TEACHING, STIMULATING, AND MANAGING CREATIVITY

Creativity is exciting but also elusive. It is not always in harmony with the more mundane, everyday tasks required in our daily lives or businesses. Education, organizations, and society force us toward conformity. Creative people want freedom of action and time to think. They disdain supervision and often dream of ideas or provide solutions that require going against the established order and the status quo. Taking time to reflect is considered a luxury, and innovative ideas are often disruptive, as they do not easily fit into the bureaucratic mode of operation of most organizations. Creativity requires change, which goes against a bureaucracy's striving to maintain stability. Can we allow and even encourage creativity in schools or firms? What will be the consequences of such a policy on discipline, the performance of day-to-day tasks, or the relationship between employees and management?

We know that some creativity comes easily to us. We can adapt to new environments, we can come up with new ideas, and we are capable of solving new problems. At the same time, we have all occasionally felt, "How could I not have thought of that?" or "How could I have been so stupid?" when we were unable to think of an extremely obvious idea or an easy solution. The teaching and stimulating of creativity becomes an interesting possibility, assuming that organizations would like to encourage more creativity in their members.

TEACHING CREATIVITY

There are schools for painters, musicians, and dancers, just as there are schools for bus drivers, airplane pilots, and electronic engineers. Although all such schools have something in common (they provide information and teach some basic skills, prerequisites for one's future job), the outputs expected from them vary greatly.

Learning to be a bus driver takes a matter of days. Driving a bus is easy for most people, even though it requires solving a lot of small problems.

Training airplane pilots takes much longer. Learning to take off, fly, and land a large airplane requires specific knowledge about the plane and a great deal of practice. An important aspect of pilots' training is that they must follow exact procedures. They are not allowed to do things differently; creativity is a punishable sin. Yet the biggest benefit of having pilots in airplanes comes when something goes wrong and they find a creative solution and eventually land the plane.

Electronic engineers, as well as those in other fields, have to go to school for many years and take many courses on a lot of different subjects. Most of the knowledge they acquire is theoretical. Its purpose is to provide them with general knowledge and teach them how to learn. When they finish, they know little about doing specific tasks, which they learn once they start working on their first jobs. Those jobs require the knowledge they have acquired in school, but in addition demand that they find new and better ways of accomplishing certain tasks.

Artists (painters, musicians, dancers) also go to school and learn skills. However, they know that applying such skills will not get them far. For artists to succeed they have to be creative in their ideas and style. What they are taught are skills, not creativity. If creativity could be taught it would not help artists much. To be creative they would still have to do something different or new in order to distinguish themselves from the others.

In all the situations examined we see that creativity is not and cannot be taught directly. Teachers can only impart knowledge and skills. Small, incremental creativity is expected and can be achieved, with some effort, as part of our everyday lives and jobs. Significant creativity or breakthroughs, however, cannot be taught or learned. Someone either has the talent or personality to achieve them or not.[15] Creativity in management presents both a paradox and a challenge. If it is to provide benefits, it must be unique; at the same time, if it could be taught or stimulated, and everybody could learn to be more creative, it would lose its uniqueness. The challenge, therefore, is to encourage creativity *in a unique fashion,* knowing full well that no recipes or rules can be found for doing so.

STIMULATING CREATIVITY

Some tasks do not require creativity. We can even say that different or new ways of performing them might be inefficient or even dangerous. Think, for example, of the procedures required to inspect a nuclear plant and the need to follow them down to their tiniest detail, because the risk of error can have tremendously dangerous consequences. Procedures must be followed to the letter, until it can be proven beyond doubt that improvements can be made and implemented, in which case the procedures are changed.

Other tasks require more creativity, and still others a great deal. The interesting question then becomes when creativity should be encouraged and when it will be useful. Dealing with this question is not easy. Creativity requires novelty and therefore change, but, as we have seen in Chapter 2, not all change is beneficial. Inconsistency can be as big a problem as lack of change and conservatism. Our minds (like organizations) deal with this conflict between inconsistency and conservatism by devising procedures that discourage change. Our minds use heuristics that rely on stereotypes, rules of thumb, and short cuts acquired through long years of experience. This process provides quick solutions but at the same time encourages conventional ways of thinking and discourages creative ones.

Try finding the answer to this grim riddle:

A father and his son were driving to a ball game when their car stalled on the railroad tracks. In the distance a train whistle blew a warning. Frantically, the father tried to start the engine, but in his panic, he couldn't turn the key, and the car was hit by the onrushing train. An ambulance sped to the scene and picked them up. On the way to the hospital, the father died. The son was still alive but his condition was very serious, and he needed immediate surgery. The moment they arrived at the hospital, he was wheeled into an emergency operating room, and the surgeon came in, expecting a routine case. However, on seeing the boy, the surgeon blanched and muttered, "I can't operate on this boy—he's my son." [16]

What can be made of this riddle? Who was the surgeon?

Some people find the answer the moment they finish reading the story. Others can take half an hour and still not come up with the right answer. When I give the riddle to my class of executives or MBAs, only a few discover the right answer (the doctor was the boy's mother). Why? Most of us know that there are a lot of women doctors. Yet we think in stereotypes. Deep down we still associate doctors with men, so we cannot find the obvious solution. Are those who find the right answer more creative than those who don't? Although we cannot generalize, it is true that some people find a solution others cannot recognize. If such a riddle were in a different context, figuring out the answer could bring benefits (e.g., in recognizing a new need others did not see). Those who had found the solution would have made gains for themselves or their organizations.

Unfortunately, it is not obvious how to stimulate creativity. When, for instance, I ask the executives and MBA students who came up with the right response how they found it, they answer, "It was obvious," "I don't know, it just came to my mind," or "It could not have been anything else." Similarly, when highly creative people are asked about the sources of their inspiration the most common answer is, "I don't know." Some respondents claim to be inspired by such peculiar experiences as smelling rotten apples or orange peels or else by being in a bathtub, sitting on the toilet, having their feet in cold water, daydreaming, sleeping, or jogging.

Scientists have been trying to gain a better understanding of how our minds work and to determine whether or not the mind can be encouraged or stimulated to become more creative.[17] Their conclusions about creativity, based on scientific research, are usually in disagreement with commonly held beliefs and the writings of popular authors. Apart from the prerequisites (mentioned above) for anything greater than incremental creativity, there is not much we know or can assert with certainty. When great artists, scientists, writers, creative people in advertising, and people who have brought forth great ideas are asked what makes them successful, their answers include thinking in the abstract, avoiding stereotypes, questioning assumptions, and disliking supervision (see Exhibit 10–3). However, it is not clear how such advice can be generalized or used by other people who want to be creative. Finally, researchers have also found that creative people cannot be identified beforehand through socioeconomic background study, personality analysis, training, or other factors. Long years of education in the "right" schools are not good predictors of significant creative output either. The great majority of inventions that made personal computers a reality, for instance, came from young kids with little formal education who had dropped out of high school or college.[18]

An area that has been studied extensively is chess and chess grandmasters. Such studies dismiss popular beliefs that grandmasters are extremely intelligent, superlogical, have an incredible memory, and are

Exhibit 10–3 Factors That Facilitate Creativity

1. Thinking in abstractions, conceiving ideas in images
2. Examining all (or as many as possible) combinations of basic ideas and/or existing products/services
3. Avoiding stereotypes
4. Searching outside one's area of business or field of study for fresh ways of looking at old things
5. Questioning assumptions
6. Rejecting conventional wisdom
7. Disliking

   a. Being supervised or told what to do
   b. Being criticized or told to hurry up
   c. Being promised rewards for accelerating current progress

extremely fast at calculation (see Exhibit 10–4). Instead, grandmasters are not any different from other people of the same socio-economic background in terms of intelligence, memory, or the speed at which they calculate. What makes them great at playing chess is a combination of other factors (or talents), which, although they can be described (see Exhibit 10–5), cannot be attributed to any specific traits in their respective backgrounds, personalities, educations, or environments. They are grandmasters because they practice a great deal, love playing chess, and

Exhibit 10–4 Myths and Reality About Chess Grandmasters

Myths	*Reality*
1. They are extremely intelligent and have an astronomically high IQ.	They are no more intelligent than people of similar socio-economic background and education. Great skill at chess is *not* a good predictor of high IQ.
2. They are superlogical.	They score high on spatial-imaginative tests but are no more logical than people of similar background and education.
3. They have an incredible photographic memory.	Average, not photographic, memory.
4. They think and make calculations at lightning speed.	They think and make calculations no faster than other people.

Exhibit 10–5 Factors Involved and Characteristics of Chess Grandmasters

1. They practice a great deal.
2. They love to play chess.
3. They can understand the logic of the game but store little in their memory.
4. They formulate a unique strategy for each game and strive to bring it to fruition.
5. They are capable of recognizing potentially great moves.
6. They are capable of considering many global and situation-specific factors in deciding which moves are great and which should be their next one.
7. They cannot explain which factors they take into consideration or why some of their moves are great (that is, their decisions are intuitive). However, they follow these two basic principles:

    a. *Focused search*. Consider only a few great moves and select the best among them (without knowing why it is the best).

    b. *Multiple hypotheses*. Continuously reevaluate strategy (goal) in and of itself and in comparison with alternative goals. Strategies are not thrown away when met with resistance. Grandmasters are extremely persistent, and even if sidetracked for a while will reevaluate and return to their initial strategy.

8. They are highly sensitive to positive and negative feedback.
9. They have an extremely selective memory of chess moves and patterns.
10. They have tremendous ability to know what to remember.
11. They are psychologically stable.

are highly creative when it comes to recognizing a few great moves and studying them in depth before choosing the best among them. They are extremely competent in formulating a strategy early, and then they are persistent in bringing it to completion. However, scientists do not know and cannot explain why only the grandmasters, and not other players who also practice a lot and love chess, have or develop these qualities. Why certain chess players with a higher IQ than grandmasters play average chess—all other factors, like practicing and love of the game, being equal—remains an enigma to this day.

THE MANAGEMENT OF CREATIVITY

Organizations like Merck, Bell Labs, 3M, Hewlett-Packard, Martin Marietta, Apple, Du Pont, Citicorp, Wal-Mart, and Compaq have managed consistently to outperform their rivals in creative output either as technological research or as ideas. Other companies have been less successful even though they have spent equivalent or larger amounts on R&D and high-paid managers and staff. Similarly, some organizations (business and nonprofit) have consistently produced more creative output in the form of imaginative solutions, advertising campaigns, new theories, successful movies, plays, or songs, and so on. The obviously successful organizations are ones that can develop and maintain an environment supportive of creativity. But how they do it while others cannot is not clear. Creative companies have in common certain policies, which range from spending a high percentage of their income on R&D and providing complete freedom and flexibility to their scientists, to having first-rate lab facilities and promoting the concept of "champions" who make sure the new ideas reach completion (see Exhibit 10–6 for additional policies). Although such practices are not exactly the same from one company to another, they seem to be present across the board. Unfortunately, there is no guarantee that other companies that follow the policies and practices in Exhibit 10–6 will also produce above-average creative output.

Managing creative people necessarily means little management, which presents another paradox and challenge. For instance, R&D money must be spent as effectively as possible; conventional wisdom dictates that management must select research projects, judge their potential usefulness, decide on the people who will work on them, monitor their progress, and, in short, be directly involved in all aspects of planning and research. However, active supervision might destroy initiative and creativity. Thus managers must manage without getting involved. They must agree to spend huge sums of money without concrete, analytical information about returns on investments. Objective analysis must give way to the capacity to evaluate individuals' potential correctly and then hold firmly to the belief that they can succeed.

An area that has received considerable attention is creative breakthrough, which both illustrates and confirms the paradox and challenge of managing creativity. Nayak and Ketteringham have studied a dozen breakthroughs. They confirm that breakthroughs are not originally "believable" except to one person or a few people.[19] The problems to be overcome are insurmountable. Breakthroughs require huge amounts of money before it is at all clear that they are technically feasible or that they will ever be economically profitable. There seems to be no market for them even if they could be achieved, which at the time seems impossible. Thus, management cannot judge the potential benefits in any rational, analytical manner. Market plans, forecasts of potential profits, market

Exhibit 10–6 Successful Practices and Procedures of Companies Producing Above Average Creative Output

1. Devote at least 10% (or any similar percentage) of sales to R&D.
2. Allow creative people an exceptional degree of freedom.
3. Create and maintain a college campus atmosphere.
4. Provide the best lab facilities and leading-edge technical equipment.
5. Bring leading academics from the outside for internal seminars and interaction with inside people.
6. Provide a great deal of flexibility while minimizing paper work.
7. Ensure that at least one-third (or some other proportion) of sales comes from products that did not exist five (or some other number) years ago.
8. Spend half (or some other proportion) of the R&D budget on brand-new products.
9. Encourage competition among different units of the same company or different teams of the same unit.
10. Allow a researcher to spend 20% (or some other percentage) of his or her time developing new ideas or products other than those required by his or her normal duties, even when it means working with scientists or nonprofit insitutions outside the firm.
11. Give yearly prizes for the best idea in different categories as well as grand prizes.
12. Promote the concept of the ''champion'' who will get behind an idea and carry it forward to its completion.
13. Choose an ''executive champion'' to protect the product or idea ''champion'' and facilitate his or her dealings with the corporate bureaucracy.
14. Assign a team of experts in different areas to assist the product/idea ''champion.''
15. Assume ''champion's'' idea/product is potentially profitable unless someone can prove otherwise beyond any reasonable doubt.
16. Create independent task forces to operate outside normal bureaucratic channels and give them unlimited leeway to conceive and implement specific tasks.
17. Do not judge people by how they look, what they wear, or how they behave, but by their creativity, enthusiasm, and hard work.
18. Encourage close cooperation between research labs and marketers.
19. Couple product development with manufacturing design.
20. Encourage scientists to take up managerial positions where they supervise fellow scientists and become the link between them and top management.
21. Product champions who develop and market new products get the chance to manage them as if they were their own business.

Exhibit 10–6 (*Continued*)

22. Management is not intolerant or excessively critical when mistakes are made.
23. Get customers involved in brainstorming sessions on how to improve existing products or develop new ones.

penetration, and the like are of no value. Breakthroughs create markets. People cannot be asked if they will use a brand-new product. They cannot see the need for it. Thus, the decision to go ahead or not has to be made intuitively on the basis of trust and the potential ability of the champion of the breakthrough to succeed. There is great risk involved, for few projects become breakthroughs, while the remainder either fail or provide marginal benefits. The paradox facing management is to decide to go ahead with the required outlays knowing well what risks are involved, or to do nothing and risk allowing competitors to come up with their own breakthroughs and to gain advantages.

Despite the potential risks, Bell Labs, IBM, Philips, Merck, and Du Pont spend huge sums on basic research. There is a great deal of corporate pride when such research results in a breakthrough or a Nobel Prize. Still, the costs involved are enormous, and basic questions have to be answered concerning the benefits versus the costs of such research. It is obvious that R&D departments are difficult to evaluate by monetary criteria alone.

Exhibit 10–7 summarizes and analyzes seventeen highly successful creative ideas or products. With a few exceptions they were all originally considered impossible. Experts thought they were not feasible, newspapers wrote that they were a waste of precious time and scarce resources, and the general public ignored them initially. Banks refused financing, and when venture capitalists or bigger companies had the chance to buy the new product or idea they refused, even though the price was ridiculously low. Only a few individuals and a handful of creative companies were willing to take the risk and do things differently. They succeeded in a big way, while others still regret the opportunities lost by having refused to buy or produce the ideas or products.

Not all companies *want* to be creative. Reactive or responsive companies want to imitate innovators in a creative manner. Their strategies are based on flexible organizations and small R&D departments capable of successfully copying competitors' new products or ideas and making small, marginal improvements where necessary. Japanese companies are considered extremely successful in this type of incremental creativity.

Exhibit 10–7 Seventeen Highly Successful Creative Ideas or Products

1. *Razor blades:* Gillette could not get financing for six years. Experts insisted it was not possible to put an edge on sheet steel that would shave.

2. *The affordable car:* Henry Ford was considered a radical with no business instincts, but he managed to manufacture a reliable car costing no more than a horse and buggy.

3. *Television:* An April 8, 1927, news item in the *New York Times* read: "FAR OFF SPEAKERS SEEN AS WELL AS HEARD IN A TEST OF TELEVISION—Commercial Use in Doubt."

4. *Mainframe computers:* Even as late as the early 1950s a market study concluded that the maximum demand for computers would be 100 units.

5. *The transistor:* In 1953 Japan's MITI did not see the benefits in allowing Sony to import transistors. It took six months to convince MITI of the potential value.

6. *Fast-food franchising:* In 1954 Mac and Dick McDonald saw no need to expand their single restaurant selling hamburgers and milkshakes. Ray Kroc did, and created a multibillion-dollar business and a huge fortune for himself in less than a decade.

7. *Video recorders:* Until the early 1950s, it was thought impossible to make a device so small and inexpensive that consumers could afford it and use it.

8. *Overnight mail delivery:* The U.S. Postal Service, Emery Air Freight, United Parcel, and many other companies had seriously considered the possibility of delivering mail overnight and all rejected it.

9. *Tagamet ulcer drug:* Discovering the drug took immense resources and a very long time, which made those involved extremely doubtful about the forthcoming discovery or its potential commercial success.

10. *Swatch watches:* Initial market tests showed that consumers did not like them because they were too unusual.

11. *The Walkman:* In 1979 the marketing people at the tape recorder division of Sony were openly saying that the Walkman was a dumb product with not the slightest chance of succeeding.

12. *Post-it note pads:* At the end of 1978, 3M conducted a market test of "post-it note pads" in four cities. The results showed that the product was a big flop.

13. *The personal computer:* In 1976 Jobs and Wozniak tried to sell Apple to Commodore Computers for $100,000. Commodore refused the offer, as did Atari and Hewlett-Packard.

14. *Jogging shoes:* American sporting goods companies repeatedly turned down the proposition to produce jogging shoes, telling Bowerman (the originator of Nike shoes) to stick to his own expertise and stop telling them how to produce what they knew best: shoes.

Exhibit 10–7 (*Continued*)

15. *Just-in-time:* The idea of just-in-time was contrary to the conventional wisdom of the production line, which at that time was that it must be kept working at all costs. Thus just-in-time was considered impractical and very uneconomical. Today it is widely used throughout the world.

16. *The microwave oven:* Between 1953 and 1967 fewer than 10,000 microwave ovens were sold, mostly to airlines, cafeterias, and hospitals; no one forecast the huge market demand that developed in the 1970s.

17. *Photocopying:* In 1938, after six years of work, Chester Carlson invented the modern photocopying process but was unable to sell his invention. Until 1945 he got no response from such companies as IBM and Kodak. Only a nonprofit institution—Battelle—was willing to invest additional resources to improve the process.

Companies in mature industries require different forms of creativity from high-tech industries, where brand-new products and completely new technologies can be conceived and commercialized. Moreover, producing creative ideas and commercializing them successfully require much more than large R&D departments made up of high-level scientists or huge outlays for basic research. In all cases, creative people must be managed in a special way, which necessitates little supervision and much flexibility. Many business organizations are not familiar with this type of management and might learn a great deal from the organizational structures of universities, symphonies, theaters, or movie productions, which need to combine the management of creative people with that of administrative staff. In universities, for instance, organizational structures are flat. There is little or no supervision of professors, who are left on their own to do whatever they want when they want. At the same time (at least among first-rate universities) there is a clear, objective criterion: publish or perish. Professors are self-motivated, and most of them work very hard, even after they get tenure, not because they have to, but because they like their work. In universities, as in all other fields involving creativity, most of the output is of marginal significance: small, incremental additions to existing knowledge. Occasionally a major theory is advanced or an exceptional book is written. The cost of such breakthroughs is high, but universities are willing to bear it. The same is true of large symphonies or theater and movie productions. A lot of actors play small, marginal roles, and even leading actors do not often make substantial artistic contributions. Moreover, most plays and movies lose money. But occasionally a big breakthrough comes along and smashes all records, earns huge sums for the producers and makes the actors superfamous. Identifying breakthroughs beforehand is not possible; much can be learned, on the other hand, about better ways of managing actors and staying within imposed budgets.

Much less attention has been paid to marginal improvements and incremental creativity. Yet the majority of innovations in business come from small improvements in existing products or in services already provided. Some companies manage this sort of creativity superbly and produce a constant stream of ever more perfect output. Those companies are usually very close to their customers, whose suggestions for refinements, extensions, and new uses are carefully studied and implemented where possible.[20] In addition, they are good in exploiting new technological developments in order to improve their daily operations rather than accumulate advanced technology for its own sake. Finally, they encourage employees' suggestions for improving the efficiency of operations, consider such suggestions carefully, and implement those believed to be useful.

CONCLUSION

Creativity is an important area we do not know much about. Its value is clear, but dealing with it and making decisions concerning ways of improving creative output and its commercial benefits are not easy. Management is faced with several paradoxes and challenges concerning creativity.

PARADOXES CONCERNING CREATIVITY

1. Creativity must be encouraged and stimulated, yet it is not clear how that can be done.
2. Creative people do not like to be supervised, yet organizations want their resources utilized efficiently.
3. Some projects undergo setbacks, yet in the end they can succeed commercially in a big way if management persists.
4. Breakthroughs can bring huge benefits, yet they cannot be identified beforehand.
5. Creativity requires huge sums, yet decisions concerning creative projects cannot be judged in any objective fashion.

THE CHALLENGES AHEAD

1. To realize that highly successful products/ideas were not recognized as such even a few years before they became huge commercial successes
2. To recognize the importance of creative ideas and encourage them
3. To be willing to take risks
4. To accept that only a small percentage of creative ideas (no matter how brilliant they might seem) are technologically feasible and will end up commercially profitable
5. To be capable of abandoning ideas or products (no matter how much money has already been spent on them) once it is clear that the given idea/product is not technologically feasible or economically profitable (However, creative ideas must not be abandoned too early or too easily.)
6. To know that no creative ideas can be successful unless they are backed by a champion, hence the investment is made not in brilliant ideas but in first-rate people who embrace such ideas and make sure they are developed to completion
7. To understand and accept that it usually takes a long time between the conception of a project and its successful commercialization (Awareness of the high costs involved is necessary, but organizational or cost constraints must not stop the development of promising ideas/products.)
8. To be willing constantly to abandon obsolete products, services, or practices and redirect energies to new ones, although introducing new products is costly and risky
9. To try constantly to improve products and/or services in order to maintain creative advantages
10. To encourage and act upon employees' suggestions
11. To solicit and act upon suggestions for improvements from customers

Avoiding or Delaying Failure

A good part of American business has to do with that most un-American of ideas: failure.

ROBERT BOYDEN LAMB, *Running American Business:*
Top CEOs Rethink Their Major Decisions

Failure is a natural process, observed in both biological and organizational systems. In this chapter, different types of failure are illustrated and the most common factors that contribute to failure described. Delaying or avoiding failure is discussed as a conscious organizational process requiring a clear understanding of the factors that cause failure and the ability and willingness to do something to avoid their negative consequences. The need to recognize permanent environmental changes and the critical tasks of learning and adaptation to such changes are stressed. Finally, the statement that success breeds its own failure is explored and the implications discussed.

Charles Babbage was a genial British engineer. He created the speedometer, the actuarial tables for the insurance industry, the cowcatcher for railroads, and several other important inventions. In 1822 Babbage started building the first computer. The principles of his computer were the same as those of modern computers, yet Babbage had neither electricity nor electronics at his disposal to put his theoretical design into operation. That did not prevent him from building a full-scale computer, which consisted of an intricate collection of steam-powered cranks, gears, pulleys and levers. It is exhibited in a museum in London. Babbage's mechanical computer was ingenious. It included the idea of programming, a central processing unit, memory, and means of information input and of printing the output. Babbage worked on his computer until he died in 1871. He spent all his money, a $34,000 grant (the equivalent of about $10 million in today's dollars) from the government and large sums made available through his friends, to build his computer. His house was full of a series of half-completed models of his visionary creation.

Babbage's work on mechanical computers was a total failure, as the tolerances required for accurate processing of information were far beyond the capabilities of the best of machinists and metallurgists of his time. Babbage was a prophet of the modern computer. More than a century and a half ago he foresaw the value of such a machine and tried his best to build it. Unfortunately, his timing was off by a little more than 120 years. Had he lived a century later, Babbage might have been successful and ahead of everyone else in producing a workable computer.

AM (Addressograph-Multigraph) International was created in 1930. It developed, manufactured, marketed, and serviced a wide variety of business machines and related equipment, including embossed-metal address plates and duplicators capable of printing a whole page in a single stroke. Until the early 1960s, AM was considered one of the best-managed companies in the business annals of the times and a darling of Wall Street, included in most blue-chip portfolios. In 1946, for instance, AM's sales were close to one-fourth of those of IBM and seven times those of Xerox.

The management of AM International first ignored photocopying and the changes being brought about by electronics during the late 1950s and the 1960s. The executives considered photocopying too expensive to replace their cheap duplicating machines and concluded that the new technology in electronics was but a passing fad with little practical value for their own business. They were convinced that no competitor could uproot them; after all, they had a formidable network of suppliers and maintenance centers both in the United States and abroad, providing them with impressive competitive advantages. In the middle 1960s photocopying started making series inroads into AM's business, and its management suddenly realized that something had to be done. Its response was to overreact to the emerging technological threat. New products (automatic duplicators, copiers, electronic communicators, automatic printers, and others) were rushed to the market. They were misconceived, barely tested, mispriced, and targeted to the wrong segment. The results of the R&D and marketing efforts were disastrous, further aggravating AM's financial problems, as sale had stagnated and profits flattened. In an effort to show growth, AM's management went on an acquisition spree, but that did not help either. The companies bought were not carefully chosen and were scattered in too many unrelated fields. They had to be resold to raise needed cash and to retrench to AM's main business: duplicating. By then it was too late. The new photocopying technology had rendered mechanical duplicators obsolete, and with them AM International, which filed for bankruptcy under Chapter 11 in April 1982.

Western Union was founded in 1856. Its telegram business was a monopoly that grew and flourished for most of the first half of our century. It also provided a high rate of return and substantial dividends for its shareholders. Western Union was *the* high-tech company in the early part of this century and did reasonably well until the 1960s. The decline started in the early 1960s. It was slow and persistent, as long distance telephone rates dropped and new forms of communication were discovered (telex, electronic mail, overnight delivery, fax). More aggressive companies appeared, and Western Union lost its monopoly position and its accrued competitive advantages. Management did little to correct the situation. Somehow it was felt that nothing could be done or that there was no need to do anything, because nobody could threaten Western Union's basic business. The company managed to show reasonable profits during the 1960s and 1970s. In the early 1980s Western Union's problems started accumulating and its cash flow deteriorated. In 1984 the prospect of bankruptcy first appeared on the horizon, but reorganization was averted when a group of banks agreed to lend the corporation $100 million. At that time stock dropped to $9 from a high of $47 less than a year earlier. The attempted turnaround was not successful. The downhill trend continued until December 10, 1987, when Western Union's slow, steady decline led to bankruptcy proceedings under Chapter 11.

A somewhat different story of failure is that of WOW (Worlds of Wonder). In 1986 WOW's revenues from toy manufacturing were close to $100 million after only six months of existence. In 1987 revenues jumped to $327 million. Stock was valued at $29 a share when the company went public in 1986. WOW was growing fast in a high-margin market. It became a Wall Street favorite because of its imaginative toys that kids loved to play with and its marketing skills in distributing and pushing such toys. By early 1987 WOW employed 900 people and was planning to market more than a hundred new toys. Success ended abruptly, even faster than it had started. In March 1988 WOW went into Chapter 11 proceedings. Its staff was cut to 130 and its stock plummeted to one dollar. Early success had made WOW management overly optimistic and resulted in overstretching the company's resources and capabilities. Had WOW managed its growth and set more realistic goals, it would probably have remained a highly successful toy manufacturer.

EXTENT OF AND REASONS FOR FAILURE

Failures abound. Even though they might outnumber successes, they are somehow less well known. People obviously do not like to talk about their failures; often they hide or rationalize them, or they pretend that nothing has happened. Writing about failures is not as easy as publicizing successes; the person blamed for failure can sue the writer. The public does not want to read about failure, having far more interest in heroes and success stories. Apart from failures that bring laughter (the Woody Allen type) and some spectacular ones that get a lot of publicity, little is made of the phenomenon. From a rational point of view, failures should be publicized even more than successes. It might even be worthwhile to create a "museum" of failures where they can be studied with a view to helping future generations learn how to avoid similar ones.

The extent and pervasiveness of failure can be inferred from the following statistics collected from various sources:

- Between 35 and 80 percent (depending on the specific study) of new products fail ever to make a profit.
- More than half of spending on new products is used for products that never make it to the market.
- On average it takes eight years until corporate ventures become successful, while the majority of new ventures never make a profit.
- There were close to half a million business bankruptcies in 1988, a number that increases substantially during periods of recession.
- Personal bankruptcies grew more than two-thirds between 1980 and 1988, with about one person in every 250 declaring bankruptcy.
- For every successful corporate turnaround there are two that fail.
- In the automobile industry alone more than 1,500 firms have failed, including that of Charles Duryea, founder of the first automobile company; that of William Durant, the creator of GM, who founded his own company after he was ousted from GM; and that of John De Lorean, the charismatic auto executive.
- In the computer industry more than 300 firms have failed in the last twenty years.

- Texaco was fined $10.3 billion by a court, and in the end it had to pay $3 billion as an out-of-court settlement to Pennzoil.
- GM lost 12 percent of its market share between 1978 and 1987 (worth about $24 billion).
- In 1987 there were twenty-six U.S. companies with losses of more than $100 million.
- In 1987 U.S. banks lost a staggering $5 billion—close to 8 percent of their equities.
- In 1987, among the largest thousand global corporations, there were forty companies that accumulated more than $10 billion in losses.
- At least three people committed suicide following the stock market collapse of October 19, 1987.

FACTORS THAT CONTRIBUTE TO FAILURE

Exhibit 11–1 presents sixteen prominent failures. It also summarizes the factors most likely to have contributed to failure and the consequences involved. In this section, the factors that contribute to failure are classified and elucidated, although the causes of failure are sometimes so diffuse that they can hardly be attributed to a single factor. In the remainder of this chapter various ways of delaying or avoiding failure are discussed.

FAILURE AS A NATURAL PROCESS

In the biological world failure is synonymous with death and is considered a natural event. There are no exceptions to biological failure. Living systems are born, mature, age, and die. Death cannot be avoided, although life expectancy among humans has almost doubled during the last hundred years. In organizational systems, however, failure or death is not as certain or as regular. Some organizations (both profit and nonprofit) manage to survive and prosper much longer than others, although until now no organizations have managed to avoid the effects of aging and actual or relative decline. There are few organizations whose life span extends more than a few centuries. Failure seems to be as natural among organizational systems as it is among living ones, although it does not show the same degree of regularity. Avoiding or delaying failure seems to be the exception rather than the rule. Large size, excellent manage-

Exhibit 11-1 Sixteen Prominent Failures

Name	Industry	Event	Consequence	Main Contributing Factor
ALCOA (Aluminum Company of America)	Metal	Other materials edged into and diminished the aluminum market.	Lack of growth and increased competition	Natural causes
Bank of America	Banking	President could not remedy misguided policies of predecessors, caused by unexpected loan losses, expensive computer breakdowns, and high interest rates.	Bank grew too big to manage. Bank lost $3.5 billion, $955 million in 1987 alone.	Overextension, overoptimism, preoccupation with the short term, CEO
Beech-Nut Nutrition	Baby food manufacturer	Stripped of its profitable chewing gum division. Sells only baby food. To save costs it used a synthetic concentrate, which it described as 100% pure (but it was not perceived as such).	Fines estimated at $25 million as well as legal costs, slumped sales, and negative publicity caused a 20% drop in market share during 1987-88.	Quick-fix belief

Burlington Northern	Railroad	Longest U.S. railroad, operating in a mature industry	Misguided diversification into oil, gas, and pipelining so as to compensate for the pitfalls of railways	Natural causes, organizational arteriosclerosis, overoptimism, quick-fix belief
Eastern Air	Airline	$182 million loss in 1987; hostile management–labor relations.	Poor performance; labor detesting CEO; no solution in sight	Quick-fix belief, CEO
E. F. Hutton	Financial	Disorganization and mismanagement; CEO wielded absolute power for a long time; extravagance in both investing and spending	Profits slipped since 1981; in 1985 firm was found guilty of 2,000 counts of fraud; in 1986 firm lost $90 million.	Organizational arteriosclerosis, preoccupation with the short term, CEO
Exxon	Oil giant	Diversified into office automation market—the growth industry	Spent $2 billion, never made any money; new company sold for a pittance in 1985	New technology overdazzle, taking risks, incompatibility
Ford's Edsel car model	Automobiles	A medium-priced car (Edsel) conceived and designed using the best of marketing and design techniques	An estimated loss of $200 million during 1957–60	Poor judgment, overoptimism, unforeseen recession

Exhibit 11–1 (*Continued*)

Name	Industry	Event	Consequence	Main Contributing Factor
Genex	Biotechnology	Developed an unpatented product that could be made cheaply using biotechnology	Clients started manufacturing the product themselves; Genex had not secured a long-term supply contract; sales tumbled; idle plants added to costs	New technology overdazzle, overoptimism, ignoring competition
IBM Japan Ltd.	Computer manufacturer	Since 1979 has progressively lost its market dominance	Reacted with an atypical IBM strategy that included joint ventures, discounts and system integration; IBM seemed not to realize that it had to compete in Japanese style	Ignoring competition, quick-fix belief, overreaction
International Harvester	Machinery/truck manufacture	Decades of weak management	Insolvent; sold farm machinery firm; represented today by Navistar in the truck market	Natural causes, organizational arteriosclerosis, CEO

Company	Industry	Description	Outcome	Causes
Osborne Computers	Computers	Founded in 1980; produced the first "portable" computer; sales of $100 million in 1982	Filed for bankruptcy in September 1983	New technology overdazzle, overextension, ignoring competition, CEO
Penn Central	Railroad	A three-way merger among three East Coast railroads	Three-way merger burdened with huge labor costs and flat dividends; in 1970 rail operations went bankrupt; nonrailway assets were sold to public at a huge loss in 1987	Natural causes, organizational arteriosclerosis, others
Texaco	Oil	Acquired Getty Oil in 1984; $3 billion out-of-court settlement for buying Getty, which Pennzoil had arranged to acquire	Most valuable company to go to Chapter 11 bankruptcy proceedings	Taking risks, overoptimism, CEO
Time Inc.	Publishing	Launched TV *Cable Week.*	After five months and $47 million loss it closed the magazine	Overoptimism, ignoring competition, quick-fix belief, CEO
Union Carbide	Chemicals	Cloud of toxic gas spewed from the Bhopal plant, India killing about 3,000 people	Simultaneous failures in design, systems, safety, decision-making procedures; firm subject to global protests and sanctions; stock price fell; compensation still to be settled	Organizational arteriosclerosis, taking risks, overoptimism, quick-fix belief, bad luck

SOURCE: Compiled from published sources in the business press.

ment, and monopolistic or other advantages are not guarantees for continued survival and actual or relative prosperity.

In an article entitled "It's Tough Up There," *Forbes* concludes that only twenty-two of the one hundred largest companies in 1917 were also included in the 1987 list. Of the remaining seventy-eight, the majority had ceased to exist as companies, while the remainder had dropped well below the top hundred.[1] For companies below the largest hundred on the list, survival becomes even tougher and prosperity more difficult, as smaller companies are swallowed by larger ones or fade away for lack of sufficient resources to attain economies of scale in production, marketing, and R&D.

In addition to a considerable turnover among firms, whole sectors and industries also are born, mature, age, and die. Until the turn of the century agriculture was the most successful sector. It was then replaced by manufacturing, which in turn is being overshadowed by services. Within sectors, there are also growth, mature, and declining industries. In the last century small textile firms prospered. In the earlier part of this century mining and automobile companies did well, followed later by chemicals, steel, tool manufacturing, construction, aluminum, and airplane construction companies. Today the "best" industries are high-tech, including computer, pharmaceutical, and service industries. In the future the growth industries might be biochemical or genetic engineering, artificial intelligence, superconductors, high-speed trains, supersonic airplanes, or space industries. In the service sector, the growth industries might be entertainment, vacations, tourism, education, caring for the old, and research. As new technologies emerge, the growth patterns shift and new industries and firms appear and prosper. At the same time the older ones become less competitive and lose their real or relative advantages. Although many of the older industries can operate for a long time after new technologies appear or consumer attitudes change, they lose their dynamism and their potential to generate adequate returns on investments. As they eventually slow down, they are merged into other companies, are bought out, or stop operating anything. This S-curve pattern of birth, steep growth, plateau, and eventual decline can be observed in a great many cases, including technologies, products, services, companies, and, as we have said, even industries and whole sectors. S curves, the equivalent of biological birth, maturity, old age, and death, seem inevitable unless something is done to reverse their natural course.

Western Union, mentioned earlier, is a perfect example of a failure brought about by "natural" causes. Western Union was unable to adapt to environmental changes. It became obsolete and basically died. As a group, the steel industry has also declined because of "natural causes," as new technological developments have provided cheaper and better-quality substitutes for steel.

Organizational Arteriosclerosis

As organizations grow older, their managements and the organizations themselves usually become more conservative and more bureaucratic. Conservatism results in resistance to changed established ways of doing things. That is particularly true for successful organizations whose founder or top management see little reason to change established goals and directions or the way the organization operates. Henry Ford's insistence on continuing to manufacture the model T when consumer preferences had changed is a prime example of the inability to recognize the need to alter goals and perceptions when the market or the economic environment has changed. In addition, increased size brings more bureaucracy, which diminishes individual initiative and emphasizes control and formal procedures over effectiveness and efficiency. The examples of GM, AT&T, IBM, and many other large companies come readily to mind. Although formal policies and written procedures are necessary to improve control, overemphasizing them hampers decision-making and results in diminished dynamism, which in turn becomes the point of departure for eventual relative or absolute decline.

Organizational arteriosclerosis accelerates the failure brought about by natural causes. Conservative and bureaucratic organizations often ignore technological or environmental changes by believing they are temporary fads that will not affect them. Exhibit 11–1 contains failures caused by inability or unwillingness to innovate and compete effectively with companies using new technologies or new ideas. For instance, a common response of conservative, bureaucratic organizations is to wait until others innovate so as to determine whether or not there are economic benefits to be obtained by following the innovators. Although such a strategy is much better than ignoring changes altogether, it is not without potential long-term problems, as early innovators can accrue advantages and shape the market in desired directions. IBM's difficulties stem partly from its unwillingness to be a technological innovator, letting others play that role. As the cases of Cray and Digital Equipment in the mainframe market and Apple and Compaq in microcomputers have illustrated, such a strategy is full of long-term dangers. As Cray, Digital, Apple, and Compaq have established their reputation for technological excellence, they have been able to translate that reputation into higher sales. At the industry level, the steel companies lost their ability to innovate and let aluminum and other lightweight materials take away demand for steel. That could have been avoided had the steel companies started much earlier to compete actively with steel substitutes by reducing costs and innovating with new manufacturing processes and higher-quality products.

General Motors provides a good example of a company that is failing because of conservatism/bureaucracy. GM, the biggest and most integrated of all the automobile companies, cannot effectively compete in today's fast-changing car market. Its decline, which started much earlier,[2] has greatly accelerated during the last decade. GM's ambitious business strategy of redesigning each of its cars and modernizing each of its factories failed miserably. Eight years and $70 billion later, GM is no longer the lowest-cost manufacturer among automobile companies but the highest-cost. Its integrated factories and high technology are hardly more efficient than the old system, and all its cars look alike. Locked into heavy investment plans, GM continued spending in the expectation of profits and a recapture of its lost market share instead of questioning whether its modernization strategy made sense. Today things are changing at GM, but whether they are changing in the right direction and fast enough to keep up with competition still remains to be seen. GM's bigness, bureaucracy, and conservatism have decreased its flexibility and have brought to this once-excellent company what I have been calling organizational arteriosclerosis.

Being Dazzled by New Technologies

Although some organizations are unable to innovate, others fail by attempting to innovate too much or too early. It can be done by introducing new products or new technologies that are not economically viable. Schnaars regards this as the main reason for what he labels managerial megamistakes: decision-makers seduced by the alleged wonders of new technologies and the potential profits they will bring if exploited faster than by competitors.[3] Consumers are resistant if changes are not justified by lower prices or added benefits. But the advocates of new technologies (picturephones, moving sidewalks, three-dimensional TV, three-dimensional cameras, dehydrated foods) have tended to overestimate their concrete benefits in comparison with existing products while underestimating the costs, which depend heavily on the amount being sold. Demand cannot increase until prices go down, which creates a chicken-or-egg situation in which prices must decrease in order for demand to increase, but costs (and prices) cannot go down unless sales go up and thus reduce costs and decrease prices. Hence organizations must walk a tightrope: They must determine when it is profitable to innovate while at the same time guarding against premature or uneconomical technologies.

Once they are commercially profitable, new technologies increase demand and provide large opportunities for growth and profit. Such growth and profit potential inevitably attracts competition and causes many failures. In the computer industry alone more than 300 major firms have failed in the last twenty years. Today the computer industry is concentrated in a handful of firms, which hold large market shares and make huge profits. But failures have been legion. A good illustration of this point is Xerox.

In 1968 Xerox bought SDS (Scientific Data Systems) in an attempt to diversify into computers. It paid $900 million, ninety-two times the 1968 SDS earnings, to purchase the company. Poor management, inadequate resources, and open rivalry destroyed SDS's envisaged role and resulted in poor results. SDS lost considerable sums in 1970 and 1971. The losses increased in 1972, 1973, and 1974 (totaling more than $130 million). Xerox's venture into the computer business proved exorbitantly expensive. In July 1975 the board unanimously resolved that the purchase of SDS was "a mistake" and decided to get rid of its prominent investment. The writeoff necessary to get rid of SDS amounted to just under $1.3 billion.

TAKING RISKS

Taking risks is usually necessary in order to succeed, particularly if success on a big scale is sought. At the same time, risk-taking can lead to financial and other difficulties and can result in big failures. New and smaller firms must do something different from established or larger companies if they want to establish themselves and gain advantages over their powerful competitors. This often involves trying new, untested technologies, investing in new markets, and taking higher risks than seasoned firms. At the same time, new firms are usually hard-pressed for working capital (cash). Everybody is aware of the successes of Polaroid, Xerox, Compaq or Apple today, but those companies had to take considerable risks and overcome huge obstacles at the initial stage. Large, profitable companies can also get into serious difficulty or even go bankrupt by taking risks, pursuing new products, or going after untested technologies. The pressure to maintain high growth rates is usually responsible for such risk-taking among large, successful companies.

Bank of America, once the dominant firm in the world banking system, also fell victim to too many unnecessary risks. Its management gave priority to size and growth at the expense of quality and soundness of investments. During the 1970s Bank of America reaped record profits by globalizing its reach and lending to giant corporations and Third World countries. Gambling on a fall in interest rates during 1979 and 1980, it increased its mortgage sales. The rates rose, which resulted in a $3.5-billion loss. Unexpected loan losses, expensive computer breakdowns, unsuccessful takeover attempts, and employee involvement in consumer fraud cases all contributed to ethical problems and enormous overall losses. On top of that, many of the bank's loans to Third World countries had to be written off or discounted, which further increased its heavy losses. Today the bank's share of loan problems is still proportionately higher than that of most other big banks. The bank faced a $915-million loss for 1987 and continued having serious problems in 1988 and 1989.

OVEREXTENDING RESOURCES AND CAPABILITIES

Initial success can lead to grandiose goals of uninterrupted success and rapid growth, which can either overextend the organization's resources and capabilities or lead to a situation of unmanageable growth, both of which can contribute to problems and eventual failure. The example of WOW, listed earlier in this chapter, and several other failures listed in Exhibit 11–1 fall into this category. A prominent recent case is Carlo De Benedetti, the Italian financier, who launched an acquisition campaign in the 1980s using the booming European stock exchange to assemble a multi-billion-dollar empire. Using small equity holdings, he grabbed control of extensive assets, ranging from computers (Olivetti) to pasta (Buitoni). At the end of 1987 the sales of his empire were about $14 billion and its market value, despite the crash, was almost $10 billion. However, Benedetti's raid on Société Générale de Belgique, the Belgian holding company, which he hoped to make the center of his vast European industrial holding, failed. Although he invested $1.6 billion, he emerged with only 45 percent of the company's shares, making him a minority shareholder with no board representation. A rival, Compagnie Financière de Suez, managed to take control of Société Générale. Benedetti misjudged his opposition. Some associates expressed the opinion that Benedetti had "spread himself too thin," and others said they felt he was overconfident. At the same time the European Corporate Community bitterly resisted his brash, American-style hostile takeover tactics. Rivals were surprised at how poorly the bid was executed, since he had a head start by beginning in January and by paying more per share than the stock market value. But he lost big in terms of management time, money, and prestige by overextending his resources and capabilities while underestimating his opponents.

BEING OVEROPTIMISTIC

As was discussed in Chapter 2, being overoptimistic is a common judgmental bias that can lead to serious problems as difficulties are underestimated and future uncertainty ignored. Successful entrepreneurs often see themselves as gamblers and feel that they must take risks in order to succeed in situations where the odds are against them. Such success becomes a special reward of its own and an external recognition of their ability to recognize and exploit opportunities. Thus they can defend their unnecessary risk-taking with an overoptimistic outlook: They underestimate the dangers and overestimate the benefits. They say otherwise they would never have attempted to take such high risks and built successful empires.

Genex was commonly believed to be destined for great success in genetic engineering. The idea was to use genetic engineering techniques to make specialized chemicals needed in the manufacture of consumer and industrial goods. The idea helped the firm to raise $50 million in venture capital. Genex's board of directors came from IBM, Scott Paper, Emerson Electric, and other leading companies. After going public in 1982 and becoming a "hot" stock to buy, Genex saw its market value fall from $300 to $30 million in a few months. Genex had hoped initially to sell to Searle Corporation the key ingredients of its sugarless sweetner in bulk quantities. By doing so, Genex expected to generate quick cash, which it could use for working capital while at the same time starting to work on other specialized chemicals for long-term profitability. But Searle decided to manufacture the sugarless sweetner itself, as Genex had not secured a patent for its new products and had also failed to secure a long-term supply contract from Searle. Without a buyer, Genex's sales fell 39 percent in 1985, and the firm lost $16 million. In 1986, burdened with idle capacity, Genex lost $12 million more on sales of only $3.3 million, all of which came from contract research. Using high technology to produce an unpatented commodity product that could be made just as easily and cheaply elsewhere proved to be overoptimistic behavior.

IGNORING OR UNDERESTIMATING COMPETITION

Ignoring or underestimating competition can lead to serious problems and eventual failure. First, it must be assumed that existing competitors will constantly attempt to gain market share or other competitive advantages, especially at the expense of successful, profitable firms. Second, it must be accepted that new competitors can enter the industry, taking market share away from existing firms. Third, it must be recognized that technological developments (aluminum replacing steel, or plastics replacing aluminum) can allow substitution effects and in so doing change the boundaries of the market, thus bringing in new competitors from outside of what was considered to be a certain industry. Fourth, it must be acknowledged that foreign firms and the globalization of trade can change competitive forces and patterns in fundamental ways.

Examples of companies that underestimated the response of their competitors abound: the Pepsi-Coke, McDonald's–Burger King, and Gillette–Bic wars are examples. Yamaha underestimated Honda's response when it decided to challenge Honda's leadership and become the world's top manufacturer of motorcycles. Honda counterattacked furiously by introducing many new models and slashing prices so drastically that the weaker Yamaha could not respond. When the war was over, not only had Yamaha gained nothing, but it had lost its second position to Suzuki and become a distant third. Similar counteractions can be provoked even from much weaker opponents whose response is underestimated. The military defeat of the U.S. army in Vietnam and the forced Soviet "withdrawal" from Afghanistan were mostly due to an underestimation of an opponent's will to respond to superior force.

PREOCCUPATION WITH THE SHORT TERM

Too much preoccupation with the short term can create serious problems in the long term that could lead to failure. Many critics mention this as the main reason for the decline of U.S. firms in relation to Japanese ones. Investing in people, improving the quality of products or services, nurturing long-term customer relationships, adequate R&D spending, introducing new technologies, and the like might reduce short-term profits and put a strain on cash flows, but they are necessary to maintain or improve long-term competitive advantages. Critics argue that there are areas emphasized by the Japanese which frequently become the critical determinants of their success. Along the same lines, critics charge that U.S. companies are too concerned with, and driven by, short-term financial performance and how Wall Street will react to their short-term earnings.

Revco D.S. is an illustration of how short-term motives can lead to failure. In the hope of improving short-term profitability, Revco's management embarked on an uncontrolled expansion drive and took too many risks. In 1983 its vitamins were blamed for the deaths of thirty-eight infants. In 1984 another company was bought to avoid a hostile takeover, but the takeover danger was not eliminated by its short-sighted actions. Revco's CEO was obliged to arrange a leveraged buyout, which greatly increased Revco's debt and eventually forced it to apply for chapter 11 proceedings.

BELIEVING IN QUICK FIXES

Many problems facing organizations cannot be corrected easily and quickly.[4] Some of them are deeply rooted in the corporate culture. Others might involve managing and rewarding people, managerial skills, or the organizational structure and strategy, while others might stem from the fact that the firm is operating in a mature or declining industry. A belief that a new theory or a highly paid consultant can quickly correct such problems is naïve and can even further aggravate them. Solving these problems requires a long-term outlook, persistence, and some fundamental changes in what Kilmann calls the five areas (organizational culture, management skills, team building, strategy-structure and reward system) that determine organizational success or failure in the final analysis.[5]

Pan American World Airways is just one example of the quick fix's failure to work. Pan Am suffered huge losses as a result of the deregulation of the airline industry. Deep in debt and with little prospect of making a profit from its airline business, Pan Am chose to sell off most of its profitable assets, which included a centrally located New York building and the Intercontinental hotel chain. As its losses continued, it sold off some of its profitable routes to other airlines and was ultimately left with no non-airline assets and only highly competitive routes. Management failed to realize that selling the airline business might have been the best way of getting rid of losses and achieving long-term profitability.

BELIEVING IN BARRIERS TO ENTRY

Large, successful organizations believe that their size and financial might are adequate deterrents to competition. Firms with monopolistic or oligopolistic advantages also think they can keep competitors away. History has shown that no barriers can be effective in the long run, as competitors, attracted by high profits, will always find ways of overcoming them. IBM's great advantages and formidable barriers did not stop competition. The oligopolistic power of the U.S. automobile firms did not stop imports. OPEC did not manage to impose its will and maintain high oil prices, although it could control a large part of oil production.

OVERREACTING

Once things start deteriorating and the prospect of failure becomes real, overreacting is a common response. The actions of AM International, described earlier, are typical of firms that suddenly realize the magnitude and severity of the problems facing them and attempt to solve them without thinking carefully about the consequences of their actions. In the same category are high-growth companies that see their growth flattening and the price of their stock suddenly falling because of forecasts predicting reductions in the future growth of their earnings. To reverse the trend, such companies often overreact by diversifying into high-tech industries or introducing new products aimed at exploiting new needs or creating new markets. Such actions often fail, however, because acquired companies are bought at a high price and new products do not live up to the expectations of the desperate managers looking for quick fixes. The example of Xerox, mentioned earlier; the search for new high-growth, high-profit ventures made by ITT; the entrance of many companies into the computer market; and the expensive acquisition of biotech firms are typical of the urge to maintain high growth rates at any cost, often without proper consideration of the consequences.

THE PERSONALITY AND ABILITY OF THE CEO

In an extensive study of the decision-making process among top executives of large U.S. companies, R. B. Lamb explores the principal reasons why some of their decisions lead to failure. According to Lamb, the most crucial factor of all is the personality of the CEO and his ability to translate essentially simple ideas into workable strategies.[6]

Some executives can destroy their organizations through autocratic management, which leads to high turnover among top executives (Lamb cites the example of James Dutt of the Beatrice company, who had a hand in changing three presidents in one division over a two-year period and three in another in a single year). Others cannot recognize or are incapable of changing the deeply rooted culture of their organization (for example, John de Butts's attempt to change AT&T's culture after the deregulation of telecommunications in the late 1970s). Others can pursue unrealistic or misconceived strategies despite clear evidence that such strategies will lead to disaster.

Top management can also be responsible along with the CEO for failure. Groupthink and the inability to accept threatening evidence can lead to failure. The debacle of *TV-Cable Week* is an illustration of involvement of the CEO and top management in a failure.[7] *TV Cable Week* was the most heavily promoted magazine startup in Time Inc.'s history. The company was planning to spend more than $100 million to make the project a big success. After five months of publication, Time Inc. closed the magazine. The direct cash flow loss was approximately $50 million, but the indirect damage was far greater: In less than two weeks Time Inc. stock lost $750 million in market value. The magazine was developed in an effort to maintain high growth rates and earnings by pursuing new, potentially profitable, and high-growth projects. However, disconfirming evidence was ignored, as top management was not willing to accept the fact that its "pet" project was not going to be profitable. Grandiose goals were pursued. Top management rejected market testing and pushed hard to publish a magazine that had no chance of ever making a profit. In doing so, they transformed a failure into a disaster.

THE ROLE OF LUCK IN FAILURE

Such events as new technologies, new products, new competitors, recessions, changes in customers' preferences, political unrest, physical catastrophes, and the like that cannot be predicted can sometimes lead to failure. Because planning for such events is impossible or impractical, the failure they bring can be, at least partly, attributed to bad luck. Malcolm Mclean, the man who pioneered the concept of container shipping and changed the world of shipping with his company, Sea-Land Corporation, typifies what bad luck can do. He sold Sea-Land to RJR in 1969, created a holding company, Mclean Industries, and bought another company, "U.S. Lines." Betting on a rising demand for oil, Mclean bought twelve supertankers for $570 million. They were slower but more fuel-efficient vessels than his competitors were using. However, luck deserted him. The oil market collapsed starting in the middle of the 1970s, and oil prices increased, giving faster ships an advantage. Mclean Industries filed for Chapter 11 protection from creditors in late 1986, almost $1.3 billion in debt.

INCOMPATIBILITY

The fashion for diversification and large conglomerates that brought together diverse firms under a single corporate umbrella in the 1960s and early 1970s was reversed in the late 1970s and 1980s, when streamlining and restructuring to reduce costs became necessary. Examples of mergers and acquisitions that created incompatibility and thus led to failure are legion. The examples of LTV, ITT, and other monstrous conglomerates come easily to mind. Companies buying their way into the computer, aerospace, biotechnology, and other high-tech industries are also relevant examples of the inability to avoid failure through incompatible acquisitions. Diversification did not provide opportunities for synergy. Few benefits could be gained through these acquisitions. There was little or no know-how for running the firms being bought. If corporate top management interfered with the running of the acquired company, it had no expertise to contribute and could even make things worse. If it did nothing, no synergy could be gained, and its firms could go their own ways.

CAN FAILURE BE AVOIDED OR DELAYED?

Very few business and nonprofit organizations have managed to survive for long periods. Most importantly, only a tiny percentage of them have maintained above-average performance for considerable spans of time. Organizations must therefore take concrete steps to reverse what seems to be the natural process leading to organizational arteriosclerosis and eventual failure. Some of those steps are described below. Others are the equivalent of maintaining success and are dealt with in the next chapter.

UNDERSTANDING THE NATURE OF FAILURE AND THE FACTORS THAT CONTRIBUTE TO IT

Failure must be accepted as a natural process affecting all organizations unless some conscious efforts are made to avoid or delay it. That is not always easy to accept, as top executives tend to believe that their organizations are different from the majority and therefore cannot fail. Ways of rejuvenating organizations must be conceived and implemented. They should include fighting bureaucracy, continuously injecting dynamism into managerial and other personnel, and in general avoiding the factors that contribute to failure described in the preceding section.

RECOGNIZING MISTAKES

Along with accepting the inevitability of failure, unless conscious efforts are made to halt its natural progress, mistakes must be recognized in order to avoid making similar ones in the future.[8] Recognizing mistakes is not an easy task. For one thing, in our Western culture mistakes are considered shameful and those making them rationalize them or hide their existence; for another, in many managerial decisions feedback is neither precise nor frequent, making it difficult to identify mistakes; finally, undesired outcomes do not always imply mistaken decisions, since unforeseen events and factors outside a company's control can be responsible. Learning about mistakes therefore requires an open attitude similar to that of managers in Japan, where mistakes are publicized so that others can learn to avoid them. Moreover, it must be accepted that those making them should not be penalized. Instead, procedures for evaluation of past decisions must be set in place and ways of learning from mistaken ones established.

Failure can result from the type of judgmental biases discussed in Chapter 2, which must also be recognized so that steps can be taken to eliminate or minimize their negative impact. The consequences of such mistakes (or judgmental biases) are amplified when committed by CEOs or top managers. In this case, recognizing these mistakes is more difficult, for few people in the organization are willing to tell top executives that they are wrong or that their judgment is faulty and biased.

DOES SUCCESS BREED ITS OWN FAILURE?

It is natural for success to produce arrogance and similar psychological attitudes among the executives of successful organizations. Such arrogance, in combination with the factors listed below, can slow down success, foster mediocrity, and eventually lead to failure.

- *Inviting Imitation.* Successful companies must attract attention and become models for imitation by other firms in their industries, which attempt to reproduce their success and the factors that contribute to it.

- *Motivating Competition.* Successful companies earn higher than average profits, which attract new entrants on the markets and encourage existing ones to increase their capacity or more forcefully compete for products and markets.

- *Encouraging Segmentation.* Existing competitors and new entrants might not be able or willing to compete directly, particularly if successful companies have accrued substantial advantages. They often choose instead the indirect approach of carving out a segment of the market in which they can specialize. Often such a segment is small and unimportant to the big company, but with time its importance grows or it serves as a base for obtaining experience and expertise, which are then used to expand to other segments and possibly the entire market.

- *Stimulating Higher Fixed Costs and Possible Conservatism.* Once organizations become successful, they must take several steps to maintain their advantage. Success might entail (1) paying higher salaries to keep their managerial and scientific personnel or hire new recruits; (2) investing more in R&D; (3) increasing fixed expenses by establishing structures and procedures to manage growth and maintain success; and possibly, (4) becoming more bureaucratic in order to be able to maintain and control their success.

- *Cultivating Arrogance.* Successful companies are often "impressed" by their own achievements, which tends to exaggerate their confidence in their ability to continue to be successful. It also leads them to underrate dangerously the capacities of their competitors to threaten or overtake them. They are likely to drop the low end of the market from strategic consideration as not profitable enough, which opens the door to segmentation as competitors move in to cater to the neglected part of the market.

Even when successful companies do not fail outright, there is a tendency toward average performance. Regression toward mediocrity is a historical fact that can be observed not only among business firms but also among non-profit organizations, the military, and, most notably, nations. To be avoided, it requires conscious, concerted efforts aimed at reversing the natural effects of organizational aging and neutralizing the other potentially negative factors discussed in this chapter.

THE PARADOXES OF FAILURE

1. At the societal level failure is a natural process allowing for renewal and continued dynamism, yet from an individual firm's standpoint failure leads to permanent problems and eventual bankruptcy or halting of operations, which must be avoided at all costs.
2. Organizations must adapt to environmental changes, yet they cannot be sure beforehand whether a change will be temporary or permanent.
3. Organizations must often take risks in order to succeed, yet risk-taking, by its very nature, can lead to failure. On the other hand, not taking risks can also lead to failure, as more aggressive competitors will be willing to take such risks and might succeed.
4. Organizations must innovate, yet premature innovation can lead to serious financial problems and other difficulties if the espoused innovation turns out to be uneconomical.
5. As organizations become successful and grow they have to become more bureaucratic to maintain adequate control, yet bureaucracy lessens individual initiative and hampers the effectiveness and efficiency of decision-making.
6. Organizations must use their accrued competitive advantages to achieve desired objectives, yet they should not overestimate their own importance or underestimate the ability of competition to overcome such advantages, especially over the long term.

THE CHALLENGE AHEAD

1. Reverse the natural tendency of organizations toward aging and eventual decline.
2. Take calculated risks in order to succeed, but at the same time protect the organization against failure.
3. Understand the major factors causing failure and take steps to avoid or delay their negative influences.
4. Overcome organizational resistance to change.
5. Avoid rigidity and bureaucracy without losing control.

CONCLUSION

Business executives must always walk a tightrope. Taking too many risks can be as bad as taking no risks at all. Failing to fend off competitive attacks might be as fatal as seeing danger everywhere. Delaying or preferably avoiding failure is a challenge of the highest order that must, along with success, strategy, and creativity, engage the time and efforts of top executives. The possibility of failure must not be ignored or downgraded just because it is an unpleasant subject. In my view failure requires as much consideration as strategy, creativity, and success. It is a natural process caused by organizational aging and decline. History has clearly shown that organizational failure is almost inevitable unless something is actively done to delay or avoid it. Organizations must therefore constantly innovate and adapt. The greatest challenge facing executives is to know *when* and *how fast* to innovate and *what* changes to adapt to. Another serious challenge is overcoming the resistance to change present in most organizations so that the desired program can be implemented.

12

Achieving and Sustaining Success

*S*how me a chief who's happy with his lot and I'll show you a
guy who's going to blow it.

LEE IACOCCA, Talking Straight

Success is the ultimate objective of individuals and business or-
ganizations. Not everyone can be successful, for success requires
special skills or talents and an ability to do relatively better than
others. In this chapter success is defined and the factors that
might contribute to it are explored. Successful individuals are dis-
cussed and the reasons for their success analyzed. Finally, the
myths about success are outlined, together with the essentials of
organizational success.

Thomas Watson, Sr., the founder of IBM, knew nothing about mathematics, engineering, or computers. Yet in the late 1930s he had a clear
vision of the need for a computer suitable for business applications. He
saw computers not as simple calculators but as machines capable of
storing, retrieving, and processing information. Watson put substantial
resources into research in order to produce a ''computer'' that fitted his
vision of the future. He did so in 1937, in the middle of a depression,
when his company could hardly afford it. With Watson's insistence,
vision, and financial backing, Harvard's Howard Aiken produced a high-
power calculating machine in 1942 that resembled the first all-purpose
computer built a few years later, in 1946. Aiken's expertise provided
IBM with the know-how to get started in the computer business when
most other companies had not even heard of computers.

About ten years later IBM began selling its 650 model, the first commercial computer, which was highly successful. The 650 model sold close to 2,000 units and allowed IBM to become the leader in the computer industry and one of the most successful companies ever built. Watson's vision and willingness to gamble close to half a million dollars produced results by giving IBM an early lead and a strong competitive advantage. Where Babbage had failed to build a computer more than a hundred years before, Watson succeeded by being "in the right place at the right time," having a vision, and being willing to act upon it.

Watson, with little formal education and no technical talents at all, started his career as a salesman and made no contribution to the development of computers other than supporting research through his company. Watson picked up information available to everybody about computer technology and potential business needs and interpreted it in a unique way. He came up with a vision of the modern computer while everyone else was seeing computers as machines to do calculations faster. Most important, Watson was willing to act on his vision and invest (gamble, really) considerable resources to achieve his goal. Unlike AM International, a competitor of IBM at that time, he not only adapted to changes in the environment but also actively anticipated them. In fact, he even speeded them up through his decisions and actions. Unlike WOW, the toy manufacturer mentioned in the last chapter, he did not overextend his company. Instead, he managed its growth wisely and created an effective organization capable of harvesting the fruits of the new technology—computers. In the process he achieved a share of close to 50 percent of the lucrative computer market, which in 1988 reached $150 billion.

In 1988 William H. Gates III, at thirty-two, was the world's youngest self-made billionaire. He had been chairman of Microsoft ever since 1975, when he founded it. Microscoft is the largest independent software company in the world, with sales estimated at close to half a billion dollars, an undisputed leader in the field of programs for personal computers. Gates dropped out of Harvard in 1975 at the age of nineteen to devote all his time to writing programs for personal computers, which were just starting to be used by hobbyists at the time. He quickly realized the need for new programs if personal computers were to become useful tools for everyone. He therefore founded Microsoft, which went public in 1986, trading at $21.50. In March 1987 the value of the stock hit $90.75, making Gates, who owns 40 percent of the shares, a billionaire. In 1988 his stock in Microsoft and his other assets were estimated to be worth more than $1.5 billion, making Gates the richest self-made billionaire ever at the age of thirty-two. His success and that of Microsoft derive from his perception that personal computers would become popular and that there would be a huge demand for software, which represented a great opportunity. This was at a time when personal computers were just being invented, and when Xerox was failing to capitalize on having built the first microcomputer, Alto, in its Palo Alto research facilities. Not long afterward, company after company would reject the offer of the founders of Apple Computers to buy their new invention (the personal computer) for $100,000.

But Gates saw the future clearly and created a company to exploit the huge opportunity that the future was offering, namely, writing computer programs for micros. Gates succeeded where many failed, including some large companies, thanks to his technical skills in designing and writing computer programs, his extremely hard work (often until 4:00 A.M.), and his ability to build and manage effectively a team of people. His information about computers and his vision about computer programs did not come from many years of education or from privileged sources but rather from his interest in computers and his interpretation of information available to everyone.

Gates, like Watson and such other hi-tech entrepreneurs as Packard, Perot, and Jobs, found himself with a great opportunity which he exploited to create a highly successful multibillion-dollar company. An interesting question is how all these people became so successful. Are there any common factors that contributed to their success and permitted them to remain successful while others stumbled and fell after having reached considerable heights?

Succeeding is definitely not easy. The vast majority of individuals, companies, and nations would naturally like to succeed, which is arithmetically impossible, because most of the time success is a zero-sum game. At the same time some people, firms, and countries do succeed. Why them and not us? After all, achieving success is equally difficult for everyone. How then did Bill Gates become a billionaire after dropping out of college? Why are Merck's shares worth more in the stock market than those of GM, whose revenues are eighteen times higher? What made Japan and Germany two economic giants after they were reduced to ruins in World War II? At the other extreme, why do individuals commit suicide? Why do companies go bankrupt? What makes countries decline?

Success, failure, and mediocrity (the most common condition of all) are tightly interwoven. One person's outstanding success is someone else's mediocrity or failure. In real life only one, or at most two, can be outstandingly successful in competition. For new companies to succeed, some of the existing ones must produce average results, or fail. Thus success, mediocrity, and failure are relative concepts depending upon each other and the specific situation involved. Outstanding success, like that of Watson, Gates, Merck, or Japan, becomes part of popular folklore, as does spectacular failure. There is not much interest in what goes on in between. We hear little about the more than one million millionaires in the United States or the millions of mediocre ("average") large or small businesses. They are "no news," like a dog who is not barking. Yet they represent the vast majority, the key to a country's well-being, which clearly points to a strong need for more attention.

WHAT IS SUCCESS?

Success is the ultimate objective behind the vast majority of individual and organizational decisions and the motivation for a great deal of behavior. Its meaning is elusive, however, because there are as many interpretations of success as there are individuals and situations. A father who kills his entire family and then commits suicide or a mother who feeds her children all the food she has and dies from hunger have both succeeded in fulfilling their objectives. Success is achieved with the reaching of a desired, favorable, or satisfactory outcome. That makes the meaning of success highly personal, as it depends very much upon the objective of the person involved, the situation, and the standard of comparison. What seems like success to one person (the person succeeding in his suicide attempt) might seem the ultimate failure to another (his psychiatrist or priest).

Examples of the relativism and subjective character of success abound. In a poor Third World country, a firm that makes $100,000 profit is a super-success story, whereas such a sum would represent petty cash to a corporation in the industrialized West. For a kid who grew up in a ghetto, being accepted at an Ivy League college is a big success, while admission to the same college for a kid who went to the best of private schools is considered normal. Few people questioned the quality of Detroit's cars until the arrival of Japanese imports with which to compare them.

Success is relative, refers to specific situations, and is not easy to attribute, but that does not prevent people from making quick judgments about successful individuals, companies, and countries. Efforts to quantify success and to rank successful individuals or organizations abound. Some of them have gained wide public acceptance as symbols and absolute certification of success: a gold medal in the Olympics, a Nobel prize, and an Oscar are indisputable tokens. Among business organizations, measuring success goes beyond large profits, big market shares, or high rates of return on equity. In our days, for instance, GM is not commonly considered a success story, although its revenues are a stunning $110 billion (the biggest of all American companies), while its U.S. market share is a commanding 36 percent. Many business observers have questioned the recent success of IBM (it was ranked twenty-third in the annual survey of CEOs conducted by *Fortune* magazine), although its 1988 earnings of $5.5 billion were the highest of all American corporations.

DETERMINING SUCCESS

Success can be determined objectively, subjectively, or through a combination of objective and subjective procedures and criteria. Winning the 100-meter race in the Olympics is accomplished through an objectively measured procedure that involves direct competition in groups of six athletes drawn randomly from those who have been preselected to participate in the games. In the end, the top six winners run against each other. The gold medalist is the one who finishes first. To eliminate any element of subjectivity a photo of the finish is taken to determine the order in which the athletes pass the 100-meter mark. The winner of the singles in the U.S. Open tennis tournament is selected after the successive elimination of all those who lose in matches played between two players. Those matches are governed by specific rules and an explicit scoring system.

In other sports (ice skating, gymnastics) there is an element of subjectivity, although few will dispute the success of the victor. In such sports the procedure and criteria used to judge the athletes are objective, but scores are given by a panel of experts who inevitably use their (at times) different judgments to evaluate the performances of the various athletes. In order to introduce objectivity, the scores of judges are averaged, but this assumes that their opinions are not influenced in any systematic way.

In cases where both criteria and judgments are subjective, the global opinions of many experts are sought to quantify success and rank those being evaluated, when sportscasters are asked to vote for the most valuable college football player, when deans of business schools are asked to rank the five best business schools; or when CEOs are asked to determine the ten most and ten least admired corporations. The reasoning behind this type of evaluation of success is that experts cannot be wrong, and that by averaging their answers one can arrive at as objective a result as possible.

Apart from competitive sports, where winning occurs through direct competition or successive elimination, all other ways of determining success involve an element of subjectivity in the procedure employed, the criteria used, or the opinion of the judges. A 1988 survey conducted by *Business Week* to determine the best of business schools produced very different results from previous surveys, because the criteria used to evaluate the various schools included the students' satisfaction and that of prospective employers along with the opinions of business school deans, the only group being surveyed in the past.[1] About the same time a survey of European executives conducted by the *Economist*[2] produced results that differed from both the previous studies and the *Business Week* survey.

The success of business corporations can be assessed in several ways other than surveys. The assumption behind the *Fortune* list of the 500 largest corporations is "the bigger the better." Another way is to evaluate companies according to their profits, their rate of return on equity, their average growth rate, or the gains in their share price. Yet another is to rank companies according to the ratio of the price of their shares divided by their annual earning per share. The larger such a ratio, the higher is people's opinion of the value of a company: They are willing to pay more now because they expect future earnings of the company to grow fast enough to compensate them. Thus, people consider Merck more than 150 percent as valuable as IBM, because the price–earnings ratio of Merck is 19 while that of IBM is 12. IBM, in turn, is valued twice as much as GM, with a P/E ratio of 6.

Do people (professional stock market analysts and the general public) show good enough judgment in the stock prices they are willing to pay? It can be argued that as long as many thousands of people are willing to pay their money to buy certain shares rather than others, this is the most objective way of valuing a certain company. We can therefore say that the higher the price–earnings ratio, the more successful the company *in the judgment of professional stock market analysis and the general public* who buy the shares of these companies.

Although stock prices might provide some measurable insight about the success of business corporations, they fail to provide an objective way of measuring success agreed upon by all. That can be seen in the fact that the price of certain stocks might double in a few days when another company, or a group of investors, makes a bid to buy the stocks of the company involved. Such offers are based on criteria other than earnings per share. They might include book or breakup values or the earning power of the company after it has been bought and reorganized. If large discrepancies exist between different evaluations of the same company, it means that one or the other is wrong. As was noted in Chapter 2, judgments about the present and future values of companies are not independent, as people read the same publications and are provided with similar and not necessarily adequate information. Furthermore, judgments are influenced by factors that are interpreted in a similar (because of the dependent nature of the information being used), but not necessarily correct, fashion. Hence, the fact that many people agree on a certain evaluation is not indisputable evidence about the objectivity or correctness of such an evaluation.

Determining the success of business firms is not a simple task. The outcome depends heavily upon the procedure used to make the evaluation, the criteria on which the evaluation is based, the available information, its interpretation, and the judges themselves. Most evaluations use a procedure that combines analysis of historical performance with the prediction of anticipated future accomplishments. The criteria used are a combination of short- and long-term performance measures, which include profits, growth rates in assets and revenues, market and book values, average rate of return on equity, average rate of return per employee, productivity gains, and management ability. The information itself can come from many sources and be interpreted in many different ways.

The Paradox of Determining Success

In addition to satisfying curiosity (people are impressed with and fascinated by outstanding success and those who achieve it), determining success can bring concrete benefits that influence decision-making and further improve or at least maintain success already achieved. In theory, eliminating subjectivity in measuring results can provide an objective way of determining success (or progress toward success) and help in making rational decisions. In practice, the procedure, criteria, information, and measurement of results become a game of bending the rules and taking actions aimed only at improving the scores. The goal of those involved becomes a matter of getting high quantitative scores in the various areas evaluated instead of achieving or sustaining "real" success. There are numerous examples.

During the Vietnam War success was measured by how many of the enemy were killed (body count). Once that became the criterion, over-estimation of enemy bodies was widespread, because promotions and other rewards were based on that statistic. Soon body count lost its value as a measure of success and even diminished the quality of decision-making, as those using the information were not aware of (or chose not to believe) the cheating that was going on at the front.

Similarly, the stock market's preoccupation with short-term profits obliges management to concentrate its efforts on improving short-term performance. Whether or not the company will also do well in the long term is not of immediate concern, as managers switch jobs within the company or move to other firms. Hence a particular way of determining success can have a negative impact on the real, long-term value of a company (or even a country), as short-term decisions aimed at improving short-term profits can impair long-term performance. Many critics cite this as an important reason for the decline of U.S. companies and the rise of their Japanese counterparts, which show more concern about long-term performance.

Along the same lines, student grades are a way of measuring success, namely, how much they have learned. However, as anyone who has gone through school knows, students "learn" how to get good grades instead of devoting their time to real learning. They might spend many hours finding old exams given by a certain professor, talking to students who have taken the same course, copying old papers that received A's in previous years, or memorizing notes and parts of books in order to do well on the exam. Such devices might improve their chances of getting a higher grade but contribute little or nothing to real learning, the main objective of education.

Unfortunately, any attempt to quantify and measure success leads to Heisenberg's uncertainty principle, mentioned in Chapter 1. The simple fact that a criterion exists corrupts the measurement procedure and renders the evaluation of success questionable. At the same time, abandoning all attempts to evaluate success objectively is no more acceptable; judging success on purely subjective grounds can be even more easily manipulated to prove one's point of view.

Dealing with the paradox of how to determine success objectively while avoiding the various problems just described is not easy. The whole area of determining success becomes even more complex as one looks below the organizational level to divisions, departments, projects, or individuals. In such cases, we must add problems of accounting and of allocating fixed expenses to the costs of various units or projects. Finding satisfactory, realistic solutions is extremely important and becomes a prerequisite for achieving or maintaining success in organizations.

THE ZERO-SUM GAME OF SUCCESS

Humans rarely question their ability to succeed. They attribute success to their own abilities and blame bad luck for failures (in psychology this is called "attribution theory"). However, if objective criteria are used, success is neither automatic nor pervasive. Maintaining success requires a different mentality and different skills from those needed for achieving it. Success often reduces motivation, encourages arrogance, and provokes imitation by others who are also eager to succeed.

THE RELATIVISM OF SUCCESS

Success depends upon one's goals and reference group. The higher the goals and the wider the reference group one aims at competing with, the more difficult it is to achieve objective success and sustain it. By definition, objective success judged by a peer group will mean that half of those competing are below average (that is, they are failures). As the first accompanying graph shows, it also means that a small percentage will achieve above-average success, a smaller percentage "excellent" success, an ever smaller percentage outstanding success, and only one, or a handful at most, unique success.

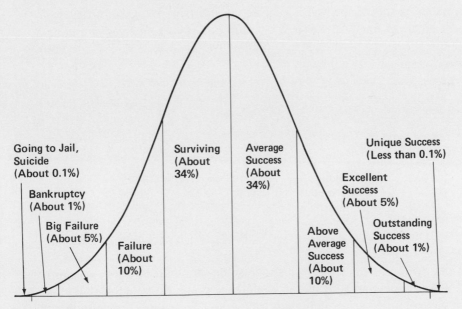

Exhibit 12–1 Various Types of Success (and Failures)

The reference group one is compared with can range from the family and neighborhood to national and international levels as the second graph shows. Obviously, the farther an individual or company wants to move to the right-hand side of both graphs, the harder it will be; the number of spots available becomes progressively smaller, and competition becomes progressively stiffer.

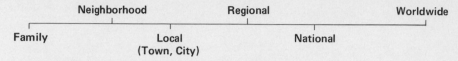

Exhibit 12–2 The Reference Group Judging One's Success

Finally, the third graph shows a progressive reduction in the number of spots available as one moves to competition at a higher level.

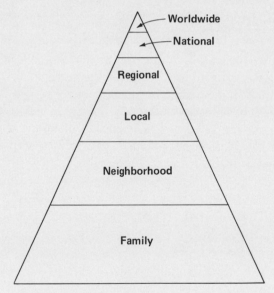

Exhibit 12–3 The Numbers of Successful Individuals as a Function of Their Reference Group

FACTORS AFFECTING SUCCESS

Studying success requires distinguishing among the various types of success and placing ourselves in a reference group. The factors that influence success may vary widely with each type and group. They might even be contradictory: Factors that facilitate success of a certain type might be useless or even a serious handicap for another (the positive attributes of an entrepreneur, for example, might be a handicap for a manager). At the same time, there is one consistent finding: There are many alternative ways of succeeding but behind successful companies there are always successful individuals.

UNIQUE AND OUTSTANDING SUCCESS

Exhibit 12–4 gives a brief résumé of highly visible individuals who have been the driving force behind the creation of large and very profitable corporations. It also lists their major accomplishments, major ideas and some related information, as well as the major reason for their successes—assuming that success can be equated to high visibility and large, extremely profitable companies. Exhibit 12–4, as well as a study of many more highly successful individuals, reveals almost as many reasons for success as there are successful individuals:

1. *Persistence*. In most cases the ideas that led to success were not originally accepted as potential breakthroughs. The ideas and their orig-inators were often rejected outright, and bankers or other investors ap-proached for funds thought that the ideas were impractical and uneconomical and had not a remote chance of making a profit. Often the originators of the ideas were ridiculed and told to stop dreaming and concentrate their efforts on some worthwhile practical tasks.

2. *Endurance*. Exhibit 12–4 shows that most of the successful indi-viduals listed had to face and solve formidable financial, technical and other problems. Their success was achieved as much by their ingenuity in solving such problems as by their persistence against formidable odds. Most often the road to success was long and bumpy. In some cases abandonment was repeatedly suggested by outsiders and bankruptcy threatened. Only through superhuman efforts and untold forbearance did these individuals manage to overcome obstacles and ultimately succeed.

3. *Motivation*. Most importantly, the successful individuals exhibited an ability to motivate themselves and their associates continuously, never contenting themselves with some initial success or being satisfied with the monetary or other gains they achieved. Instead, they wanted to continue reaching higher and higher levels of performance, which brought addi-tional success and contributed to their extraordinary accomplishments.

4. *Irrelevance of Background*. The majority of the successful individ-uals listed in Exhibit 12–4 were immigrants or came from poor families.

Exhibit 12–4 Successful Individuals, with Major Achievements, Ideas, Reasons for Success, Family Situation, and Education

Person	Major Achievement	Major Idea	Major Reason for Success	Successful Until End of Career (or Today)?	Major Idea Initially Accepted?	Family Situation	Education
Elisabeth Arden	One of the largest cosmetics companies	Taking bold approach to product development	Shrewd businesswoman who understood demand for beauty products	YES	YES	Poor; father an immigrant truck driver	No formal education
Alan Bond	Founded global empire—focuses on brewing, media, real estate, energy, mining on 5 continents	Takeover artist	Strong, loyal management team	NO	YES	British immigrant	High school dropout at 14
Richard Branson	Empire of music-related products	Products (including records) appealing to the young	Entrepreneurial drive	YES	NO	Family of lawyers	High school dropout

Andrew Carnegie	Founded steel and iron empire	Investing in iron rail manufacturing business	Good salesman and clever businessman	YES & NO	YES	Poor; father a linen weaver	No formal education
Serge Eastman	Invented simple, cheap camera that anyone could use (Kodak)	Revolutionized film texture and introduced a simple camera to go with it	Highly practical, inventive mind	YES	YES	Poor; father died when he was eight	No formal education (left school at 14)
Thomas Edison	Invented electric light and other popular products	Practical inventions with commercial value	Unflagging curiosity and entrepreneurial mind	YES	YES	Modest	No formal education (left school at 12)
Henry Ford	Established largest car company of his time	Produced a reliable, affordable car	Putting most of profits into expansion	YES	NO	Modest: farmer's son	No formal education
King C. Gillette	Invented safety razor	Made cheap razors that can be used once, thrown away	An innovator and clever salesman	YES	NO	Impoverished	No formal education

Exhibit 12-4 (*Continued*)

Person	Major Achievement	Major Idea	Major Reason for Success	Successful Until End of Career (or Today)?	Major Idea Initially Accepted?	Family Situation	Education
Armand Hammer	Successful entrepreneur and trader	Use barter in commercial deals with Eastern countries	An able wheeler-dealer	YES	YES	Modest: immigrants	Medical degree
Lee Iacocca	Launched and promoted series of successful cars	Innovated and introduced new management techniques	Super salesman	YES	YES & NO	Poor: immigrants	University engineering degree
Ralph Lauren	Created Polo Inc. in 1967	Classic, superb quality clothing	"Have a strong point of view that you believe in and stand by"	YES	YES	Russian immigrant parents	None

William Lear	Created Learjet, used by corporate executives	Reliable, fairly inexpensive plane for corporations	Inventive mind, prodigious energy	YES	NO	Working class	No formal education
Simon Marks	Britain's largest retail chain	Self-service at cheap prices	Innovating retailing by eliminating wholesaler and creating a brand name	YES	NO	Poverty-ridden; Russian immigrants	Illiterate
Aristotle Onassis	Shipowner, inventor of flag-of-convenience ships	Using flags of convenience as a way of cutting red tape and avoiding taxes	Shrewd entrepreneur with courage to take risks	YES	YES & NO	Humble background, immigrant	No formal education
Helena Rubenstein	Cosmetics industry	Adapting cosmetic products to every kind of skin	Shrewd businesswoman	YES	YES	Polish immigrants	University degree in dermatology
Gilbert Trigano	World's largest organized holiday resort chain (Club Med)	Providing an exotic, organized holiday resort at reasonable prices	Remarkable organizational skills	YES	YES	Modest	High school dropout

Some were illiterate and had little formal education, while many others were high school or college dropouts. Thus, background, family situation, and education appear not to determine success, as highly successful individuals come from all walks of life and all levels of formal education—from illiterate to Ph.D.

5. *Hard Work*: A study of the lives of the highly successful individuals listed in Exhibit 12–4 suggests that they work extremely hard, at least during critical periods, that they are driven by the belief that they will ultimately succeed, and that they have a great deal of enthusiasm, which they manage to transmit to their collaborators and employees. They are also capable of building an organization, controlling growth, and consolidating initial success. Organization-building and consolidation constitute a critical stage where many fail by overextending themselves or by being unable to create a viable and effective organization (of course, they are not listed in the exhibit).

Many successful businessmen have written accounts of their lives and business successes.[3] Some of their books provide insight into the factors that contributed to their success. In one such book Warren Avis,[4] the founder of the car-rental company that bears his name, advocates the following personal and business qualities for those who want to become successful entrepreneurs: (1) an unencumbered personal life, (2) a severe case of monomania and personal commitment, (3) plenty of staying power in order to overcome obstacles and eventually succeed, (4) a high energy level, nurtured by periods of relaxation, (5) good judgment about people, (6) the belief that nothing in one's business is impossible, (7) willingness to take risks, (8) the determination to make the first product profitable, and (9) a pragmatic approach to business and life rather than living in an ivory tower. Iacocca says there is nothing mysterious about success, that there are no magic formulas. His advice is simple: "Start with good people, lay out the rules, communicate with your employees, motivate them, and reward them if they perform."[5]

Michael Meyer, in *The Alexander Complex: The Dreams That Drive Great Businessmen*,[6] studied six empire builders. His conclusion was that although each one is driven by different motives they have something in common: a vision to change the world and make it a better place. Meyer writes that "because they are talented and convinced they can change the world, they often do."

Sustaining success for long periods is a challenge as difficult as attaining it. As discussed in the last chapter, there is a natural tendency (regression) toward mediocrity. Moreover, successful entrepreneurs (those who usually achieve the initial success) are not necessarily successful managers capable of sustaining it. In order to maintain success, effective organizations must be not only built but also managed. Growth must be controlled, and the natural tendencies that lead to mediocrity overcome. Organizations and their top management must never become self-satisfied or complacent. Instead, they must be supermotivated all the time, never stop being creative, and always be ahead of competition. Flexible organizations must be capable of recognizing changes and of adapting to them. Even the slightest relapse in motivation or the smallest mistake in reacting to an important change in the environment is enough to reverse unique or outstanding success. As we move from outstanding to unique success, these factors of supermotivation, creativity, keeping ahead of competitors, flexibility, and recognizing changes become all the more crucial.

An element that will always exist and may hamper continued unique or outstanding success is imitation. Successful companies receive a great deal of attention, and it is natural for competitors to take a close look at the successful company's achievements and to attempt to imitate them. A good example is in the People's Express airline, which started offering no-frills flights at a cost much lower than that of scheduled airlines. Reduced fares attracted large numbers of students and others who wanted to fly cheaply. People's Express planes could be utilized at full capacity, thus providing nice profits and ample opportunities for further expansion. It did not take long, however, for other airlines to imitate the People's Express strategy. They offered deep discounts for advanced-purchase tickets to lure students, and promotional giveaways (the frequent fliers' program) to attract businessmen. They also reduced their fixed expenses to bring them closer to those of People's Express lower cost advantage and force it into a broad acquisition strategy in order to become a national carrier instead of a local one. That increased People's Express's fixed costs and reduced its flexibility, thereby destroying its competitive advantages. In 1986 People's Express was obliged to merge into Texas Air to avoid bankruptcy.

EXCELLENT SUCCESS

Little is known about successful individuals and companies below the unique and outstanding categories. Not much is written about individuals and companies that attain excellent success, for they are numerous, and there is little interest in their activities or performance. How many tennis fans, for instance, know or care about the tenth- or nineteenth-ranked tennis player? On the other hand, achieving excellent success is no small accomplishment; only 1 percent do better than the individuals or companies in this category.

Excellent companies, like outstanding, ones must be creative and self-motivated and must work hard to maintain their gains. The difference between the two lies in the degree of their creativity, self-motivation, and other capacities. Excellent companies rarely try for big success or major breakthroughs. Instead, they are satisfied with small improvements, marginal extension of their product lines, or logical expansions of their products or businesses. To a great extent, their success lies in their ability to use existing technologies effectively (rather than inventing new ones) and to make small, marginal improvements rather than come up with dazzling breakthroughs. Many excellent companies remain so because they possess considerable competitive advantages resulting from their size, experience, or network of contacts (suppliers, agents, distributors, customers). Because of such advantages they are able to avoid taking risks. Instead, they wait for others to innovate and then enter the market when they judge the situation ripe. They can do so by acquisition or by using internal company resources to enter the new market when the time is right. Because of their huge resources, experience, and contacts, they often succeed. Many large corporations like Philip Morris, General Motors, IBM and several Japanese company follow this strategy. George Weissman, president of Philip Morris, describes it as follows: "We have not often been first with a new cigarette . . . an essential element in our success is our ability to react rapidly to changes in market or competitive position."

OTHER SCENARIOS

Some excellent companies were once unique or outstanding, but they regressed toward the average as they became more bureaucratic and more conservative and their management grew older. Others were overtaken by new, more dynamic firms capable of being more creative or more willing to take risks.

Still other excellent companies never managed to climb to higher levels of success either because top managers became complacent with their success and therefore lost the motivation and drive to continue, or because they were unable to overcome the stronger competition they encountered as they climbed on the ladder of success.

The leader of an excellent company does not need the charisma and creative genius of the leaders of unique or outstanding ones. Needless to say, he or she must be capable of motivating people, maintaining a climate of excellence in the organization, and avoiding too much bureaucracy and too many interpersonal rivalries among management. Leaders of excellent companies have to concentrate on being consensus makers, consolidators, and efficient managers (on top of those qualities, leaders of unique or outstanding companies must be entrepreneurial, inspiring, and visionary).

THE MYTHS ABOUT EXCELLENT, OUTSTANDING OR UNIQUE SUCCESS

Exhibit 12–5 lists twelve myths about success. Studying these myths and the reality of success can help avoid some common misunderstandings about achieving or sustaining success. Success comes not only from new ideas but also from seeing things from a different perspective. Moreover, it does not always require huge resources. Fairy tales and movies to the contrary, achieving success is a long process and requires a great deal of insistence.

The literature on how to succeed is voluminous. The vast majority of the serious books and articles on the subject describe successful countries (like Japan), companies (IBM), or individuals (Trump), listing the factors that led to their success and often drawing conclusions as to how others can achieve similar results. Although reading success stories is exciting, it provides only historical accounts of what happened in the past. It cannot guarantee future success for those who imitate the success stories described. For one thing, conditions are rarely the same, but more important, even perfect duplication of the factors that lead to success for one person or company cannot ensure the same success for another. Moreover, besides what can be described and quantified there is another element in success that eludes description and quantification. This ''something extra'' can be called talent, the right organizational climate, the right moment in time, charismatic leadership, or intuition. In the end, it is what makes all the difference and distinguishes highly successful individuals or companies from average ones. This is true in all fields, not just business.

Exhibit 12–5 Twelve Myths About Excellent, Outstanding or Unique Success, and the Reality

Myth	Reality
1. Success comes from ideas nobody had before.	What seems new is something others may have devised before but could not figure out what to do with. Alternatively, what seems new might really be a new twist to an old idea.
2. Big success requires large resources.	The critical factor is not the resources themselves but the right mix of resources at the right place and time.
3. Success comes overnight.	In the vast majority of cases success requires considerable effort and overcoming myriad obstacles.
4. Success comes from identifying unfulfilled needs.	Success often comes from new ideas that open new markets rather than satisfy existing needs.
5. To succeed one needs to be an innovator.	Pioneers do not always succeed (they are often killed in the process of opening new frontiers). Early imitators can often avoid the initial mistakes made by pioneers and succeed.
6. Big success requires big companies or special types of environment.	Big success can be achieved in all types of companies (from garage-type operations to giant firms) and in all types of environments.
7. There are secret formulae or recipes for success.	Success always requires uniqueness and a personal touch that cannot be put into formulae or recipes.
8. Success requires appropriate education or family connections.	Many successful individuals have had no formal education and come from poor families.
9. Successful ideas can be recognized immediately.	Often successful ideas are so new that they are not recognized as such even by the experts.
10. Once initial success has been achieved, the person involved can relax and reap the fruits of his or her success.	Continuous effort is required to exploit initial success and maintain achievements.

Exhibit 12–5 (*Continued*

Myth	Reality
11. To succeed one must be lucky.	Although luck (being there at the right place and time) can be extremely useful, it usually favors those who are prepared to seize the opportunities presented and who have the abilities to exploit them to achieve success.
12. Success, once achieved, brings happiness.	Most often highly successful individuals get used to the money, fame, or power brought by their success. Instead of being satisfied, they attempt to achieve higher levels of success.

International prominence in sports is an example. To be among the top hundred tennis players in the world, one must have the right build and be physically strong, be smart and self-confident, be a good strategist, and be willing to travel around the world and spend most of the time away from home. In addition, he or she must be perfect in the execution of the various strokes in tennis and must practice many hours a day. However, at this level of outstanding or unique success there is something extra that distinguishes super champions from the rest of the great players. That something extra is hard to describe. It differs from one world champion to another, as there are few similarities among such great tennis players as Borg, McEnroe, Agassi, Becker, Lendl, and Wilander. The same can be observed among great dancers, painters, musicians, or actors. They need talent, but talent cannot be described, taught, or imitated. One has it or does not.

Success requires additional nonquantifiable factors, which include a cohesive society, group spirit supportive of excellence, and a government willing to be a partner rather than an adversary of those striving to succeed. At the internal level, organizations must motivate their employees, who must feel that they are an integral part of an organization whose success depends entirely upon their hard work and correct decisions. In such circumstances organizational goals are put above personal ones and the prevailing common purpose facilitates excellence and success. How some countries, industries, or companies manage to develop such a high group spirit and climate for excellence while others cannot is impossible to explain, but differences can be observed even among companies that are only a few blocks apart.

THE PARADOXES OF SUCCESS

1. Everyone wants to succeed in a big way, yet such success is impossible, because success is relative, and by definition not everybody can succeed.
2. Everyone looks for recipes for success or wants to be told the factors that determine success, yet beyond a certain level the factors that bring outstanding or unique success cannot be identified or quantified.
3. Success brings psychological gratification and real benefits, yet when it results in satisfaction it reduces the motivation for achieving higher levels of success or sustaining such success.
4. Success requires experimenting, making mistakes, and taking risks, yet many of those acts inevitably lead to failure.

THE CHALLENGE OF SUCCEEDING

One of the biggest challenges facing those in search of success is to choose the right level and geographical region for competing. Attempting to succeed above the level and region where one is capable of competing usually results in frustration and disappointment, as results are below expectations. On the other hand, aiming below the level and region where one is capable of competing provides few challenges and inevitably leads to boredom. Moreover, it is difficult in our day to succeed in a big way without going "global." Although it may not be possible to know at what level and where to compete at the outset, it becomes a critical part of the journey toward achieving success. Targeting the right level and region to compete requires a continuous adjustment of the level or region where one is competing in such a way as to balance potential difficulties with the challenge of doing more, competing at a higher level, and eventually achieving a greater degree of success.

The biggest opportunities for excellent, outstanding, or unique success come during periods of change in new, growing markets. Thus, correctly identifying such opportunities becomes the highest of challenges and the most common way to attain big success. Although pioneers were often killed by the Indians, the few who succeeded extended the known frontiers and opened up new territories. In the process they managed to succeed in a big way, to harvest large riches, and to accumulate competitive advantages that others could not nullify.

In order to succeed in business, pioneers must see opportunities others have not recognized. That requires challenging assumptions and going against conventional wisdom. The challenge is therefore to think creatively and differently from others but at the same time to be realistic and possess good business sense in order to avoid major mistakes or giving up prematurely, as Ron Wayne did when he sold his 10 percent stake at Apple for $1,700 in January 1977. Less than three years later his stock would have been worth about $100 million.

Sustaining success is a different challenge. The question, "How can I do better what I am doing already?" must be asked all the time. Ways of improving existing products, services, production processes or procedures must be considered at all times and practical solutions found. Ways of extending existing products and services must also be continuously sought, and the search must be successful. Otherwise, competitors make inroads and force successful firms toward average performance.

$\boxed{13}$

Conclusion: Toward a New Management

*P*lacebos can be more powerful than, and reverse the action of potent, active drugs. The incidence of placebo reactions approaches 100% in some studies. Placebos can have profound effects on organic illnesses, including incurable malignancies. Placebos can often mimic the effects of active drugs.

A. K. SHAPIRO in Spiro, *Doctors, Patients, and Placebos*

This concluding chapter provides a summary and a synthesis of the principal paradoxes and challenges facing management in decision-making, forecasting strategy, and creativity. The possibilities of learning from experience gained outside the management field are summarized, and learning from the mistakes of others as well as our own is examined. Finally, the emerging business organization is discussed and the future challenges for management are outlined.

Placebos are a big mystery to modern medicine and science. In innumerable clinical tests that have covered practically all ills, it has been found that patients who receive placebos do as well as patients who receive active drugs. In other clinical studies patients who receive placebos report side effects practically the same as the side effects of the active drug itself. Moreover, reports indicate that billions of dollars' worth of prescriptions are for drugs considered ineffective by the FDA. Those drugs may have harmful side effects.

H. M. Spiro, an M.D., asks some penetrating questions in a book that summarizes research findings and the current debate about placebos.[1] He says that the basic question is not the percentage of patients healed by each (60 percent for placebos and 70 percent for active drugs) but rather what the implications are as far as scientific medicine is concerned. For instance, are the healing effects of the real drugs incidental to the psychological benefits of taking a pill, any pill, that is thought to be of medical value? Is the symbolic nature of the meeting between the patient and the doctor as important as any active drug? Is it possible that most sickness goes away on its own, and that the patient sees the doctor and takes the prescribed medicine when he or she feels the worst, just before the trouble begins to wane? Medical doctors mainly ignore placebos, do not acknowledge their healing value, and rarely make use of them. Their medical training and their self-image as scientists go against the empirical findings of the healing effects of placebos. Such findings are therefore ignored, and the potential value of placebos is not exploited, because it does not fit with the preconceived notion of medicine as a scientific discipline governed by rational Cartesian principles.

In comparison with medicine, management is a very new discipline. Yet attempts to make it a science abound. There are no widely accepted theories today, nor have there been any lasting ones during management's short history. Claims of value derived from theories have been grossly exaggerated, and high expectations have gone unfulfilled. Recipes and magic formulas have not (and could not have) worked. Yet business organizations must be managed; they must strive to succeed and must do everything possible to delay or avoid failure. It is imperative, therefore, that we do the utmost with the little we know. At the same time we must remain realistic as to what the field of management can offer, which means we must be aware of the limitations of managerial theories and tools. We must accept the fact that we know little and find ways to enlarge our knowledge and apply it as intelligently and realistically as possible. The placebo effects of an espoused theory, a well-written book, or a well-paid consultant must be separated from their real value. Unlike our bodies, where there is a natural healing process that allows placebos to cure disease, the value of placebos in the business world depends not only on a single firm but also on its competitors who can believe in them too. In such cases the business placebo can prove to be illusory and lead to unpleasant surprises unless its real value can be separated from the psychological one aimed at motivating or guiding the organization toward achieving certain desired goals.

ASSUMPTIONS AND BELIEFS
ABOUT MANAGEMENT

Managerial activities can be divided into strategic and operational, although the distinction is not always neat. There is an overlap between the two. Strategy requires dealing with a lot of new situations, including competition, which require creative solutions and original ideas. Operational tasks involve many day-to-day, repetitive decisions. My belief (and assumption) is that we know little concerning how best to deal with the interaction between strategic and operational decisions. An understanding of the difference between the two is a first step.

Operational decisions are repetitive. They can be systematized to obtain maximum benefits. The shorter the forecasting horizon involved in them, the more accurately we can forecast, the better we can deal with the uncertainty that surrounds the future, and the less competitors can influence future events. For those reasons, and because feedback indicating the effectiveness and usefulness of such decisions can be objectively obtained, operational decisions can be formalized. With the use of modeling techniques, for instance, optimal solutions can be found for scheduling the pilots and air crews of a major airline; the optimal utilization of oil tankers can be computed; and how much and what grades of oil have to be refined at various factories can be found; and so on. Operational decisions of this sort can be made automatically (and mechanically) by the computer. Even less well-defined day-to-day decisions can be systematized and expressed in terms of decision rules, since people are not necessarily more effective in making such decisions than are well-thought-out and consistent rules (Chapter 2).

Strategic decisions, however, cannot be modeled or systematized. They are unique. They require a deep understanding of the factors involved, the competitors, and the future and how it might change, as well as an objective assessment of internal capabilities. There is always an element of uncertainty that cannot be estimated objectively. I believe we know next to nothing about the best way of making strategic decisions, and that whatever we assume we know can turn out not to be true after all (Chapter 1).

Strategic decisions cannot be made analytically. They must be creative and intuitive. A great deal depends upon uncontrollable factors such as competitors, future technologies, and the consumer. Strategic decisions must therefore be unique, and they always involve a considerable element of risk. There is a perfect duality in all strategic decisions, as competitors would also like to succeed by formulating and implementing their own strategies, which, in addition to being unique and creative, will attempt to outsmart their competitors' strategy.

We must understand and accept the limitations of managerial tools, theories, and knowledge in general, as well as the uncertainty and risks involved in future-oriented decision-making. Doing so might require a radical rethinking of what the field of management is able to offer in its present state. The time has come to be realistic and to learn through a better understanding of managerial practices, experience, and past mistakes. We can also go outside the field of management in search of relevant, useful ideas which we could subsequently apply to management.

THE KEY INGREDIENTS OF MANAGEMENT

In this section, managerial decision-making, strategy forecasting, and creativity will be briefly summarized, together with the paradoxes and challenges they present.

HUMAN DECISION-MAKING

On one hand, judgmental psychologists tell us that human judgment is limited and biased (Chapter 2); on the other hand, highly successful business people maintain that their decisions are mostly intuitive. The same is true of great artists, chess grandmasters, and other creative geniuses. They cannot tell us why their decisions, creations, or actions are so successful. Their secret is their intuitive ability to recognize potentially great directions and choose the most critical aspects on which to focus their search and to come up with a successful outcome. Management is faced with a paradox: being intuitive and running the risk of bias versus being analytical and worrying that the outcome will be sterile. Although part of the paradox can be resolved by systematizing routine, day-to-day decisions, it is not at all clear how to be intuitive while at the same time being reasonably unbiased. That is the biggest challenge facing top management. There is no doubt that a lot of intuitive decisions have failed, even some made by highly successful business people, and nothing indicates that this state of affairs will necessarily change in the future. However, intuitive decisions *must* be made since analytical tools are limited in their capacity to deal with complex, less quantifiable, and longer-term strategic decisions or issues.

THE FUTURE AND PREDICTING IT

There are three things we know with certainty about the future. First, the future will be different from today, and the farther away from today we aim at, the bigger the difference will be. Second, many forecasts have been (and will continue to be) made; some went wrong in foretelling events that did not occur and others in not predicting things that happened, in some cases only a short while later (e.g., the appearance and widespread usage of computers). Third, knowledge of the future might be of little or no value if it refers to events external to the organization and is shared by one's competitors.

Forecasting the future also presents a paradox and a challenge. To be of value forecasts must be accurate, but no such accuracy can be assured. Even if accurate, they would be of little or no value for the majority of strategic decisions if their competitors' were accurate too. At the same time, almost all strategic decisions require some predictions of how the future might be. That means strategists must come up with unique forecasts or unique interpretations of how the future might change and what competitors will do based on their own forecasts of the future. Strategists therefore need to understand current technologies, forthcoming inventions and their implications, the market place, and their organization's skills and capabilities (as well as those of their competitors). As with the other tasks related to strategy, forecasting of that sort cannot be delegated or modelized, because strategic decisions require dealing with changes that cannot be predicted statistically. The challenge for strategists is therefore to predict such changes, how they might affect their organizations, what can be done to anticipate them, and what the most likely competitive actions and reactions will be. Those are not easy predictions to make. No matter how much effort or care is invested, uncertainty cannot be wholly eliminated.

COMPETITIVE AND OTHER STRATEGIES

Competition in business is not exactly the same as in war, but that does not make competitive business strategy any easier. In military conflict the opponent is known, although estimates of its strength might not be accurate. In business, however, new opponents can appear, and technology can drastically change the industry boundaries, destroy barriers to entry, or make products, processes, or even whole markets obsolete. Worse yet, an existing or new opponent can choose to attack any part of the market at any time, where and when it is least expected. In military terms this means defending a concentrated attack with dispersed forces, which creates yet another paradox and another challenge for management. Since an attack can come at any place and time (e.g., through segmentation and positioning), organizations are obliged to be on guard all the time. But that is not possible, for one cannot be prepared for a possible attack at all times. The cost and resources required to do so would be enormous, and the organization would be totally distracted from its day-to-day strategic tasks. At the same time, effective means of defense against attack must exist.

On the noncompetitive side, the challenge for strategists is to develop unique skills attained through specialization and perfected through experience. Organizations that become overspecialized, however, run the risk of becoming obsolete in the face of environmental changes. Dealing with this challenge requires anticipating future changes, but, as we know, there are serious limitations to predicting such changes and benefiting from the predictions. One alternative is to become proactive and attempt to shape or control the environment in desired directions so as to avoid the negative consequences of unanticipated change. Another alternative is to develop flexibility, allowing for quick reactions and rapid adaptation once it is confirmed that a certain environmental change is permanent. On a different track, organizations can develop a capacity for excellence that would allow them to compete without being directly concerned with competition. Great athletes and artists, as well as first-rate organizations, have this ability. Once it exists, they can outdistance their competitors while making it hard for them to close the gap and compete directly. How the drive for excellence is encouraged, achieved, or maintained is not something we can put our hands on. Some organizations (or individuals) have it, others do not. At the same time it seems that the drive for excellence slows down or disappears in most organizations that have had it in the past. Thus, unless top management is aware of these problems and makes a conscious effort to slow down or reverse the natural decline toward mediocrity, the organization will not be able to remain excellent for long.

CREATIVITY

Creative ideas, original solutions to problems, and new products or services are essential to business organizations and a key ingredient for success. Creativity presents yet another paradox and another challenge. If creativity could be taught or produced at will through appropriate encouragement or specific actions, everyone could become creative. In that case, what was creative before would become commonplace, while "real" creativity would always remain something more original than the majority of people or organizations could achieve. Thus, creativity will continue to be a relative concept where "new," "original," or "creative" will always be measured in relation to a norm established by the majority. That is true for creative ideas and solutions as well as for new products and services. It is therefore illusory to search for general methods to teach creativity or universally applied rules for bringing it out. Encouraging creativity in organizations will continue to be a unique challenge defying rules or analytical treatment.

Another paradox and challenge relating to creativity is the amount of effort or resources required to generate creative output and the extent of creativity that *can* be generated. By definition, creative output is hard to come by; if it were easy it would already have been produced by someone else. Moreover, the harder it is to discover, the rarer the chance of doing so and the greater the effort, resources, and creativity required.

Although there might be some exceptions, creative ideas, solutions, products, or services that are easy to recognize and bring to fruition result in small returns. The contrary is also true, which means that the greater the difficulty and the larger the resources required to produce some creative output, the greater the chance of more than average returns or even achieving some kind of breakthrough. At the same time, a newer and more original idea will be harder to evaluate and will always require taking bigger risks. Management must therefore commit substantial resources when objective evaluation is impossible. Evaluating creative ideas and deciding upon their levels of risk and potential returns is yet another important challenge for management.

In addition to new ideas and breakthroughs, the majority of organizations grow and prosper through small improvements in quality or tiny decreases in costs, which require creativity exercised in research labs, in engineering departments, or among managers. This type of marginal creativity is continuous and must not be confused with breakthroughs, which happen once, or at most on a very few occasions, in a lifetime.

Managing creative people represents another challenge. R&D and other creative departments require huge sums of money, which necessitate better supervision, clear objectives, and more structure. However, structure often kills creativity, which raises the paradox of having to manage something which seems at first glance unmanageable.

In the final analysis, the production of above-average creative output and the management of creativity are intuitive, unique tasks. There are no rules or set formulas telling us how above-average results can be achieved or maintained. What brings such results is something more often described as "the right climate," "the right spirit," or "the right leadership." Thus, the challenge for top management in this instance is to discover its own unique approach and develop the right climate in which creative output can flourish.

LEARNING

What can a top manager do to deal with the paradoxes and challenges inherent in management? Can anything be done to facilitate success and discourage or avoid failure? First and foremost, no one should expect miracles, recipes, or magic formulas. Miracles, recipes, and magic formulas do not work in competitive environments, while formulating strategies, or with creativity. The only realistic alternative is to look inward, to grasp the situation at hand as well as possible, and to come up with clever, creative approaches or solutions. That requires serious thinking. Six facts must be understood: (1) Each situation is unique; (2) competition is not static, and competitors will try to outsmart each other; (3) competitive actions and reactions cannot be predicted although their existence, and the uncertainty they introduce must be incorporated into strategy; (4) competitors are faced with the exact same situation—they encounter the same difficulties, uncertainty, and doubts. (5) since everyone has the same information, in order to gain advantages over competitors such information must be interpreted in a unique way. To quote Beaufre:

> One of the most important factors in classical military strategy has always been the ability of the general to grasp the changing conditions of war *faster* than the opponent and, therefore, to be in a position to anticipate and act on the new factors.

Finally (6) managers must not rely too heavily on accurate forecasting, in particular for longer-term predictions, while at the same time knowing that only if they plan ahead of time they can get a head start and gain competitive advantages.

LEARNING FROM OTHER DISCIPLINES

A manager's success and that of his or her organization will depend on his or her ability to understand the uniqueness of the situation he or she is facing and to devise the best way to deal with it. For that a manager needs to acquire a competitive advantage with respect to knowledge or information.

Advanced Living Systems. Advanced living systems are successful, beyond a doubt, as they have survived several hundred thousand years of evolution. How do they do it? Can managers learn from them? Advanced living systems are both super-specialists and super-generalists. All their functions relating to routine operational matters are highly automated. No one worries about how his or her heart or digestive system works, since they do so superbly and efficiently on their own with a minimum of supervision (except in cases of serious illness). The brain controls everything but pays little attention to operational details; the best way of automating these details has been found, which allows complete delegation of all routine, day-to-day functions. The structure of internal control and external scanning to get information and act on it is not, however, hierarchical (as in business firms). The brain controls everything directly, while at the same time receiving all information and making all decisions. Such organization is flat, efficient, and interactive.

Military. Military strategy, both in war and in times of peace, aims at impressing the opponent through the display of real or psychological advantages. An opponent who is impressed enough will not go to war or, if threatened, will accept our conditions. If he is not impressed, a war might start.

Military history has shown that psychological advantages over the opponent (many of which might come through the display and deployment of psychological power) are crucial. Victory must be assured with a minimum of force by cornering the opponent and taking away his freedom of action. Strategy becomes a game of wills where opposing generals try to put each other at a psychological disadvantage. This is the utmost of what in the military is called the indirect approach.

Sports. Great athletes practice a great deal, constantly work to better their own game, and strive for excellence without worrying much about competitors, who can spring up in any place at any time.

Arts. Great artists (dancers, actors, musicians, entertainers) have great talent or creativity. Contrary to popular belief, however, they work extremely hard to reach the top. Once there, it also takes a great deal of effort to remain there, a task that can be achieved only through constant practice or many hours of work.

There are a few great artists, as there are few great athletes. Thus, getting to the top is not easy. It cannot be done by imitation, nor can it be learned, as teaching is available to many. Furthermore, the criteria of excellence change over time, making imitation and teaching insufficient means.

Outstandingly Successful Individuals. Success can come from many diverse sources, which cannot be categorized or predicted beforehand. In the overwhelming majority of cases, however, highly successful individuals have a great idea and a vision of the future, are superbly motivated, can transmit their enthusiasm to their associates, do not give up in the face of formidable obstacles, and work extremely hard to achieve success. They are doers, are willing to take risks to succeed, and can function at their best when the going gets rough.

Failing does not follow set rules either. However, the factors that contribute to failure can be categorized. They include natural causes, a tendency toward bureaucracy, overoptimism, misjudging competition, judgmental biases on the part of the CEO, incompatibility, and plain bad luck. Delaying or avoiding failure might be even more difficult than achieving success. Although there is some advice to follow, this is no guarantee that failure can be delayed or avoided, in particular when one takes risks in order to succeed.

MANAGING CREATIVE PEOPLE

Managing creative people like actors, scientists, advertising personnel, or university professors requires different management techniques from those used in business organizations. Creative people usually disdain all forms of supervision and produce their best output in conditions that do not fit into the daily nine-to-five mode. The manager of creative people (theatrical producer, impresario, research director, advertising executive, dean) is a facilitator who smoothes over problems and interfaces between creative people and the formal organization they work for. In such situations, the role of the manager is critical. He or she has a specific task to accomplish while at the same time being unable to reward or punish the members of his or her group. He or she therefore needs to motivate the members with means other than those typically used in business organizations.

PAST MISTAKES

It is important to understand common mistakes made in the past by people in general and managers in particular so as to try to avoid them. Here are the most common and critical mistakes:

1. Overconfidence
2. Inability to adapt to change
3. Inability to distinguish temporary from permanent changes
4. Believing the future can be accurately predicted
5. Underestimating competition
6. Being dazzled by technology
7. Underestimating uncertainty

LEARNING THROUGH FEEDBACK

Learning requires precise and frequent feedback. That is why operational, repetitive tasks can be improved. However, strategic decisions usually refer to the longer term, and the feedback they provide is not precise or frequent. Thus, evaluation is difficult. Judging the effectiveness of creative output is also hard, as the criteria for evaluation are not clear. Besides, people find many excuses to rationalize their mistakes and attribute them to bad luck.

THE EMERGING BUSINESS ORGANIZATION

Business organizations will continue changing in a fundamental way.[2] For one thing, if the trend toward more automation combining mechanical and computer technologies continues, all repetitive operations will be completely automated. At the same time the majority of repetitive decisions will be replaced by decision rules and expert systems. Competitive advantages will not be derived from technology alone or from people making repetitive decisions. The use of new technologies and expert systems will eventually render those decisions as automatic as the smooth running of our digestive systems. In such an environment, where will competitive advantages come from?

Today's organizations must be capable of producing the goods or services that customers want in a competitive environment where other firms are trying to predict and satisfy those needs too. Until recently, businesses' main concern was to build organizations capable of efficiently producing and effectively distributing such goods or services at as low a cost as possible. All of that is changing, however. If the goods can be produced automatically and repetitive services made available with a minimum of human interference, far fewer people will be required to work in organizations. Maximum automation will be achieved in both operations and the gathering of information.

At this first level, line management will solve problems or deal with unexpected, exceptional situations by using information that has been gathered, summarized, and made available to them automatically. In most cases line managers will be able to monitor operations, evaluate the information received, and solve problems while sitting in front of their display screen in a control room. They will be the white-collar line managers and in many cases the only workers.

The ability of top managers and the CEO to implement an effective strategy and come up with new products and services will be the *only* means of gaining competitive advantages. At a time when competition is keener and environmental conditions are changing rapidly, hiring, keeping, and motivating creative people will be a continuous challenge. Creativity will become the scarce resource. Since only people can provide creativity, the battle will be to find such people and manage them best.

WHAT NEXT?

What comes next is up to each manager. To paraphrase Beaufre, strategy is an idea that requires creativity. To be effective, it must be simple but also powerful, as it will greatly affect the firm's existence. Most information is available to everyone. It is only those who can find the right information, interpret it correctly, and act decisively before their competitors do who will gain from using it. The same is true with management tools or theories. Few are the managers who will dig deeper, understand the assumptions of proposed management theories, and correctly calculate their advantages and limitations. Cookbooks make the same recipes available to everyone, but there are few great chefs. To quote one of them, Roger Vergé:

> A recipe is not meant to be followed exactly—it is a canvas on which you can embroider. Add a zest to this, a drop or two of that, a tiny pinch of the other. Let yourself be led by your palate and your tongue, your eyes and your heart. In other words, be guided by your love of food, and then you will be able to cook.[3]

CEOs and top managers must always think "What next?" Having succeeded in restructuring the organization, rationalizing and globalizing its operations, and streamlining and automating its functions (so have the competitors), what next? To stay ahead in the competitive game, CEOs and top executives must always try to be a step ahead of their competitors. But to do so they must search for and interpret information about the present and the future in a unique way and come up with novel ideas and new, original ways of staying at the top. Here they are on their own. No one and nothing can help them but their own creativity, vision, strategic wisdom, and leadership.

Appendix

Computers:

Their Advantages, Limitations, and Implications

Computers are changing all aspects of business organizations, governmental operations, and the military, and will continue to do so. They will have a profound effect on education and entertainment as well. In the final analysis, they are about to produce huge social changes going right to the core of our social fabric.

Computers are made up of hardware and software. The former provides the structure and the parts (the cranium and the neurons of the human brain), the latter the processor of information (the equivalent of the thinking part of the brain). Computers can also access memory devices from which they can retrieve information and in which they can store new data. Such memory devices can be huge, containing the equivalent of many times the information in the *Encyclopaedia Britannica*. In addition, many such storage devices, scattered geographically, can be addressed by a computer so its capacity to retrieve and store information is practically unlimited.

At the same time, computers are morons. They have no intelligence of their own. They cannot understand or think even the simplest of thoughts. However, they can be programmed to perform complicated tasks requiring a great deal of ingenuity and intelligence. How is it possible that stupid machines can be made to behave intelligently? This question might bother those not familiar with computers, but answering it is fairly simple. Computers can think through computer programs (the software), which tell them what to do step by step, very explicitly, including the slightest of details. If the programmer is creative, he can instruct the computer to perform highly intelligent tasks. If the task is complicated, the program may be large and difficult to develop and test. Such a program may require many man-years to develop.

A simple task, like playing tic-tac-toe, can be programmed by an average programmer in less than a day. It can be written in such a way that a human player can never win (at most he or she can draw). The rules of tic-tac-toe are simple and do not change, the objective is clear, and the available moves are few. Thus it is possible to tell the computer what to do in any and all circumstances, ensuring that it will never lose.

In chess the program must be much more complicated. The rules of chess are more complex and the number of possibilities almost infinite. A computer program to play chess therefore can be written only by experienced programmers who are also experts in mathematics and logic. In chess, as in tic-tac-toe, the rules are known and do not change. Furthermore, the objective of chess is clear (you play to win), as are the criteria for achieving that objective (try not to lose any pieces, or lose one of less rather than more value, and try to capture the highest-valued of our opponent's pieces).

What makes chess difficult is that there is no way to instruct the computer to do something specific in each of the billions of situations that can develop in any single game. Humans cannot examine all the possibilities either. However, they can easily figure out where to concentrate their attention and what strategy to follow in order to win. A computer cannot do that. Instead, it can consider several million of the possibilities (but not all) and choose the best among them. In so doing, it uses simple brute force (examining each one of millions of alternatives) but not thinking or strategy. Its advantage is that it is many million times faster than humans in examining and evaluating various alternatives. Its disadvantage is that it cannot figure out where to concentrate its attention so that it will not have to evaluate every single alternative.

As time passes programmers (or the experts who conceive and design the programs) are becoming smarter, more experienced, and more creative. Thus, they can incorporate into the programs techniques that mimic the way people play chess or make decisions in general. Although the programming for such a task is not trivial, it can be done. Experts in mathematical combinations and logic are discovering efficient short cuts that allow programmers to devise optimal algorithms (specific procedures to achieve specific tasks) that can greatly increase the computer's capacity to evaluate and come up with the best move at each stage of the chess game. But in the end the computer can play and win at chess only because of its ability to evaluate millions of possible moves in the allowed playing time.

Computers process information at an incredibly fast rate. Today's fastest supercomputer can perform 10 billion multiplications a second. Imagine the speed of such computational power. If you had to do 10 billion multiplications with a pencil and paper it would take you 5,000 years, assuming that you could do a multiplication every five seconds, that you could work ten hours a day, three hundred days each year, and make no mistakes. An ability to do multiplications, you might say, does not make computers worth much. However, equivalent high speeds can be achieved with all types of tasks a computer performs when processing information (e.g., in making simple yes or no decisions or storing and retrieving information). Thus, computers hold a huge competitive advantage over people in this domain; their power of processing information is phenomenal in comparison with a human's.

Then why can't computers be smart? It is one thing to be superfast in processing simple information and another to be intelligent—not to mention the capacity to learn, be creative, solve new problems, or adapt to changes. For instance, the human eye passes to the brain billions of bits of information every second. The brain knows which of this information is important and where it has to concentrate its attention. Someone driving on a mountain road therefore can look out the window for one second and admire the magnificent view. The next second concentration focuses on avoiding a passing car; after that the driver can admire the beauty of the snowy mountain top. The information passed to the brain in a few seconds is more than any computer can process in months. Most importantly, however, the brain can go back and forth effortlessly, knowing what information it needs, where to concentrate, how to evaluate each situation, and what to do. Computers cannot do those tasks. Even the biggest and fastest of today's computers has great trouble walking down a staircase.

It is not likely that computers will be capable of competing with people in any tasks that involve senses or the ability to discriminate, learn, solve new problems, be creative, adapt, and perform similar highly intelligent functions. On the other hand, computers can process simple information (doing arithmetic, making simple yes/no decisions, searching for a particular piece of information) at phenomenal rates in comparison with humans, who are slow in dealing with such information, get bored easily, and make mistakes when working for extended periods.

It is possible that eventually computers will be programmed to become intelligent, but that is not going to happen overnight. Making a computer see and understand what it is seeing will take tens if not hundreds of years. Making a computer learn and exhibit real human intelligence might require thousands of years. Getting computers to reproduce humanlike creativity might take even longer, if it can ever be done.

Computer costs are decreasing exponentially while their power (speed and memory capacity) increases exponentially. The improvements are phenomenal and are likely to continue. What computers are still lacking is the appropriate programs to exploit their capabilities. Once those programs are developed, we shall have a revolution in terms of the benefits we can obtain by using computers.

For a concrete example of the evolution and potential capability of computers, think of a wrist watch made by Casio today and selling at $70. Such a watch can tell the time, the day of the week, and the date (day, month, and year); can store 100 telephone numbers or the equivalent number of memos or appointments; and has an alarm and a calculator. That watch has more memory, and its calculator is faster, than the first computer (ENIAC) built in 1946, which filled a room, weighed 30 tons, and required enough electricity to run all the battery-operated digital watches in existence. Its cost was $2 million in today's prices. Thus, while computers cannot even come close to competing with the higher of human intellectual powers, they have made great strides since 1946. They are certainly much faster, much smaller, and a great deal cheaper than those of even a decade ago. A lap-top computer the size of a notebook, weighing a couple of pounds, with higher speed and more memory than the biggest of today's supercomputers, costing around five thousand dollars, is well within the realm of possibility by the year 2001.

The greatest competitive advantage of computers comes from their ability to process information superfast and carry out speedy computations. Scientists, engineers, and others with huge computational requirements have found the perfect tool to assist them. Computational problems that were unthinkable even ten years ago can now be successfully solved. Spreadsheet programs, like Lotus 1,2,3, present only trivial computational tasks for even the smallest of today's microcomputers.

Another great competitive advantage of computers relates to their ability to store specific pieces of information and then retrieve them in any form one might desire. Suppose, for instance, that I wanted to find all the papers and books predicting depressions that have been written in the past (indeed, I needed to use such information in Chapter 4). Although I knew of several such papers and books, I wanted to find them all. I used four data banks that included all published papers of all important journals in economics and management and all books published since 1950. I indicated a search for the word "depression" in the title of the journal or among the keywords that journal articles contained. The computer came up with a list of almost 400 titles. However, about 250 of them referred to personality or psychological depression or to topics related to the Great Depression of the 1930s. The computer was not capable of distinguishing between economic and psychological depressions. The same was true with the 330 book titles: About two-thirds of them were not about the prediction of economic depressions. The computer took less than two minutes to search hundred of thousands of titles and keywords and come up with 730 of them. Incidentally, I was not the only person using the computerized library search service (there were probably hundreds of others searching at the same time), which was located in England and the United States while I was sitting in front of a computer terminal in a small town in France.

An extension of the computer's ability to search for appropriate information is the area of expert systems, where the way information is retrieved is much more involved than using simple rules. In expert systems the computer will be able to use many rules, as well as conditional ''if this . . . then that'' types of decisions and several verification checks. The result will be a refined search procedure focusing on small, specific areas of the data so that the appropriate information or knowledge can be found and used as a basis for the decision made by the computer. If the information found is judged to be of doubtful value, the computer will be instructed not to make a decision and instead to ask for human help. In the case of searching for articles and books on economic depressions, an expert system would be able to check if the words ''economic,'' ''economy,'' ''business,'' ''profits,'' and so on were in the title and thus select the paper or book. On the contrary, if the words ''psychology,'' or ''psychological,'' ''personality,'' ''personal,'' and so on were there, it would reject the paper or book. Similar words denoting ''Great Depression,'' ''historical evaluation,'' ''1929–1941,'' ''New Deal'' would have told the computer to reject the paper or book. Such computerized searches are not possible today but will definitely become available in the near future as expert systems are developed.

Another area in which computers possess important competitive advantages is monitoring and controlling situations. The only constraint is that the data needed for monitoring must exist in digital form (that is, in numbers) and the output for controlling must be provided in digital form too. Thus, a computer can continuously monitor whether the pressure of a chemical process is within an acceptable range and can take corrective action to either increase or decrease the pressure when it is outside allowable limits. Similarly, computers can be used to monitor complicated instruments or automatically inspect items in quality control situations.

They can continually verify that an airplane stays on its course, fuel is efficiently burned, and the best speed—given the payload and wind direction—is maintained. As computers become smaller, faster, and cheaper, the range of repetitive applications they can be used for is unlimited, and so are the advantages we can obtain through such uses. It is estimated that by the year 2000 as much a one-third of the value of a car will be made up of the computers installed under its hood to monitor its running and make it more efficient.

Computers can also be used like elementary brains performing simple tasks. They can substitute mostly semiskilled operators whose job is to do repetitive, routine tasks. Such an ability adds elementary intelligence to machines in the sense that they can make simple decisions and can be guided and controlled internally. As was mentioned, robotics and high-level automation fall into this category, in which growth has just started but will continue.

Finally, computers are powerful tools for mental work. Their superb graphic capabilities, precision, speed, memory, unlimited stamina (they never get tired), and inability ever to get bored have opened up vistas unimaginable even a few decades ago. The computer as a mental tool will become as indispensable to future generations as books are to us today. It will revolutionize thinking, learning, and education in its way just as much as the printed book once did.

Revolutions affect society, and the Information Revolution[1] is no exception: It will change relative wealth, experience, mental skills, amount of free time, entertainment, consumption habits, and almost all aspects of our personal, family, and business lives. When those changes will take place, how deep they will be, and how much they will affect specific groups are not certain, but there is little doubt that such changes will arrive and that they will create problems of transition, as did, for many groups of people, businesses, and industries, the Industrial Revolution. On the positive side computers will remove the repetitive, boring tasks that humans have to perform today. They will help improve productivity, lower the cost of goods, raise disposable income, and create more free time.

The biggest loss to the Information Revolution will be experience and skills in performing repetitive mental tasks, which will slowly become obsolete. The Industrial Revolution made manual experience and expertise unnecessary by designing machines that could reproduce repetitive and manual skills. The Information Revolution will do the same for mental tasks. Machines can now produce shoes and most other products. The constraint is not the skills (expertise) required to make the shoes but money to buy the necessary machinery. Better-quality products are not the province of experienced (through many years of apprenticeship and actual work of making shoes) craftsmen but rather of superanalytic engineers. Furthermore, since everybody can make shoes now, competitive advantages are gained through organizational capacities to produce them at the lowest cost and market them in the most effective way. Finally, shoe styling, conceived by creative people, has become a critical factor in succeeding. The Information Revolution is creating similar changes, which will reduce and eventually eliminate the value of experience and expertise in a wide range of mental tasks. A quote from a foreman of a newly computerized company best summarizes what is in the making. "The computer is programmed to do all the thinking for me. . . . It has become my job. . . . The computer has become an extension of the supervisor. It is the law now, black and white. There is no question there about what you have to do."[2]

Will tomorrow be the turn of middle managers to see their jobs taken over by computers?

TECHNOLOGICAL TRENDS

Computers, microelectronics, lasers, and communications technologies are already creating trends toward the following:

- *Diminution*. Products get smaller and smaller as tiny components are being built. Miniature TV screens, the Walkman, lap-top computers, and multifunction digital watches are examples of the trend, which is likely to continue or even accelerate as we move toward the twenty-first century.[3]

- *Digitalization*. As memory chips become cheaper and can store larger amounts of information, it becomes technically and economically feasible to digitalize everything. Music, voices, photographs, books, and practically everything else can be transformed into digital form (that is, zeros or ones) and stored, transmitted, or retrieved electronically. Once so transformed, the original (music, voice, photo) can be reconstructed at practically the same level of quality.

- *Computerization*. Computers and microprocessors can and will eventually be used to guide, control, or make more efficient all aspects of machine operations, climate control, communications, and so forth. Personal computers will become as widespread as telephones are today.

- *Globalization of Communications.* As telecommunications become more reliable and cheaper, it will be possible to communicate with any point in the world and transmit or receive not only voices but also images and computer messages. Electronic or E-mail is becoming commonplace and will eventually replace regular mail except for sending bulky packages or products. Also personal computers that can send and receive faxes will become commonplace.

- *Instantization.* Through the above four advances instant access to a great variety of information and services will be possible. Airplane reservations and orders for products or services can be made twenty-four hours a day from a home computer.

- *Customization.* Once two-way communication with home computers is economically practical, firms can provide a wide variety of personalized products or services geared to specific customer needs. Again, such products and services can be ordered from home at any time of the day or night.

- *Automation.* The trend toward higher levels of automation will continue and even increase as mechanical and information technologies are combined and computers and microprocessors become smaller, more powerful, and cheaper.

- *Robotization.* As with automation, the trend toward more powerful, more versatile, and cheaper robots will continue as computers and microchips become smaller, more powerful, and cheaper. Robots will increase the amount of automation and considerably extend its limits.

- *Leisurization.* As automation increases and computerization makes the daily chores of life easier, more free time will be available, accelerating the trend toward more leisure activities (sports, entertainment, vacation, travel).

Notes

CHAPTER 1
The Rise and Fall of Management Theories

1. Eight factors were found to be common to the great majority of the "excellent" companies: a bias for action, closeness to the customer, autonomy and entrepreneurship, productivity through people, hands-on and value-driven style, sticking to the knitting, simple form lean staff, and simultaneous loose-tight properties. Tom Peters and Robert Waterman, *In Search of Excellence* (New York: Harper & Row, 1982), pp. 3–26.

2. G. D. Wallace, D. Foust, T. Thompson, J. Schwartz, G. L. Miles, and M. J. Pitzer, "America's Leanest and Meanest: Companies That Are Rising to the Challenge of Tougher Competition," *Business Week,* Oct. 5, 1987, pp. 48–54.

3. E. Schultz, "America's Most Admired Corporations," *Fortune,* Jan. 18, 1988, pp. 26–41.

4. Thomas Peters, *Thriving on Chaos: Handbook for a Management Revolution* (New York: Knopf, 1987).

5. The word "theory" is used in the broad sense to mean concepts, ideas, advice, and approaches, as well as more formal theories.

6. J. Rothchild, *A Fool and His Money: The Odyssey of an Average Investor* (New York: Penguin Books, 1988).

7. R. André and P. Ward, *The 59-Second Employee: How to Stay One Second Ahead of Your One-Minute Manager* (Boston: Houghton-Mifflin, 1984).

8. M. Kaku and J. Trainer, *Beyond Einstein: The Cosmic Quest for the Theory of the Universe* (New York: Bantam Books, 1987).

9. For a lively account of "behaviorism" as a theory and its deficiencies, see M. Hunt, *The Universe Within: A New Science Explores the Human Mind* (New York: Simon & Schuster, 1982), pp. 48–83.

10. For an excellent discussion of the topic, see T. S. Kuhn, *The Structure of Scientific Revolutions,* (Chicago; University of Chicago Press, 1962).

11. A. N. Whitehead, Science and the Modern World, (New York: Free Press, 1925), p. 23. Italics added.

12. R. Gordon, *Great Medical Disasters* (New York: Dorset Press, 1983), p. 15.

CHAPTER 2
Biases and Limitations of Our Judgment

1. Norman Dixon, 1976, *On the Psychology of Military Incompetence* (London: Jonathan Cape, 1976).

2. Irving L. Javis and Leon Mann, *Decision Making: A Psychological Analysis of Conflict, Choice, and Commitment* (New York: Free Press, 1977).

3. Kets de Vries, M. Miller, and D. Miller, *Unstable at the Top: Inside the Troubled Organization* (New York: New American Library, 1988).

4. D. Kahneman, P. Slovic and A. Tversky, *Judgment Under Uncertainty: Heuristic and Biases* (Cambridge, England: Cambridge University Press, 1982).

5. P. C. Wason, and P. N. Johnson-Laird, *Psychology of Reasoning: Structure and Content* (London: Batsford, 1972).

6. A. Morita, *Made in Japan: Akio Morita and Sony* (New York: E. P. Dutton, 1985), p. 147.

7. E. H. Bowman, "Consistency and Optimality in Managerial Decision Making." *Management Science,* 10, no. 1 (1963): 310–21.

8. P. Meehl, *Clinical Versus Statistical Prediction: A Theoretical Analysis and a Review of the Evidence* (Minneapolis: University of Minnesota Press, 1954).

9. L. H. Garland, "The Problem of Observer Error," *Bulletin of the New York Academy of Medicine,* (1960): 569–84.

10. I. L. Janis, *Victims of Group Think* (Boston: Houghton Mifflin, 1972).

11. S. Oskamp, "Overconfidence in Case-Study Judgments," *Journal of Consulting Psychology,* 29 (1965): 261–65.

CHAPTER 3
Predicting the Future: Myths and Reality

1. For a survey of historical comparisons, see R. Hogarth and S. Makridakis, "Forecasting and Planning: An Evaluation," *Management Science,* 27 (1981): 115–38.

2. An interesting account of stock market investing can be found in J. Rothchild, *A Fool and His Money: The Odyssey of an Average Investor* (New York: Viking, 1988).

3. Chaos theory talks about the "butterfly effect," that is, a butterfly that flaps its wings somewhere in the forest can be the initiator of changes in the weather pattern a few days later, a thousand miles away.

4. For a detailed account, see S. Makridakis and S. Wheelwright, *Forecasting Methods for Management,* 5th ed. (New York: John Wiley, 1989).

CHAPTER 4

Identifying Megapatterns: Trends Versus Cycles

1. J. L. Simon, *The Ultimate Resource* (Oxford: Martin Robertson, 1981).
2. E. R. Dewey, *Cycles: The Mysterious Forces that Trigger Events* (New York: Hawthorn Books, 1971).
3. R. Beckman, *The Downwave: Surviving the Second Great Depression* (Portsmouth, U.K.: Milestone Publications, 1983).
4. A popular book that describes the new theory of chaos and its implications in the physical, natural and biological world is J. Gleick, *Chaos:* (New York: Viking, 1987).

CHAPTER 7

Planning for the Future

1. P. Wack, "Scenarios: Uncharted Waters Ahead," *Harvard Business Review,* September–October 1985, pp. 73–89.
2. W. R. Huss, "A Move Toward Scenario Analysis," *International Journal of Forecasting,* 4, no. 3 (1988): 377–88.

CHAPTER 8

Competitive Strategy

1. A vivid account of how Pepsi won its war against Coke by nullifying its advantages and changing the rules of the game is provided in J. Sculley, *Odyssey: Pepsi to Apple* (London: Collins, 1987; New York: Harper & Row, 1987).
2. B. H. Liddell Hart, *Strategy* (London: Faber & Faber, 1957).
3. Sun Tsu, *The Art of War,* translated by S. B. Griffith (London: Oxford University Press, 1963).
4. J. M. Collins, *Ground Strategy: Principles and Practices* (Washington, D.C.: United States Naval Institute, 1973).
5. Clausewitz, K. von, *Clausewitz on War* (London: Penguin Books, 1968; first published, 1832).
6. André Beaufre, *Introduction à la stratégie* (Paris: Economica, 1985).
7. Material for this section has been collected from E. S. Creasy, *Fifteen Decisive Battles of the World* (New York: Dorset Press, 1987); C. Falls, *A Hundred Years of War* (New York: Collier Books, 1962); various other sources, including newspaper and magazine accounts.

8. M. E. Porter, *Competitive Strategy: Techniques for Analyzing Industries and Competitors* (New York: Free Press, 1980).

9. Falls, *A Hundred Years of War.*

10. N. Dixon, *On the Psychology of Military Incompetence* (London: Jonathan Cape, 1976).

11. See R. Durö and B. Sandström, *The Basic Principles of Marketing Warfare* (Chichester: John Wiley & Sons, 1987); D. J. Rogers, *Waging Business Warfare* (New York: Scribner's, 1987); and W. E. Peacock, *Corporate Combat* (New York: Facts on File, 1984).

12. In recent years many unlikely alliances have emerged, among them IBM and DEC against AT&T, and GM and Nissan against other car companies.

13. The creation of the EEC has been a direct response to the inability of European countries to compete on their own with their strong U.S. and Japanese business rivals.

14. P. Kennedy, *The Rise and Fall of the Great Powers* (New York: Random House, 1987).

15. S. Makridakis, *Europe 1992 and Beyond: Challenges and Dangers for Business* (San Francisco: Jossey-Bass, 1990).

CHAPTER 9
Noncompetitive Strategies

1. K. Ohmae, *The Mind of the Strategist: The Art of Japanese Business* (New York: McGraw Hill, 1982), p. 2.

2. W. T. Gallway, *The Inner Game of Tennis* (Toronto: Bantam Books, 1979).

3. See S. Makridakis and D. Héau, "The Evolution of Strategic Planning and Management," in W. R. King and D. I. Cleland, eds., *Strategic Planning and Management Handbook* (New York: Van Nostrand Reinhold, 1987).

4. *Ibid.*

5. For example, H. Mintzberg, *Mintzberg on Management* (New York: Free Press, 1989) and J. B. Quinn, *Strategies for Change* (Homewood, Ill.: Richard D. Irwin, 1980).

6. E. A. Znosko-Borovsky, *The Middle Game of Chess* (New York: Dover Publications, 1980).

CHAPTER 10
Creativity

1. A. Koestler, *The Act of Creation* (New York: Macmillan, 1964).

2. For example, G. Walles, 1926, *The Art of Thought,* Harcourt Brace, New York.

3. J. W. Young, *A Technique for Producing Ideas* (Chicago: Crain Communications, 1940).

4. J. L. Adams, *Conceptual Blockbusting*, 2d ed., (New York: Norton, 1979).

5. E. De Bono, *Lateral Thinking* (London: Penguin Books, 1970); *idem, Lateral Thinking for Management* (London: Penguin Books, 1971); and *idem, Six Thinking Hats* (London: Penguin Books, 1985).

6. A. Osborn, *Applied Imagination* (New York: Scribner's, 1953).

7. M. Ray and R. Myers, *Creativity in Business: Based on the Famed Stanford University Course that Has Revolutionized the Art of Success* (Garden City, N.Y.: Doubleday, 1986).

8. See R. W. Weisberg, *Creativity: Genius and Other Myths* (New York: W. H. Freeman, 1986).

9. Ray and Myers, for instance, say: "The creative techniques from the 1950s, such as brainstorming, do little to deal with this basic conflict—a conflict that keeps you from being consistently creative." *Creativity in Business,* p. 9.

10. H. Simon, "What We Know About the Creative Process," in R. L. Kuhn, ed., *Frontiers in Creative and Innovative Management* (Cambridge, Mass.: Ballinger, 1985).

11. M. Minsky, *The Society of Mind* (London: Heinemann, 1985).

12. I. Asimov, "Creativity, Computers and Cooperation," paper presented at the 17th Biennial Executive Forum: Leadership in 2001—Technology and Markets, sponsored by Arthur D. Little, Boston, 1988.

13. J. Gleick, *Chaos: Making a New Science* (New York: Viking, 1987).

14. S. Levy, *Hackers: Heroes of the Computer Revolution* (New York: Dell, 1984).

15. A good example of a creative genius and his personality characteristics are provided in A. Stassinopoulos-Huffington, *Picasso: Creator and Destroyer* which describes how Picasso became a painter with little formal education (London: Pan Books, 1988).

16. D. R. Hofstadter, *Metamagical Themes: Questions for the Essence of Mind and Pattern* (New York: Basic Books, 1985).

17. J. Baron, *Thinking and Deciding* (Cambridge, England: Cambridge University Press, 1988); A. R. Luria, *The Working Brain: An Introduction to Neuropsychology* (London: Penguin Books, 1973); M. Hunt, *The Universe Within: A New Science Explores the Human Mind* (New York: Simon & Schuster, 1982); and H. Margolis, *Patterns, Thinking and Cognition: A Theory of Judgment* (Chicago: University of Chicago Press, 1987).

18. Levy, *Hackers.*

19. P. R. Nayak and J. M. Ketteringham, *Breakthroughs!* (New York: Rawson Associates, 1986).

20. E. Von Hippel, *The Sources of Innovation* (Oxford and New York: Oxford

University Press, 1987), for instance, reports 75–90% of incremental innovations coming from customers' demand.

CHAPTER 11
Avoiding or Delaying Failure

1. "It's Tough Up There," *Forbes,* July 13, 1987, p. 145.

2. J. P. Wright, *On a Clear Day You Can See General Motors: John Z. De Lorean's Look Inside the Automotive Giant* (Grosse Pointe, Mich.: Wright Enterprises, 1979).

3. S. P. Schnaars, *Megamistakes: Forecasting and the Myth of Rapid Technological Change,* (New York: Free Press, 1988).

4. R. H. Kilmann, *Beyond the Quick Fix: Managing Five Tracks to Organizational Success* (San Francisco: Jossey-Bass, 1984), and M. E. McGill, *American Business and the Quick Fix* (New York: Henry Holt, 1988).

5. Kilman, *Beyond the Quick Fix.*

6. R. B. Lamb, *Running American Business: Top CEOs Rethink Their Major Decisions* (New York: Basic Books, 1987).

7. C. M. Byron, *The Fanciest Dive* (New York: New American Library, 1986).

8. R. F. Hartley, *Marketing Mistakes,* 3rd ed. (New York: John Wiley & Sons, 1986).

CHAPTER 12
Achieving and Sustaining Success

1. *Business Week,* November 28, 1988, pp. 76–92.

2. *Economist, MBA: The Best Business Tool? A Guide to British and European Business Schools* (London: The Economist Publications, 1988).

3. For example, D. J. Trump, *Trump: The Art of the Deal* (New York: Random House, 1987), and J. Sculley, *Odyssey: Pepsi to Apple* (London: Collins, 1987; New York: Harper & Row, 1987).

4. W. Avis, *Take a Chance to Be First* (New York: Macmillan, 1988).

5. L. Iacocca, *Talking Straight* (London: Sidgwick & Jackson, 1988; New York: Bantam, 1988).

6. M. Meyer, *The Alexander Complex: The Dreams that Drive Great Businessmen* (New York, Times Books, 1989).

CHAPTER 13
Conclusions: Toward a New Management

1. H. M. Spiro, *Doctors, Patients, and Placebos* (New Haven: Yale University Press, 1986).

2. P. F. Drucker, *The New Realities: In Government and Politics/In Economics and Business/In Society and World Views* (New York: Harper & Row, 1989).

3. R. Vergé, *Cuisine of the Sun* (London: Macmillan, 1979).

APPENDIX
Computers: Their Advantages, Limitations, and Implications

1. For more on this topic, see S. Zuboff, *In the Age of Smart Machines: The Future of Work and Power* (New York: Basic Books, 1988).

2. *Ibid.*, p. 333.

3. G. Gilder, *Microcosm: The Quantum Revolution in Economics and Technology* (New York: Simon and Schuster, 1989).

Index